Pro Sync Framework

Rituraj Singh and Joydip Kanjilal

Apress®

Pro Sync Framework

Copyright © 2009 by Rituraj Singh and Joydip Kanjilal

ISBN-13 (pbk): 978-1-4302-1005-4

ISBN-13 (electronic): 978-1-4302-1006-1

Lead Editor: Ewan Buckingham
Technical Reviewer: Todd Meister
Editorial Board: Clay Andres, Steve Anglin, Mark Beckner, Ewan Buckingham, Tony Campbell,
    Gary Cornell, Jonathan Gennick, Michelle Lowman, Matthew Moodie, Jeffrey Pepper, Frank Pohlmann,
    Ben Renow-Clarke, Dominic Shakeshaft, Matt Wade, Tom Welsh
Project Manager: Beth Christmas
Copy Editor: Nancy Sixsmith
Associate Production Director: Kari Brooks-Copony
Production Editor: Ellie Fountain
Compositor: Susan Glinert
Proofreader: Nancy Bell
Indexer: Brenda Miller
Artist: Kinetic Publishing Services, LLC
Cover Designer: Kurt Krames
Manufacturing Director: Tom Debolski

Distributed to the book trade worldwide by Springer-Verlag New York, Inc., 233 Spring Street, 6th Floor, New York, NY 10013. Phone 1-800-SPRINGER, fax 201-348-4505, e-mail orders-ny@springer-sbm.com, or visit http://www.springeronline.com.

For information on translations, please contact Apress directly at 2855 Telegraph Avenue, Suite 600, Berkeley, CA 94705. Phone 510-549-5930, fax 510-549-5939, e-mail info@apress.com, or visit http://www.apress.com.

Apress and friends of ED books may be purchased in bulk for academic, corporate, or promotional use. eBook versions and licenses are also available for most titles. For more information, reference our Special Bulk Sales–eBook Licensing web page at http://www.apress.com/info/bulksales.

The source code for this book is available to readers at http://www.apress.com.

I would like to dedicate this book to two special ladies in my life, my mom (Radhika Singh) and my wife (Priya Singh). Thanks for all your support and patience over the years and the years to come. Writing a book requires lot of time and thanks for allowing me to steal a large part of your time to write my first book. Thank you for all your sacrifices.
—Rituraj Singh

Dedicated to my parents and family.
—Joydip Kanjilal

Contents at a Glance

Contents

Foreword

The emergence of the Microsoft Sync Framework could not have come at a better time. Today's applications and (more importantly) the applications of the future are evolving in a manner that forces us to pay more close attention to offline data access, peer-to-peer collaboration, and other sharing scenarios. At the forefront of the revolution is the Microsoft Sync Framework—a flexible, ambitious, and amazingly powerful development kit that empowers developers to easily synchronize data.

Data synchronization plays a pivotal role in today's world. It also is an essential component in the transition of tomorrow's applications to a managed cloud environment. In short, understanding the Sync Framework and grasping its capabilities and potential will strongly position you for the next wave of applications and services.

That's why this book is so valuable. With a tremendous importance placed on practical, real-world code in a concise and easy-to-understand format, *Pro Sync Framework* will serve as a vital resource for those developers looking to comprehend and unlock the hidden gems of the framework. Rituraj and Joydip have demonstrated their ability to take complex topics and break them into smaller fragments that can be easily understood and applied.

With resources like this book, the Microsoft Sync Framework is sure to continue to develop and succeed. As you read this important manuscript, you will be preparing yourself to take advantage of the many new innovations in the years to come. Enjoy!

David Barkol
ASPInsider
Author of *Asp.Net Ajax In Action*
Principal Consultant, MCSD
Neudesic, LLC
david.barkol@neudesic.com

About the Authors

RITURAJ SINGH is a Senior Consultant for Neudesic (www.neudesic.com), one of Microsoft's leading .NET professional service firms. At Neudesic, he specializes in custom application development and Microsoft Dynamics practice. Rituraj has written articles for popular technology web sites such as Wrox and Devx on various Microsoft technologies.

Rituraj is an active participant in various Microsoft communities and user groups, and also enjoys working on cutting-edge technologies. When he is not writing code, he likes to play chess with his brother and spend time with Ashin playing cricket. Rituraj can be reached at devgeekraj@gmail.com.

JOYDIP KANJILAL is a Microsoft Most Valuable Professional in ASP.NET since 2007. He has more than 12 years of industry experience in IT, with more than 6 years' experience in Microsoft .NET and its related technologies. Joydip has authored a lot of articles for many reputable sites, including www.asptoday.com, www.devx.com, www.aspalliance.com, www.sql-server-performance.com, www.aspnetpro.com, and www.sswug.com. A lot of these articles have been selected at www.asp.net, which Microsoft's official site on ASP.NET. He was also a community credit winner at www.community-credit.com a number of times.

Joydip has authored two other books: *ASP.NET Data Presentation Controls Essentials* (Packt) and *Sams Teach Yourself ASP.NET Ajax in 24 Hours* (Sams).

Joydip is currently working as a lead architect in a company located in Hyderabad, India. He has years of experience in designing and architecting solutions for various domains. His technical strengths include C, C++, VC++, Java, C#, Microsoft .NET, Ajax, Design Patterns, SQL Server, operating systems, and computer architecture. Joydip blogs at http://aspadvice.com/blogs/joydip and spends most of his time reading books, blogging, and writing books and articles. His hobbies include watching cricket and soccer and playing chess. Joydip can be reached at joydipkanjilal@yahoo.com.

About the Technical Reviewer

 **TODD MEISTER** has been developing and using Microsoft technologies for more than ten years. He's been a technical editor on more than 50 titles, ranging from SQL Server to the .NET Framework. Todd is an Assistant Director for Computing Services at Ball State University in Muncie, Indiana. He lives in central Indiana with his wife, Kimberly, and their four children. Contact Todd at tmeister@sycamoresolutions.com.

Acknowledgments

This book is not just the work of the authors; so many people have contributed to this book as a whole that it is difficult to name them all. But if I missed anyone, it is an oversight, not a lack of gratitude.

I want to begin by thanking my director, Ashish Agarwal, for his support and inspiration. I wouldn't be an author without his encouragement.

I must thank the entire team at Apress for giving me a chance to write this book and for the support and understanding throughout the project. My heartiest thanks to Joydip Kanjilal for his support and inspiration.

An extended thank you goes to my friend and colleague, Sandeep Chanda, for helping me through every stage of the book.

I am also thankful to Steele Price, David Barkol, Mickey Williams, and Steve Saxon for their guidance, inspiration, and support.

I also want to thank my friends Ajay Yadav, Rajesh Mishra, Jagdish Mishra, Amol Gholap (Neudesic), Aneesh Pulukkul (Neudesic), Pushpendra Singh (Neudesic) and Sanjay Golani (Neudesic). A big thank you goes to entire team of Neudesic India. You guys rock!

My deepest respect and gratitude go to my parents, Ravindra Singh and Radhika Singh, for their love, blessings, and encouragement. Most importantly, I would like to thank my brother, Rishiraj Singh, and my wife Priya Singh. I am very lucky to have such a wonderful family.

Rituraj Singh

I want to thank Ewan Buckingham for providing me the opportunity to author this book. I am also thankful to Beth Christmas for her cooperation and support in this project. My heartiest thanks to my coauthor Rituraj Singh for his hard work and help to make this project a success.

I am also thankful to Abhishek Kant (Microsoft), Steve Smith (AspAlliance), Russell Jones (DevX), Steve Jones(SSWUG), Jude Kelly (SQL Server Performance), and Anand Narayaswamy (AspAlliance) for their inspiration and support.

My deepest respect and gratitude to my parents for their love, blessings, and encouragement. I also thank my other family members for their support and inspiration.

Joydip Kanjilal

Introduction

It's been almost a year since we first started playing with the first test build of Microsoft Sync Framework. It was an absolute pleasure writing this book since then and we hope that you will have fun reading it, too. However, we must admit that it was a little tough writing a book on a cutting-edge technology that was still undergoing changes. Thankfully, after a lot of hard work and many sleepless nights we are proud to share the knowledge that we have gained during last year.

As with any Microsoft technology, you will find lots of information about Sync Framework on the MSDN website. There are some really cool videos, blogs, online documentation, and forums. However, we believe that the greatest strength of this book is that it provides you a step by step guide to quickly get started with Sync Framework and slowly start increasing the complexity level of the project. Almost every chapter is equipped with a code sample, and we have focused more on code than theory. Code examples are a great way for any developer to start learning a new technology. Most of the code can be used as the building blocks of any sync application.

Each chapter introduces a concept, discusses why it is important to learn that concept, and then explains how to put that concept in use with the help of code examples.

Overview

Welcome to *Pro Sync Framework!* To help with the discussion, this book is divided into four content areas.

The first part of the book, consisting of Chapter 1 and Chapter 2, helps you understand the basics of the Microsoft Sync Framework. Chapter 1 explains the need for synchronization and how the Sync Framework eliminates some of the common problems. You will also get detailed information about the architecture and components of the Sync Framework. Chapter 2 dives into the details of the Sync Framework metadata model. The Sync Framework enables you to synchronize any type of data between any devices over any network topology and protocol, and it agrees on a common metadata model.

The second content area, consisting of Chapters 3, 4, and 5, helps you understand how to create custom sync providers. Chapter 3 discusses the need for custom sync providers and provides in-depth information about the classes available in the Sync Framework APIs for creating them. It also includes a code sample to create a custom provider. Chapter 4 explores the different options available in Sync Framework for creating custom sync providers to suit your synchronization needs. It contains a code sample to demonstrate how to create different sync providers for different synchronization scenarios. Chapter 5 explains how to create unmanaged sync providers using C++. It also provides in-depth information about built-in file sync providers.

The third part of this book, made up of Chapters 6 and 7, helps you understand Sync Services for metadata storage and RSS and Atom feeds.

The fourth content area, consisting of Chapters 8 and 9, contains information about Sync Services for ADO.NET 2.0 offline and peer-to-peer collaboration.

Source Code for This Book

The entire code sample found in *Pro Sync Framework* is written using Visual Studio 2008 and C#. The code is available online at www.apress.com/book/sourcecode.

The source code can also be run using Visual Studio 2005. The code is tested on Windows Server 2K and Windows XP.

The database for the code is compatible with SQL Server 2005 as well as SQL Server 2008. You'll find that the code has been organized in chapter format for easy location and execution.

■ ■ ■

CHAPTER 1

Introduction to the Microsoft Sync Framework

Microsoft's answer to a synchronization platform for offline data accessibility is here. The Microsoft Sync Framework (MSF) is a comprehensive framework for synchronizing offline data with its online counterpart. Using this framework, you can build applications that can synchronize data from any data store using any protocol over any type of network. It is independent of the protocol used and the data store that contains the data to be synchronized.

Microsoft says, "Microsoft Sync Framework is a comprehensive synchronization platform that enables collaboration and offline access for applications, services, and devices. It features technologies and tools that enable roaming, sharing, and taking data offline. Using Microsoft Sync Framework, developers can build sync ecosystems that integrate any application, with any data from any store using any protocol over any network."

In this chapter you will learn the following:

- The features and benefits of using the Microsoft Sync Framework and how it can resolve common problems of synchronization

- How to install the Sync Framework

- Different components of the Sync Framework

Benefits of Synchronization

Before we dig into the Sync Framework, it's important to understand what synchronization is and why it is required.

In its simple form, *synchronization* can be described as the process of bringing together two end points or data stores. When the contents of the two data stores are the same, they are known to be *in sync* with each other. For example, if you want to synchronize two databases manually, you do the following (this isn't the best way but it explains the concept in a simple way):

1. Determine changes in the source database.

2. Send the changes to the destination database.

3. Apply the source's changes to the destination database.

4. Repeat the previous steps by swapping the source and destination databases.

Why would you need to build synchronization for an application, store, or services? The following lists some of its benefits:

- *Takes the application, store, or services offline*: The biggest advantage of synchronization is that it enables you to take your application offline. If you build synchronization into your application, users of the application can interact with their local data stores until they need the items that are not contained in a local repository or until the application is back online.

- *Builds a faster and richer user interface*: Building synchronization into the application allows you to build a richer user interface without worrying about the performance of the application. Because data is usually fetched from a local store, your application can provide faster responses.

- *Reduces the network cost*: Sync-enabled applications or services upload and download only incremental changes, thereby reducing the amount of the data that needs to be sent over the network.

Now that you understand the need for synchronization, the next section examines some issues associated with synchronization and how Sync Framework can resolve them.

Life Before Sync Framework

The importance of Sync Framework can't be understood without discussing problems involved while implementing synchronization, including the following:

- *Storage and application errors and failover handling:* Imagine that you're synchronizing two databases, and an application error such as a connection timeout or a constraint violation occurs while changes to the destination database are applied. What happens to the record that needs to be synchronized? It is the responsibility of the Sync Framework to recover from such application and storage errors.

- *Network failure:* Imagine the same example of synchronizing two databases. What happens if one of the databases is downloading changes from another and suddenly the Internet connection goes down? Sync Framework can recover the network failures.

- *Conflict detection:* A conflict is said to occur if the same item was modified at both end points at the same time. The Sync Framework should be able to detect the conflicts and provide a mechanism to resolve or log the conflicts.

Obviously, you can write the code to implement the solution to the problems listed previously. But wouldn't it be nice to have a framework with built-in capabilities to handle all these problems so you can concentrate on implementing business rules instead? Well, allow us to introduce the Microsoft Sync Framework, which is the framework offered by Microsoft to implement synchronization between any data store over any protocol over any network.

Why the Microsoft Sync Framework?

The capability of the synchronization to support offline and online data is the greatest benefit that this framework offers. The major goal of the Sync Framework is to enable any data source to be integrated in the data synchronization, regardless of its type. Imagine a scenario in which the sales data entered in offline mode by a salesperson needs to be in sync with the data available online. The salesperson might be using a smart phone or a personal digital assistant (PDA) to connect to the remote corporate network to retrieve the latest data and information. It is critical for the company to ensure that the data and information are consistent and in sync, regardless of the modes in which they are looked at. This is where the Sync Framework comes into play.

The Sync Framework documentation states, "Microsoft Sync Services for ADO.NET lets you synchronize data from different sources over two-tier, N-tier, and service-based architectures. The Sync Services for ADO.NET API for client and server synchronization provides a set of components to synchronize data between data services and a local store, instead of only replicating a database and its schema."

Here are some of the salient features of the Microsoft Sync Framework:

- A powerful synchronization model independent of the underlying data store, data type, or protocol in use

- Extensible provider model

- Built-in support for filters and data conflict resolution

- Sync support for file systems, databases, and simple sharing extensions (SSEs) such as Really Simple Syndication (RSS) and Atom feeds

- Supports peer-to-peer and hub-and-spoke topologies

- Works with any number of end points over any configuration

- Can be used from managed as well as unmanaged code

Installing Microsoft Sync Framework

At the time of writing, Microsoft Sync Framework 1.0 was the latest release. You can get a copy of the Microsoft Sync Framework software development kit (SDK) in three ways:

- Sync Framework ships with Microsoft SQL Server 2008.

- Sync Framework ships with Microsoft Visual Studio 2008 Service Pack 1.

- You can download the Sync Framework from the Microsoft download page: www.microsoft.com/downloads/details.aspx?FamilyId=C88BA2D1-CEF3-4149-➥ B301-9B056E7FB1E6&displaylang=en.

The Microsoft Sync Framework SDK is available in 11 languages:

- Chinese (Hong Kong)

- Chinese (Simplified)

- English

- German

- French

- Italian

- Japanese

- Korean

- Portuguese

- Russian

- Spanish

The Microsoft Sync Framework SDK is available for three types of processors:

- AMD64

- IA64

- X86

You can download the appropriate version from the Microsoft download page. For example, if you want to download the Sync Framework for the X86 processor in English, select SyncSetup_es.x86.zip.

Before installing the Sync Framework SDK, you must uninstall all previous versions of Microsoft Sync Framework and sync services for ADO.NET 2.0.

The Sync Framework is free on Windows and Windows mobile devices. It supports the following versions of Windows platforms:

- Windows Server 2003

- Windows Vista

- Windows XP

- Windows 2000 Service Pack 3

- Windows Vista Business

- Windows Vista Business 64-bit edition

- Windows Vista Enterprise

- Windows Vista Enterprise 64-bit edition

- Windows Vista Home Basic

- Windows Vista Home Basic 64-bit edition

- Windows Vista Home Premium

- Windows Vista Home Premium 64-bit edition

- Windows Vista Starter

- Windows Vista Ultimate

- Windows Vista Ultimate 64-bit edition

- Windows XP Service Pack 2

Support for other frameworks can be obtained from other commercial licensing and portal kits. For developers who want to implement the Sync Framework on non-Windows platforms, Microsoft is licensing the specifications and source code porting kit. Visit the following MSDN page for more information on licensing: http://msdn.microsoft.com/en-us/sync/bb887636.aspx.

To install Sync Framework, follow these steps:

1. Double-click the setup file to start the installation process. Figure 1-1 shows what the screen looks like.

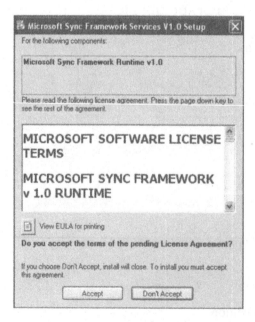

Figure 1-1. *Microsoft Sync Framework setup*

2. Click Accept to accept the license terms and conditions. The installation process for the Sync Framework runtime starts (see Figure 1-2).

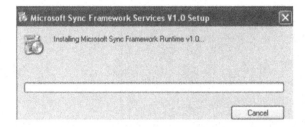

Figure 1-2. *Installing the Microsoft Sync Framework runtime*

3. After the runtime is installed, the installation process continues with the installation of the Sync Framework SDK (see Figure 1-3).

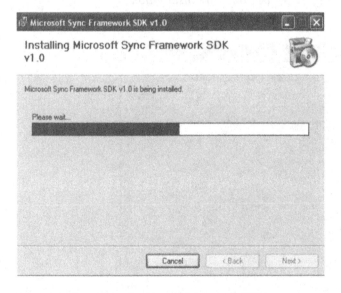

Figure 1-3. *Installing the Sync Framework SDK*

4. After the installation process is complete, you see the message shown in Figure 1-4.

5. If the Sync Framework is already installed in your system and you want to repair it, follow the preceding steps. When prompted whether you want to repair or uninstall it from your system, select the repair option and then click Finish (see Figure 1-5).

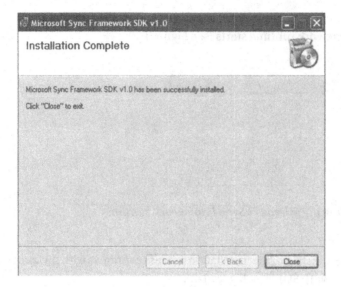

Figure 1-4. *Completing the Sync Framework installation*

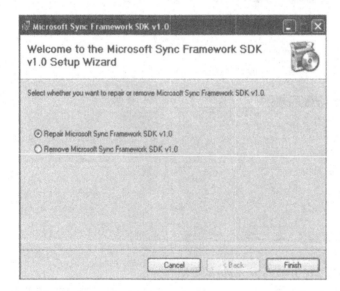

Figure 1-5. *Repairing the Sync Framework*

Core Components

The Sync Framework comes with support for ADO.NET, file systems, RSS, Atom feeds, and even custom data stores. You can divide the components of the Sync Framework into the following three categories:

- *Microsoft Sync Framework runtime*: This SDK allows developers to use the built-in sync providers and create their own sync providers.

- *Metadata services*: Provide the necessary infrastructure to store the sync metadata. Sync metadata is used by the Sync Framework runtime during the synchronization. The Sync Framework ships with the built-in Microsoft SQL Server Compact Edition (CE) that can be used to store the metadata.

- *Built-in providers*: The Sync Framework ships with the following three built-in providers:

  - Synchronization services for ADO.NET provide offline and collaboration support for ADO.NET enabled data stores.

  - Synchronization services for SSEs are the built-in providers for synchronizing RSS and Atom feeds.

  - Synchronization services for file systems are the built-in providers for synchronizing files and folders on Win32-compatible file systems.

Synchronization Providers

You can create custom providers using the Sync Framework runtime to facilitate the support for data synchronization the way you want.

Sync Framework Participants

A discussion on the Sync Framework is incomplete without understanding the participants. A *participant* refers to the location in which the data to be synchronized is retrieved. Note that any one type of participant can synchronize data from any other type of participant. Participants can be one of the following types:

- *Full participants*: Devices that have the capability to create new data stores and execute applications on the device itself. Examples of full participants are laptops, tablet PCs, and smart phones. Full participants can also store the sync metadata required for synchronization. Full participants have the capability to synchronize with any other participants.

- *Partial participants*: Devices that can create new data store and store sync metadata like full participants, but can't create or execute new applications. Thumb drives are good examples of partial participants—they can store the data, but can't execute an application. Partial participants can synchronize with full participants, but they can't synchronize directly with other partial participants.

- *Simple participants*: Devices that can't store new data or execute any application; they just provide the information if requested. Some examples of simple participants include RSS feeds and third-party web services such as those offered by Amazon or Google. Simple participants can synchronize only with full participants because they require sync metadata to be stored on full participants.

Synchronization Flow

Synchronization providers enable you to synchronize data between different replicas. Replicas are also known as end points or data stores. The actual data is stored in the replica. You need to have one sync provider for each replica for the replica to synchronize its data with other replicas. A replica synchronizes its data with another replica by establishing a sync session.

As shown in Figure 1-6, synchronization providers communicate with each other using a sync session. The two sync providers are attached to the sync agent, and the sync application initiates the communication between the two providers using the sync agent. The sync agent is responsible for establishing and managing the sync session. Sync providers can receive and apply changes to the replicas. There are two sync providers on the top of the Sync Framework runtime: the source sync provider and destination sync provider, respectively.

After being invoked by a sync agent, the destination sync provider sends its knowledge to the source sync provider. The source provider uses this knowledge to determine the changes and sends its knowledge to the destination. The destination provider compares its knowledge with the source, resolves the conflicts, and then sends the request to the source provider for changed data. The source provider sends the changes to the destination provider, and the destination provider applies the changes to the destination replica.

Within a sync session, synchronization flow is always in one direction. What this means is that the source provider and the destination provider cannot work simultaneously. At any given point within a sync session, information flows between the source and destination replicas or between destination and source replicas, but doesn't flow simultaneously between both. In its simple form, a sync session contains a sync agent and two sync providers. One of the providers is a source provider that sends the changes; the other is a destination provider that receives and applies the changes. Of course, the sync agent controls this flow.

The sync providers shown in Figure 1-6 illustrate a scenario in which the metadata is stored in the built-in metadata store provided by the Sync Framework, which is very easy to use and is built on top of the SQL Server CE. You can also store the metadata inside your own custom store.

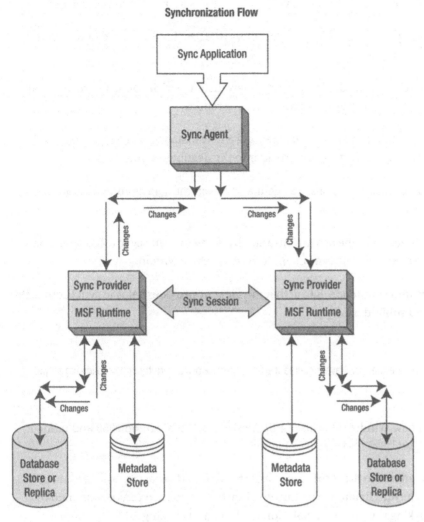

Figure 1-6. *Synchronization flow*

Synchronizing Two Replicas Using Built-in Providers

This section shows you how to synchronize two replicas using the built-in sync provider. The Sync Framework ships with the following three out-of-the-box synchronization providers:

- Synchronization provider for ADO.NET-enabled data sources

- Synchronization provider for files and folders

- Synchronization provider for RSS and Atom feeds

Using the built-in sync providers is very easy. The tasks can be summarized as follows:

1. Create unique Globally Unique Identifiers (GUIDs) for the source replica and destination replica.

2. Create a source provider by creating a new instance of the built-in provider and attaching the source provider to the source replica.

3. Create a destination provider by creating a new instance of the built-in provider and attaching the destination provider to the destination replica.

4. Create a new instance of a sync agent and attach the source and destination provider to it.

5. Set the direction of the synchronization by using the sync agent. The sync application can now use the sync agent to start synchronization.

Let's now dig into some code. Recall that the file sync provider helps to synchronize the files, folders, and subfolders.

Warning Make sure that you have installed the Sync Framework before trying the following steps!

---

1. Create a new Windows Forms application using Visual Studio 2008 and name it SyncApp_BuiltInProviders (see Figure 1-7).

2. Add a reference to Microsoft.Synchronization and Microsoft.Synchronization. Files. (The Add Reference dialog box shown in Figure 1-8 can be launched by right-clicking the project in Solution Explorer and clicking Add a Reference.)

3. Place a button on form1 and name it btnSynchronize with this text: **Synchronize**. Double-click the button to wire an event handler for the button.

4. Place a label on the form with its Name as **label1** and text as **Click on Synchronize button to start the synchronization.**

5. Add two folders in your C drive and name them TestSync1 and TestSync2. Create a new text file in TestSync1 and name it TestSync1.txt. Open the file and type some text into it.

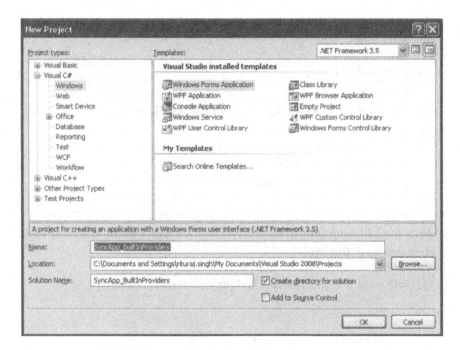

Figure 1-7. *Creating a Sync application*

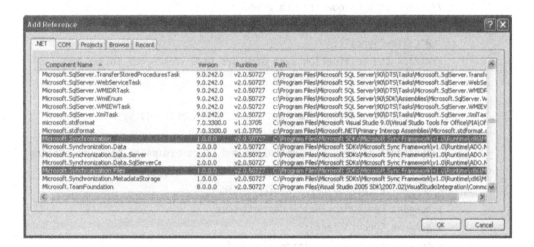

Figure 1-8. *Adding a reference to the Sync Framework*

6. In the using block at the top of the form1.cs, add the following two namespaces:

```
using Microsoft.Synchronization;
using Microsoft.Synchronization.Files;
```

7. Create two new GUIDs for the source and destination replicas, as shown in the following code:

```
Guid sourceReplicaId;
Guid destReplicaId;
private void Form1_Load(object sender, EventArgs e)
{
    //Assign Unique Guid's to the Replicas
    sourceReplicaId = Guid.NewGuid();
    destReplicaId = Guid.NewGuid();
}
```

8. Write the following code in the btnSynchronize_Click event (the main logic of the code resides in this event):

```
private void btnSynchronize_Click(object sender, EventArgs e)
{

    btnSynchronize.Enabled = False;
    //Create the Source and destination Sync provider.
    //Attach the source sync provider to C:\TestSync1 folder and
    //assign it a unique replica guid.
    FileSyncProvider sourceProvider = new FileSyncProvider(sourceReplicaId,
       @"C:\TestSync1");
    //Attach the destination sync provider to C:\TestSync2 folder and
    //assign it a a unique replica guid.
    FileSyncProvider destProvider = new
            FileSyncProvider(destReplicaId, @"C:\TestSync2");

    //syncAgent is the Sync Controller and it co-ordinates the sync session
    SyncOrchestrator syncAgent = new SyncOrchestrator();
    syncAgent.LocalProvider = sourceProvider;
    syncAgent.RemoteProvider = destProvider;
    syncAgent.Synchronize();
    label1.Text = "Synchronizing Finished...";
    btnSynchronize.Enabled = True;
}
```

The code is incredibly simple. We created the source and destination sync providers by passing the replica IDs and the folder name as a parameter. Then we created a new instance of SyncOrchestrator (also known as the sync agent) and attached the two providers to it. Finally we called the Synchronize method on it.

That's it; we wrote the code to synchronize two replicas (TestSync1 and TestSync2) using two instances of a built-in file sync provider.

Run the application and click the Synchronize button. After a few seconds, the message shown in Figure 1-9 displays.

Figure 1- 9. *Synchronization is complete*

Now check the contents of the C:\TestSync2 folder. The file TestSync1.txt is copied into the directory.

Try deleting and updating a file—it works, too! If that's not enough, the file sync provider also does conflict detection and resolution on your behalf. (A *conflict* is said to occur if the same item was modified in both replicas between synchronizations.) We will explore conflicts in detail in Chapters 2 and 3.

Try updating the TestSync1.txt with different text in the two folders and then press Synchronize. The TestSync1.txt file in both the folders is updated with the latest text (the text you updated last).We will cover the file sync provider in detail in Chapter 5.

However, there is a bug in this code. If you try to run the application a second time, you see the message shown in Figure 1-10.

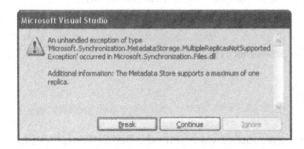

Figure 1-10. *Multiple replicas not supported exception*

When you call the Synchronization method of the SyncOrchestrator, it creates a metadata file in each of the folders (replicas) .This file is called filesync.metadata. When you run the application for the second time, it tries to create a new replica with a different GUID.

We can fix this error by persisting the GUIDS in a data store such as a database or file system instead of creating a new GUID every time. Let's try and store the GUIDs into a file within the local file system.

To fix the bug, follow these steps:

1. In the using block at the top of form1.cs, add the following namespace:

```
using System.IO;
```

2. Create a new GetReplicaGuid method in the form1.cs and paste the following code in it:

```
private Guid GetReplicaGuid(string GuidPath)
{
    if (!File.Exists(GuidPath))
    {
        Guid replicaId = Guid.NewGuid();
        using (FileStream fs = File.Open(GuidPath, FileMode.Create))
        using (StreamWriter sw = new StreamWriter(fs))
        {
            sw.WriteLine(replicaId.ToString());
        }
        return replicaId;
    }

    else
    {
        using (FileStream fs = File.Open(GuidPath, FileMode.Open))
        using (StreamReader sr = new StreamReader(fs))
        {
            return new Guid(sr.ReadLine());
        }
    }
}
```

In the preceding code, we created one more private method called GetReplicaGuid, which has an input string parameter that contains the path to store the IDs of the replica. The method checks whether the file containing a replica ID exists. If the file does not exist, it creates a new replica ID and stores it in the path provided by the input parameter. Finally it returns the replica ID. If the file exists, the method returns the replica ID stored in the file.

3. We also need to move the code for creating file sync providers in the Form load event instead of creating a new provider every time the Synchronize button is pressed, which will prevent a new instance of the sync provider being created every time you press the button. We need to declare the sync providers as a class-level variable so that we can initialize the sync providers in the Form load and use the same instances in the click event of the Synchronize button. To do this, replace the code in the Form load event with the following code listing:

```
Guid sourceReplicaId;
Guid destReplicaId;
FileSyncProvider sourceProvider;
FileSyncProvider destProvider;

private void Form1_Load(object sender, EventArgs e)
{
    //Assign Unique Guid's to the Replicas
    sourceReplicaId = GetReplicaGuid(@"C:\TestSync1\ReplicaID");
    destReplicaId = GetReplicaGuid(@"C:\TestSync2\ReplicaID");
    //Create the Source and destination Sync provider.
    //Attach the source sync provider to C:\TestSync1 folder
       and assign it a a unique replica guid.
    sourceProvider = new FileSyncProvider(sourceReplicaId, @"C:\TestSync1");
    //Attach the destination sync provider to C:\TestSync2 folder
       and assign it a a unique replica guid.
    destProvider = new FileSyncProvider(destReplicaId, @"C:\TestSync2");
}
```

4. The last step is to change the code in the click event of the Synchronize button to remove the instantiation of providers:

```
private void btnSynchronize_Click(object sender, EventArgs e)
{

    btnSynchronize.Enabled = false;
    //syncAgent is the Sync Controller and it co-ordinates the sync session
    SyncOrchestrator syncAgent = new SyncOrchestrator();
    syncAgent.LocalProvider = sourceProvider;
    syncAgent.RemoteProvider = destProvider;
    syncAgent.Synchronize();

    label1.Text = "Synchronizing Finished...";
    btnSynchronize.Enabled = true;
}
```

The complete code can be found at Sync\ChapterI\Code\SyncApp_BuiltInProviders.

Summary

The Microsoft Sync Framework (MSF) is Microsoft's answer for the increasing demand of a common synchronization platform for synchronizing two end points of any type over the network on any protocol. It guarantees an eventual convergence, regardless of common problems such as network failures, storage and application errors, and unhandled conflicts.

The Sync Framework allows developers to focus on their business requirements without paying too much attention to synchronization problems. The Sync Framework ships with built-in providers for synchronizing some very common end points such as files, SSEs such as RSSs and Atom feeds, and ADO.NET-enabled data sources. It also provides developers with the necessary infrastructure to quickly create their own sync providers. Developers can use the built-in SQL Server CE metadata store to store the sync metadata or they can choose their own metadata store.

CHAPTER 2

■ ■ ■

Microsoft Sync Framework Metadata

The Microsoft Sync Framework provides a comprehensive synchronization platform that enables offline and collaboration for applications, stores, and devices without agreeing on the following:

- Type of data to be synchronized

- Type of data store

- Transfer protocols

- Network topology such as peer-to-peer or hub-and-spoke

Instead, the Sync Framework agrees only on a common metadata model that enables the Sync Framework to do the following:

- Achieve interoperability of synchronization

- Reduce the amount of information that has to be sent between two data stores participating in synchronization

- Be independent of any network topology, data type, data store, or transfer protocol

In this chapter, you'll learn in detail about the common metadata model and its different components. We'll also discuss how the Sync Framework uses sync metadata to synchronize different data stores or replicas.

What Is Sync Metadata?

In literal terms, *metadata* means "data about the data." Microsoft sync metadata can be divided into the following two categories:

- Replica metadata

- Item metadata

In the Sync Framework, *replica* is used to refer to the actual data store. For example, if you are synchronizing two databases, each of the databases is known as a *replica* that can contain *items*. (In databases, an item can be a record in a table.)

To synchronize items between the replicas, the Sync Framework requires synchronization providers to agree on a common metadata model, which is the heart of the Sync Framework. Sync Framework providers use this metadata to communicate the changes between the replicas, but do not need to understand sync metadata (it is taken care of by the Sync Framework runtime, which can interpret the metadata for the providers). Sync providers interact with the runtime to query the metadata and find out what changes were made to the replica. They use sync metadata to determine what changes have been made to a replica since the last time the replica was synchronized. Thus, sync metadata enables providers to determine the exact changes that need to be sent from one replica to another.

Sync metadata can also help with conflict detection and resolution. A *conflict* is said to occur if the same item is modified in both replicas during synchronization. Sync providers use the metadata to determine whether an item is in conflict stage and then use the metadata to resolve the conflicts.

Sync metadata is also used by the Sync Framework runtime to solve common synchronization problems such as network failure, conflicting data, and application errors. Sync metadata ensures eventual convergence, despite these errors. For example, consider the scenario in which you have to synchronize two remote databases, A and B, on two different machines. Now imagine that while sending the changes (added/deleted/modified records) from database A to database B, your Internet connection goes down. What happens to the changes in this case? If you're using a Sync Framework that uses a metadata store, the changes are not lost. When the synchronization is initiated next time, the sync provider will use the metadata to determine changes made in database A by using its metadata. After applying these changes to database B, the sync provider will also update the database B metadata.

Metadata Store

You might be wondering where this metadata is stored. Metadata can be stored anywhere: in a file, a separate database, or a replica. The only thing you need to make sure while choosing the metadata store is that it should be programmatically accessible. The Sync

Framework invokes different methods on the sync providers, which try to retrieve and update the metadata. You should design your metadata store so you can return and modify the metadata when these methods are executed.

The sync provider is usually responsible for storing metadata, but you can also delegate this task to the Sync Framework runtime. As shown in Figure 2-1, the Sync Framework ships with a complete implementation of the metadata store. It's built on top of SQL Server Compact Edition (SQL CE), which you can leverage to store the metadata. You can store the metadata in your own custom store, but using the built-in SQL CE metadata store provides abstraction on how to store the sync metadata.

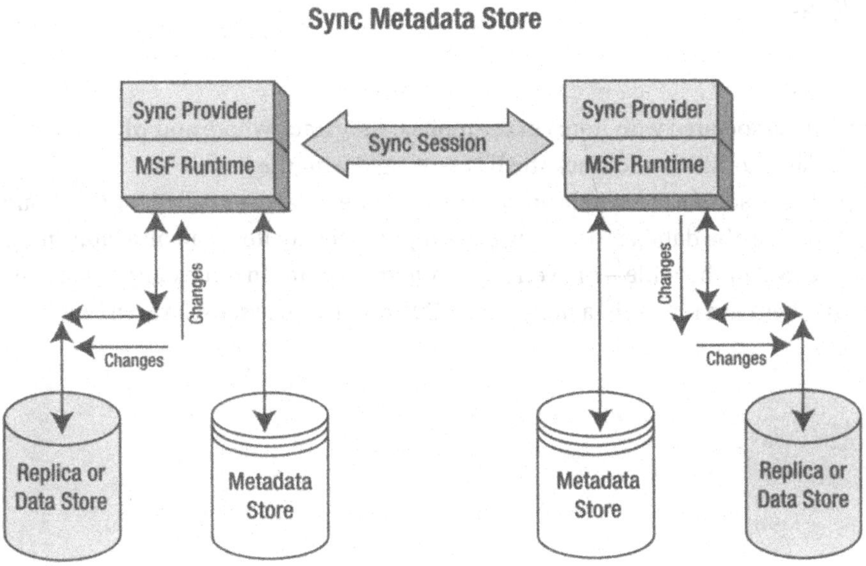

Figure 2-1. *Sync metadata store*

The decision to use the built-in metadata store or the custom metadata store is made by the developer creating the synchronization application. When selecting the metadata store, follow these two rules:

- If the replica or data store involved in synchronization is extensible, and you can change the schema, you should try to store the metadata in the application data store because it provides unified access.

- If it's not possible to change the schema of existing data store, you can leverage the built-in SQL CE metadata store. This store is very easy to use, and Microsoft Sync Framework provides an API to access the store.

The following two chapters will show you how to use the built-in and custom metadata stores, but first you need to understand the different constituents of metadata. In the remainder of this chapter, we will go into detail about each component of the metadata.

Components of Sync Metadata

Sync metadata for a metadata store can be divided into following two components:

- Version

- Knowledge

Version

Sync versions are associated with items in the replica: they track where and when an item was created or last modified, and track the ID associated with the item.

For example, let's say we are synchronizing two remote databases called replica A and replica B. In this case, the database is acting like a replica, and an item can be a table in the database or a record in the table—or even a column in a record. In our example, we will assume that the item is a record in a table called Customer whose schema is shown in Figure 2-2.

Figure 2-2. *Customer table*

Initially, let's assume that there are two records in this Customer table, as shown in Figure 2-3.

Figure 2-3. *Customer records in replica A*

Assuming that we use the ID field in the customer table as the item ID, the version information for the records in the table can be represented by the following table.

Table 2-1. *Version Information for the Customer Table*

Item ID	When		Where	
	Created at	**Last Modified at**	**Created in**	**Last Modified in**
1	1	1	A	A
2	2	2	A	A

As you can see in Table 2-1, the item version records when and where an item was modified or created, and also records the item ID linked to the item. Versions can be further classified into two types:

- *Creation version*: Records when and where an item was created.

- *Update version*: Records when and where an item was last modified.

Each of these versions is made up of the following two components:

- *Tick count*: A theoretical number that can be derived by incrementing the latest local version. Tick count is created by a logical sync clock used source-wide to uniquely identify a change. In its simplest form, you should increment the tick count whenever an item is created or modified.

- *Replica ID*: Uniquely identifies the replica in which an item was modified or created.

In our example, when the Customer1 record was created, we set the creation and update tick count to 1. When Customer2 was created, we incremented the tick count by 1, and updated the creation and update tick count to 2. Note that the creation version and update version are the same when the item is created in a replica.

Now we create a record in the Customer table in replica B (see Figure 2-4).

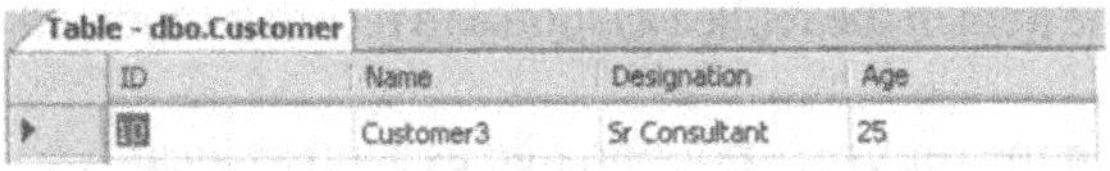

Figure 2-4. *Customer records in replica B*

The version information of the item in replica B is shown in Table 2-2.

Table 2-2. *Version Information for Replica B*

Item ID	When		Where	
	Created at	**Last Modified at**	**Created in**	**Last Modified in**
10	3	3	B	B

To demonstrate how update version works, let's update the Customer1 record in replica A (see Figure 2-5).

Figure 2-5. *Updated customer records in replica A*

Now the version information is updated, as shown in Table 2-3. Notice that the last modified column is changed to 4.

Table 2-3. *Updated Version Information for Replica A*

Item ID	When		Where	
	Created at	**Last Modified at**	**Created in**	**Last Modified in**
1	1	1	A	A
2	2	4	A	A

This process of versioning is also known as *change tracking*. To implement change tracking, the sync provider needs to update the sync versions for the changed items whenever changes happen in the replica. Change tracking can be implemented in two ways:

- *Inline tracking:* In this method of tracking, the item version in the replica is updated when a local change is made to the replica. Inline tracking is used in the scenarios when it is easy to plug in the logic for updating the replica version into the methods that change the content of the replica. For example, when synchronizing databases it can be a good idea to use inline tracking. In this case, we can use the triggers on the database to update the version of the item in the replica as soon as a record is modified.

- *Asynchronous tracking:* The item in the replica is not updated as soon as local changes happen in the replica. Instead, an external service or process is called on the replica to scan the changes and update the version of the item in the replica. This process can be made a part of a scheduled process. Asynchronous tracking is used in scenarios in which it is difficult to plug in the logic for updating the version of the item in the replica into the methods that change the content of the replica.

Both methods of change tracking must happen at least at the item level. Change tracking helps to minimize conflicts between two replicas. That said, the more granular change tracking becomes, the more change tracking information we need to store.

You might wonder whether versioning is similar to the timestamp-based synchronization technique. In timestamp-based synchronization, created and modified dates are recorded. But timestamp-based synchronization is not as smart as the Sync Framework in terms of conflict resolution or handling network and application failures. In the later sections of this chapter, you will learn how the Sync Framework uses the common metadata model to handle these problems and thereby enables developers to focus on the actual application, not on synchronization problems.

Knowledge

Knowledge is a compact representation of version or changes that a given replica is aware of. Unlike versions that are associated with items, knowledge is associated with the sync scope. Knowledge contains information about changes made directly or indirectly (via synchronization) to a replica. Synchronization knowledge is not usually directly used by sync providers; instead, the Sync Framework runtime invokes methods on the providers that manipulate the knowledge of the replica.

Sync providers use the knowledge for change enumeration and conflict detection. We will cover change enumeration and conflict detection in more detail in Chapter 3. For now, remember the following definition of change enumeration and conflict detection:

- *Change enumeration* determines changes made to a replica that other replicas don't know about.

- *Conflict detection* determines which operations were made by a replica that another replica doesn't know about.

If we go back to our examples of two remote databases, the knowledge of the replica can be represented as follows:

- The knowledge of replica A (whose content is shown in Figure 2-5) is A4.

- The knowledge of replica B (whose content is shown in Figure 2-4) is B3.

The knowledge of the replica is represented by a combination of the replica ID and the current or latest tick count of the item in the replica.

Example of Sync Metadata Use

Now let's discuss how the Sync Framework uses the sync metadata to synchronize two replicas or end points. We'll continue to use our example of synchronizing two remote databases, replica A and replica B.

Let's assume that replica A is trying to synchronize its data with replica B. In this case, replica A becomes the source replica and replica B becomes the destination replica.

Content of Replica A

Assume that there are two customer records in replica A. The content of replica A is shown in Figure 2-6.

Figure 2-6. *Customer records in replica A*

The version information for replica A is shown in Table 2-4.

Table 2-4. *Version Information for Replica A*

Item ID	When		Where	
	Created at	Last Modified at	Created in	Last Modified in
1	1	1	A	A
2	2	4	A	A

Knowledge of replica A = A4.

Content of Replica B

Assume that there is one customer record in replica B. The content of replica B is shown in Figure 2-7.

Figure 2-7. *Customer records in replica B*

Version information for replica B is shown in Table 2-5.

Table 2-5. *Version Information for Replica B*

Item ID	When		Where	
	Created at	Last Modified at	Created in	Last Modified in
10	3	3	B	B

Knowledge of replica B = B3.

The destination replica sends its knowledge (B3) to the source replica A. The source provider enumerates the changes in the source replica and determines the changes that need to be sent to destination replica B by using the destination knowledge. The source provider then sends the change batch to the destination replica. The change batch is shown in Table 2-6.

Table 2-6. *Change Batch for Replica A*

Item ID	When		Where	
	Created at	Last Modified at	Created in	Last Modified in
1	1	1	A	A
2	2	4	A	A

As shown in the table, the destination replica is not aware of any items in the source replica.

Upon receiving the versions from the source replica, the destination replica determines the items in the source replica that the destination replica does not know about. Conflict detection is also done here (a conflict is said to occur if the same record is modified in both replicas during the synchronization).

Now the destination replica requests actual records from the source replica. The source replica sends the records with Customer1 and Customer2 to the destination replica. The destination provider inserts these two records in the destination replica and updates its knowledge as well.

Content of Replica B

The content of replica B is shown in Figure 2-8.

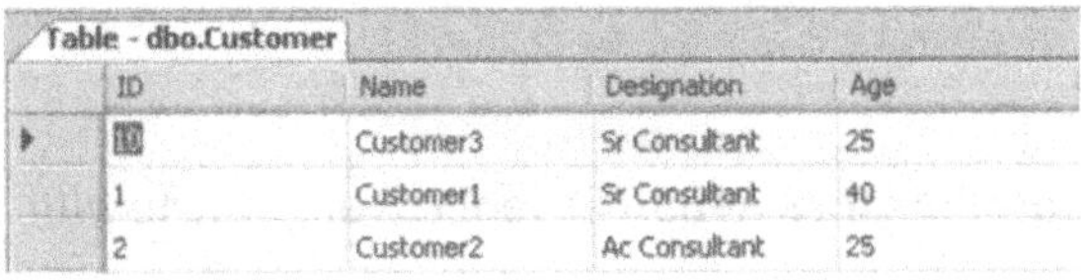
Table - dbo.Customer

ID	Name	Designation	Age
10	Customer3	Sr Consultant	25
1	Customer1	Sr Consultant	40
2	Customer2	Ac Consultant	25

Figure 2-8. *Customer records in replica B after synchronization*

Table 2-7 shows version information for replica B.

Knowledge of replica B = A4B3.

To update the records in replica A, the process is reversed.

Table 2-7. *Version Information for Replica B*

Item ID	When		Where	
	Created at	Last Modified at	Created in	Last Modified in
10	3	3	B	B
1	1	1	A	A
2	2	4	A	A

Content of Replica A

After synchronization is done, the content of replica A is illustrated by Figure 2-9.

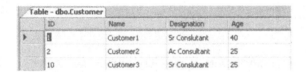

Figure 2-9. *customer records in replica A after synchronization*

Version information for replica A is shown in Table 2-8.

Table 2-8. *Version Information for Replica A*

Item ID	When		Where	
	Created at	Last Modified at	Created in	Last Modified in
1	1	1	A	A
2	2	4	A	A
10	3	3	B	B

Knowledge of replica A = A4B3.

The knowledge of replica A and B are now the same: A4B3.The replicas are in sync with each other.

Now let's see an example of how the Sync Framework uses metadata to detect conflicts.

Content of Replica A

Assume that the age of Customer1 is modified in the Customer table in both replicas. The content of the replica is shown in Figure 2-10.

Table - dbo.Customer

ID	Name	Designation	Age
1	Customer1	Sr Consultant	60
2	Customer2	Ac Consultant	25
10	Customer3	Sr Consultant	25

Figure 2-10. *Customer records in replica A*

Version information for replica A is shown in Table 2-9.

Table 2-9. *Version Information for Replica A*

Item ID	When		Where	
	Created at	Last Modified at	Created in	Last Modified in
1	1	5	A	A
2	2	4	A	A
10	3	3	B	B

Knowledge of replica A = A5B3.

Content of Replica B

The content of replica B is illustrated by Figure 2-11.

Table - dbo.Customer

ID	Name	Designation	Age
10	Customer3	Sr Consultant	25
1	Customer1	Sr Consultant	20
2	Customer2	Ac Consultant	25

Figure 2-11. *Customer records in replica B*

Version information for replica B is shown in Table 2-10.

Table 2-10. *Version Information for Replica B*

Item ID	When		Where	
	Created at	Last Modified at	Created in	Last Modified in
10	3	3	B	B
1	1	6	A	B
2	2	4	A	A

Knowledge of replica B = A4B6.

Let's now assume that replica A as the source replica and replica B is the destination replica. Initiate the synchronization, using the steps that follow, which describe the flow:

1. Destination replica B sends its knowledge A4B6 to source replica A.

2. The source replica receives this knowledge and computes the change batch that needs to be sent to the destination replica. The source provider examines the destination replica's knowledge and detects that that it does not know about the change in Customer1 made at tick count 5. It then sends the item version shown in Table 2-11 to the destination replica.

Table 2-11. *Item Version for Replica A*

Item ID	When		Where	
	Created at	Last Modified at	Created in	Last Modified in
1	1	5	A	A

3. The destination provider receives this change batch and enumerates the changes in its local replica. It detects that the same item was also modified in the local destination replica. So now it has two change versions, as shown in Tables 2-12 and 2-13.

Table 2-12. *Change Batch from Replica A*

Item ID	When		Where	
	Created at	Last Modified at	Created in	Last Modified in
1	1	5	A	A

Table 2-13. *Local Change Version from Replica B*

Item ID	When		Where	
	Created at	Last Modified at	Created in	Last Modified in
1	1	6	A	B

This is a conflict; the destination provider has the following options to resolve it:

- *Source wins*: Overwrites the destination replica's changes with the source replica.

- *Destination wins*: Overwrites the source replica's changes with destination replica.

- *Skip change*: Ignores the conflict and handles it later.

- *Merge change*: Merges the source and destination replicas' changes

- *Save conflict*: Logs the conflict for later handling.

Now that you have a fairly good understanding of what metadata is and how it is used by the Sync Framework, let's dig deeper into the details of metadata requirements and the structure of the sync metadata.

Sync Metadata Requirement

As discussed earlier in this chapter, there are two types of metadata: replica metadata and item metadata. To implement a common metadata model, the Sync Framework not only requires a set of required metadata for replica and the item but also enforces storage rules on the underlying metadata store. This section discusses the requirements of sync metadata.

Required Metadata for the Replica

A replica requires the following set of metadata to be stored in the metadata store:

- *Replica ID*: Uniquely identifies the replica participating in the synchronization.

- *Current tick count*: A theoretical number that can be derived by incrementing the latest local version. Tick count is created by a logical sync clock used source-wide to uniquely identify a change. In its simplest form, you should increment the tick count whenever an item is created or modified. The replica is required to store only the latest or current tick count.

- *Replica key map*: Efficiently stores the replica ID in the metadata store to save some storage. The replica ID is usually a 16-bit Globally Unique Identifier (GUID) and is repeated many times in the metadata store. It breaks the replica ID into two parts:

  - Replica ID

  - 4-byte keys

  These 4-byte keys are stored in another table to reduce the amount of space required to store the 16-bit replica GUID that has multiple occurrences in the metadata store.

- *Current knowledge*: Knowledge of the replica at a given stage in the synchronization process.

- *Forgotten knowledge*: Contains information about deleted items in a replica that the other replica does not know about.

- *Conflict log*: Stores the information about the conflicts detected at the destination replica. Replicas are free to choose the format of the conflict log; the only requirement is that the Sync Framework should be able to access and enumerate the log.

- *Tombstone log*: Contains information about the deleted items in a replica. Like the conflict log, replicas can choose the format of the tombstone log, but the Sync Framework should be able to access and enumerate the log.

Required Metadata for the Item

An item requires the following set of metadata to be stored in the metadata store:

- *Global item ID*: Uniquely identifies an item within a replica.

- *Current version*: Tracks when an item was last modified in the replica.

- *Creation version*: Tracks when an item was created.

Summary

In this chapter, you learned about the synchronization metadata. Sync metadata is the heart of the Sync Framework runtime. The Sync Framework relies on the common metadata model for solving various common synchronization problems such as conflict detection, network failures, and storage and application errors. The sync metadata makes synchronization using the Sync Framework independent of network topology, type of data store, types of data, and transfer protocols.

The Sync Framework ships with a built-in store for storing sync metadata. This built-in metadata store is easy to use and is built on top of the SQL Server CE. You can also store the sync metadata in your own custom metadata store. In Chapter 3, we'll create a provider that uses the built-in metadata store; in Chapter 4, we'll use a provider with a custom metadata store.

■ ■ ■

Working with Synchronization Providers: Part 1

In the last two chapters, you had the opportunity to learn what synchronization is and what are the different features offered by the Microsoft Sync Framework (MSF) for synchronizing different data stores also known as replicas. As discussed, the Sync Framework ships with three out-of-the box synchronization providers:

- Synchronization provider for ADO.NET-enabled data sources

- Synchronization provider for files and folders

- Synchronization provider for RSS and Atom feeds

In this chapter, you'll learn what a sync provider is and how to synchronize two replicas using the built-in sync providers.

You should always try to use existing providers wherever possible because they not only enable you to reuse the already existing and tested code but also reduce the development time. But what if you are trying to synchronize two replicas and there is no provider available for your replica? For example, suppose that you're trying to synchronize the data for a line of business applications or a custom application; you need to create a new custom synchronization provider using the Sync Framework.

In this chapter, you'll learn how to create your own custom sync provider. You'll also begin to understand the synchronization flow and what the different steps involved in building your own synchronization provider are. After reading this chapter, not only will you be able to use the built-in provider but you will also create your own custom sync provider.

What Is a Sync Provider?

Synchronization providers enable you to synchronize data between different replicas (also known as *end points* or *data stores*). You need to have one sync provider for each replica in order for the replica to synchronize its data with other replicas. A replica synchronizes its data with another replica by establishing a sync session.

As shown in Figure 3-1, sync providers communicate with each other using a sync session. The two sync providers are attached to the sync agent, and the sync application initiates the communication between the two providers using the sync agent. The sync agent is the one responsible for establishing and managing the sync session. Sync providers can receive and apply changes to the replicas. The figure shows two sync providers on the top of the Sync Framework runtime: the source sync provider and destination sync provider.

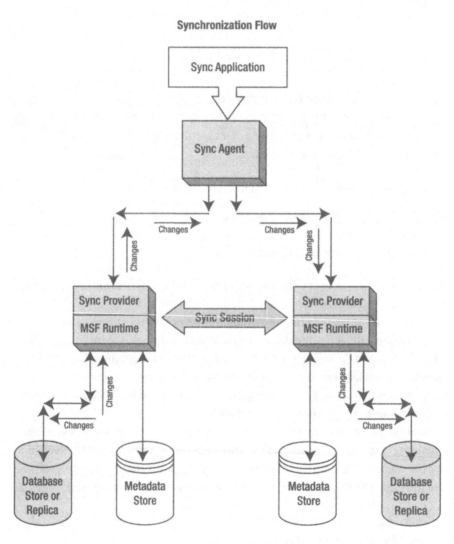

Figure 3-1. *Synchronization flow*

After being invoked by a sync agent, a destination provider sends its knowledge to the source sync provider. The source provider uses this knowledge to determine the changes and sends its knowledge to the destination provider. The destination provider then compares its knowledge with the source provider, resolves the conflicts, and sends the request to the source provider for changed data. The source provider sends the changes to the destination provider, which applies the changes to the destination replica.

Within a sync session, the synchronization flow is always in one direction, so the source provider and destination provider can't work simultaneously. At any point in a sync session, sync flows between a source and destination replica, or between a destination and source replica, but not simultaneously between both. So a sync session contains a sync agent and two sync providers in its simple form. One provider is a source provider that sends the changes, and the other is a destination provider that receives and applies the changes. Of course, the sync agent controls this flow.

Figure 3-1 shows the scenario in which metadata is stored in the built-in metadata store provided by the Sync Framework. The built-in sync metadata store is very easy to use and is built on top of SQL Server Compact Edition (CE). You can also store the metadata inside your own custom store.

Synchronizing Two Replicas Using Built-in Providers

Let's look at an example of synchronizing two replicas using the built-in file sync provider. Recall that file sync providers help to synchronize files, folders, and subfolders in NT file system (NTFS), file allocation table (FAT), and Server Message Block (SMB) file systems. (We covered an example of synchronizing files between two folders in Chapter 1. Code for this sample can be found at Sync\ChapterI\Code\SyncApp_BuiltInProviders.)

■Note Make sure that you have installed the Sync Framework before trying the following steps! (Refer to Chapter 1 for more details on installation.)

The solution structure of the example is shown in Figure 3-2.

To use a built-in file sync provider, first you need to add a reference to Microsoft. Synchronization and Microsoft.Synchronization.Files, as shown in Figure 3-3.

Figure 3-2. *Solution structure*

Figure 3-3. *Adding a reference to the MSF*

The code for synchronizing files is written inside the btnSynchronize_Click event, as shown in the following code listing:

```
private void btnSynchronize_Click(object sender, EventArgs e)
{

        //Create the Source and destination Sync provider.
        //Attach the source sync provider to C:\TestSync1 folder
        //and assign it a unique replica guid.
```

```
    FileSyncProvider sourceProvider = new
    FileSyncProvider(sourceReplicaId, @"C:\TestSync1");
    //Attach the destination sync provider to C:\TestSync2
//folder and assign it a unique replica guid.
    FileSyncProvider destProvider = new
    FileSyncProvider(destReplicaId, @"C:\TestSync2");

    //syncAgent is the Sync Controller and it co-ordinates the
    //sync session
    SyncOrchestrator syncAgent = new SyncOrchestrator();
    syncAgent.LocalProvider = sourceProvider;
    syncAgent.RemoteProvider = destProvider;
    syncAgent.Synchronize();

    label1.Text = "Synchronizing Finished...";


    }


  }
}
```

We created the source and destination sync providers by passing the replica IDs and the folder name as parameters. Then we created a new instance of SyncOrchestrator and attached the two providers to it. Finally we called the Synchronize method on it.

In the preceding code, GetReplicaGuid.method has an input string parameter that contains the path to store the IDs of the replica. The method checks whether the file containing replica ID exists. If the file does not exist, it creates a new replica ID and stores it in the path provided by the input parameter. Finally it returns the replica ID. If the file exists, the method returns the replica ID stored in the file.

Now that you have fairly good understanding of what a sync provider is, let's discuss the steps involved in creating a custom sync provider.

Creating a Synchronization Provider

Provider writers usually start writing their own providers by deriving from the KnowledgeSyncProvider, IChangeDataRetriever, INotifyingChangeApplierTarget classes.

KnowledgeSyncProvider is an abstract class that inherits from the SyncProvider class available in the Microsoft.Synchronization namespace. The following code snippet shows the anatomy of the class:

```
public abstract class KnowledgeSyncProvider : SyncProvider
    {
        protected KnowledgeSyncProvider();
        public KnowledgeSyncProviderConfiguration Configuration { get; }
        public SyncCallbacks DestinationCallbacks { get; }
        public abstract SyncIdFormatGroup IdFormats { get; }
        public abstract void BeginSession(SyncProviderPosition
        position, SyncSessionContext syncSessionContext);
        public abstract void EndSession(SyncSessionContext syncSessionContext);
        public abstract ChangeBatch GetChangeBatch(uint batchSize,
        SyncKnowledge destinationKnowledge, out object
        changeDataRetriever);
        public abstract FullEnumerationChangeBatch
        GetFullEnumerationChangeBatch(uint batchSize, SyncId
        lowerEnumerationBound, SyncKnowledge
        knowledgeForDataRetrieval, out object changeDataRetriever);
        public abstract void GetSyncBatchParameters(out uint
        batchSize, out SyncKnowledge knowledge);

        public abstract void
        ProcessChangeBatch(ConflictResolutionPolicy resolutionPolicy,
        ChangeBatch sourceChanges, object changeDataRetriever,
        SyncCallbacks syncCallbacks, SyncSessionStatistics
        sessionStatistics);
        public abstract void
        ProcessFullEnumerationChangeBatch(ConflictResolutionPolicy
        resolutionPolicy, FullEnumerationChangeBatch sourceChanges,
        object changeDataRetriever, SyncCallbacks syncCallbacks,
        SyncSessionStatistics sessionStatistics);
    }
```

To build the sync provider, we need to implement the methods from this class. Don't concern yourself with the contents of the class right now; we will cover them in detail later in the chapter.

IChangeDataRetriever is an interface available in the Sync Framework. As shown following, it contains only one method and property that we'll need to implement:

```
public interface IChangeDataRetriever
    {
    SyncIdFormatGroup IdFormats { get; }
    object LoadChangeData(LoadChangeContext loadChangeContext);
    }
```

The INotifyingChangeApplierTarget is also an interface available in the Microsoft.
Synchronization namespace that we need to implement to write our provider. The contents
of the interface are shown in the following code snippet:

```
public interface INotifyingChangeApplierTarget
    {
        SyncIdFormatGroup IdFormats { get; }
        IChangeDataRetriever GetDataRetriever();
        ulong GetNextTickCount();
        void SaveChangeWithChangeUnits(ItemChange change,
        SaveChangeWithChangeUnitsContext context);
        void SaveConflict(ItemChange conflictingChange, object
        conflictingChangeData, SyncKnowledge
        conflictingChangeKnowledge);
        void SaveItemChange(SaveChangeAction saveChangeAction,
        ItemChange change, SaveChangeContext context);
        void StoreKnowledgeForScope(SyncKnowledge knowledge,
        ForgottenKnowledge forgottenKnowledge);
        bool TryGetDestinationVersion(ItemChange sourceChange, out
        ItemChange destinationVersion);
    }
```

The next important step before writing a sync provider is to understand the flow of data
between two replicas in a sync session using synchronization providers and how the
Sync Framework makes calls to implement different methods from the classes specified
previously.

As discussed earlier in this chapter, a sync agent (also known as a sync orchestrator)
controls the sync session and thereby manages the synchronization flow. Note that the
flow is unidirectional within a sync session, and there is always a source provider hooked
to a source replica and a destination provider hooked to a destination replica. In a typical
synchronization between two replicas, the following steps are involved in the synchronization flow:

1. SyncApp creates a new instance of the sync agent (the SyncOrchestrator class) and
   attaches the source sync provider and destination provider to the sync agent. Recall
   the code that we wrote for using the file system provider:

```
//Create the Source and destination Sync provider.
        //Attach the source sync provider to C:\TestSync1 folder and
        //assign it a unique replica guid.
        FileSyncProvider sourceProvider = new
        FileSyncProvider(sourceReplicaId, @"C:\TestSync1");
```

```
//Attach the destination sync provider to C:\TestSync2 folder
//and assign it a a unique replica guid.
FileSyncProvider destProvider = new
 FileSyncProvider(destReplicaId, @"C:\TestSync2");
 //syncAgent is the Sync Controller and it co-ordinates the sync
//session
SyncOrchestrator syncAgent = new SyncOrchestrator();
syncAgent.LocalProvider = sourceProvider;
syncAgent.RemoteProvider = destProvider;
syncAgent.Synchronize();
```

2. Then SyncApp calls the Synchronize method on the sync agent, which creates a link between the source and destination provider:

```
syncAgent.Synchronize();
```

The destination provider communicates with its replica (destination replica) and sends the replica knowledge to the source provider. Recall that knowledge of a replica is nothing but a watermark; it is a compact representation of the data changes that a replica knows about. Knowledge is associated with a particular sync scope.

The Sync Framework calls the GetSyncBatchParameters method on the destination provider. If you review the signature of this method in the KnowledgeSyncProvider class, you will notice that it has two out parameters: batchSize and knowledge:

```
public abstract void GetSyncBatchParameters(out uint batchSize,
out SyncKnowledge knowledge);
```

The first parameter, batchSize, is an integer that returns the batch size; the second parameter, knowledge, is the SyncKnowledge type and returns the knowledge of the destination.

3. The source provider receives the knowledge from the destination provider. The source provider compares this knowledge with its local item versions. Recall that a version is associated with an item. The item version tells us when and where (in which replica) the item was created or last modified. By comparing the destination knowledge with local item versions, the source sync provider can determine changes the destination replica is not aware of. The source sync provider prepares the list of the changes and then sends those changed versions and its own knowledge to the destination provider. At this time the source sync provider sends only the changed versions and knowledge, not the actual items.

To perform this step, the Sync Framework calls the GetChangeBatch method on the source provider. Let's review the signature of this method:

```
public abstract ChangeBatch GetChangeBatch(uint batchSize,
SyncKnowledge destinationKnowledge, out object
changeDataRetriever);
```

This method receives batchSize and destinationKnowledge as two input parameters. After comparing it with local item versions, the source sync provider sends the summary of changed versions and knowledge to the destination provider in the form of the changeDataRetriever object.

4. After receiving the changed version and knowledge from the source provider, the destination provider first retrieves its own local versions for the items that were changed at the source. The destination provider also detects and resolves or defers conflicts. We will explore conflicts in more detail later in this chapter. For right now, understand that a conflict is detected when the same item was modified in both the replicas during synchronization. After resolving conflicts, the destination provider requests the actual items from the source provider.

The Sync Framework calls the ProcessChangeBatch method on the destination provider whose signature is shown as follows:

```
public abstract void ProcessChangeBatch(ConflictResolutionPolicy
resolutionPolicy, ChangeBatch sourceChanges, object
changeDataRetriever, SyncCallbacks syncCallbacks,
SyncSessionStatistics sessionStatistics);
```

The destination provider receives the changed versions and source knowledge in the form of two input parameters: sourceChanges and changeDataRetriever.

The destination provider also receives a parameter called resolutionPolicy of the type ConflictResolutionPolicy. This parameter defines the way conflicts are handled. If you look at the definition of ConflictResolutionPolicy given as follows, you see that it's an enumerator (enum) with three values:

```
public enum ConflictResolutionPolicy
  {
   ApplicationDefined = 0,
   DestinationWins = 1,
   SourceWins = 2,
  }
```

If the ConflictResolutionPolicy is set to ApplicationDefined, the provider leaves the handling of the conflict to the synchronizing application.

If you set the value of the ConflictResolutionPolicy to DestinationWins, the changes made by the destination replica overwrites the changes made by the source replica. In other words, no change is made to the destination item.

If you set the value of the ConflictResolutionPolicy to SourceWins, the changes made by the source replica overwrite the changes made by the destination replica. In other words, no changes are made to the source item.

The Sync Framework provides supports for callbacks. The destination provider receives an object of the SyncCallbacks class. Let's examine the content of this class:

```
public class SyncCallbacks
{
  public SyncCallbacks();
  public event EventHandler<FullEnumerationNeededEventArgs>
   FullEnumerationNeeded;
  public event EventHandler<ItemChangeSkippedEventArgs>
ItemChangeSkipped;
  public event EventHandler<ItemChangingEventArgs> ItemChanging;
  public event EventHandler<ItemConflictingEventArgs> ItemConflicting;
  public event EventHandler<SyncStagedProgressEventArgs>
   ProgressChanged;
  public virtual void

  OnFullEnumerationNeeded(FullEnumerationNeededEventArgs args);
  public virtual void OnItemChanging(ItemChangingEventArgs args);
  public virtual void OnItemConflicting(ItemConflictingEventArgs args);
  public virtual void
   OnProgressChanged(SyncStagedProgressEventArgs
   args);
  public virtual void
   OnRecoverableError(ItemChangeSkippedEventArgs
   args);
}
```

The SyncCallbacks class contains following five important events and five callback methods:

- The OnFullEnumerationNeeded method sends the FullEnumerationNeeded event. This event is raised when the forgotten knowledge from the source provider is not contained in the current knowledge of the destination provider.

- The OnItemChanging method sends the ItemChanging event. This event is raised before a change is applied.

- The OnItemConflicting method sends the ItemConflicting event. This event is raised when a conflict is detected, and the conflict resolution policy is set to applicationDefined.

- The OnProgressChanged method sends the ProgressChanged event. This event is raised periodically during the synchronization session to report progress.

- The OnRecoverableError method sends the ItemChangeSkipped event. This event is raised when a synchronization provider sets a recoverable error during loading or saving.

The last parameter in ProcessChangeBatch method is sessionStatistics, which is of the type SyncSessionStatistics:

```
public class SyncSessionStatistics
  {
    public SyncSessionStatistics();
    public uint ChangesApplied { get; set; }
    public uint ChangesFailed { get; set; }
  }
```

As the name suggests, the SyncSessionStatistics class represents the statistics about the sync session. The ChangesApplied property gets or sets the total number of changes applied successfully during a sync session. The ChangesFailed property gets or sets the total number of changes not applied or failed during a sync session.

5. After receiving the request for changed items from the destination provider, the source provider retrieves those items from its replica and sends them to the destination provider. For example, if we are synchronizing two folders, the item being tracked is a file, and the entire file will be sent to the destination provider.

To achieve this, the Sync Framework calls the LoadChangeData method that the source provider needs to implement:

```
object LoadChangeData(LoadChangeContext loadChangeContext);
```

This is the reason why we derived our provider from the IChangeDataRetriever interface.

6. The destination provider receives the items from the source provider, applies them to its local replica, and updates the destination knowledge with the source knowledge. The destination provider can also handle any failures. In case of a failure, the destination provider marks the items as exceptions so that they can be handled during next sync session.

The Sync Framework calls the SaveItemChange method, which the destination provider needs to implement (which is why we derived our provider from INotifyingChangeApplierTarget interface):

```
void SaveItemChange(SaveChangeAction saveChangeAction, ItemChange change,
SaveChangeContext context);
```

This method is called for each change in the change batch. The method has the following parameter types:

- SaveChangeAction is an enum that specifies the type of action indicated by a change. Valid values for this enum are defined as follows and described in Table 3-1:

```
public enum SaveChangeAction
{
    Create = 0,
    UpdateVersionOnly = 1,
    UpdateVersionAndData = 2,
    UpdateVersionAndMergeData = 3,
    DeleteAndStoreTombstone = 4,
    DeleteAndRemoveTombstone = 5,
}
```

Table 3-1. *SaveChangeAction Enumerator*

Action Value	What It Tells the Destination Provider
Create	The item is a new item created in the source replica that also needs to be created in the destination replica.
UpdateVersionOnly	Only the item version should be updated in the destination replica, and item data should not be updated. This action corresponds to DestinationWins in conflict resolution. So existing data in destination is *not* overwritten.

Table 3-1. *SaveChangeAction Enumerator*

Action Value	What It Tells the Destination Provider
UpdateVersionAndData	Both the item data and the item version should be updated in the destination replica. This could be caused by creating/updating an item or updating a change unit in the source replica. This situation corresponds to SourceWins in conflict resolution.
UpdateVersionAndMergeData	Existing item data in the destination replica should be merged with the updated item from the source provider. The item version at the destination should be overwritten with the version at the source. This situation corresponds to merge in conflict resolution.
DeleteAndStoreTombstone	The item data should be deleted from the destination store. The destination replica should also store the tombstone information for each deleted item. This situation is a result of an item being deleted from the source replica.
DeleteAndRemoveTombstone	The item data should be deleted from the destination store. The tombstone information for the deleted item is not stored. This situation happens during forgotten knowledge recovery and is caused by the item being deleted from the source replica where the source replica has cleaned up the tombstone.

- ItemChange contains the information about the change to an item; SaveChangeContext represents information about a change to be saved to the item store.

The preceding six steps discussed the flow within the unidirectional sync session. If we want to achieve bidirectional synchronization, we need to execute the previous process twice and swap the destination provider with the source provider.

Provider Writer Tasks

As a synchronization provider writer, your main tasks are to implement change tracking, change enumeration, handle conflict, and save changes. Let's explore each of them in detail.

Change Tracking

Change tracking happens before a sync session begins. To implement change tracking, the sync provider needs to update the sync versions for the changed items whenever changes happen in the replica. When creating a custom sync provider before a source sync provider begins to enumerate changes, we need to ensure that whatever changes are made locally to the source replica should also be reflected in its knowledge. This process, called change tracking, can be implemented using either of the following two methods:

- *Inline tracking:* In this method of tracking, knowledge of the replica for an item is updated when a local change is made to the replica. Inline tracking is used in the scenarios when it is easy to plug in the logic for updating the replica's knowledge into the methods that change the content of the replica. For example, in the case of synchronizing databases, it can be a good idea to use inline tracking. In this case we can use the triggers on the database to update the knowledge of the replica as soon as a record is modified.

- *Asynchronous tracking:* In this method of tracking, knowledge of the replica is not updated as soon as the local changes happen in the replica. Instead, an external service or process is called on the replica to scan the changes and update the knowledge of the replica before a source provider begins to enumerate the changes. This process can be made a part of a scheduled process, but it needs to be executed before the sync session begins. Asynchronous tracking is used in scenarios in which it is difficult to plug in the logic for updating the replica's knowledge into the methods that change the content of the replica. The simplest way to implement asynchronous tracking is to store the state of an item after each sync session and then compare it with the state of item before doing synchronization. For example, when synchronizing files between two folders, it might be a good idea to use asynchronous tracking. The easiest way to do this is to store the date modified and the file size after each sync session. Then check these parameters to determine whether a change was made before beginning the new sync session.

Both methods of change tracking must happen at least at the level of the items. Change tracking helps to minimize the conflicts between two replicas. That being said, the more granular the change tracking becomes, the more amount of change tracking information we need to store. A provider writer has to make this decision based on the scenario.

Change Enumeration

Change enumeration happens at the source provider. Change enumeration involves retrieving changes from the source replica that are unknown to the destination replica. The source provider uses the destination replica's knowledge to determine changes that the destination replica doesn't know about.

As shown in Figure 3-4, the destination provider invoked by the sync agent sends its local knowledge to the source provider. The source provider receives this knowledge and compares it with its own local version to prepare a list of changes that the destination replica is not aware of. This list is called a *change set.*

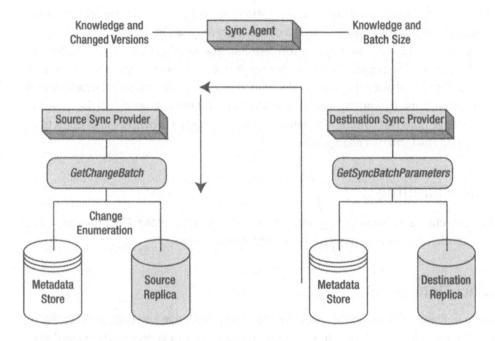

Figure 3-4. *Change enumeration*

Each change set contains the following information:

- The global IDs for the changed items that the destination replica is not aware of.

- Changed item versions.

- Knowledge of the source replica. Destination provider uses this knowledge to determine what items need to be retrieved from the source replica.

- Tombstone information for the items deleted from the source replica but present in the destination replica.

The Sync Framework automatically excludes obsolete changes from the change set while adding changes to the change set. Changes that are already contained in the destination replica's knowledge are called *obsolete changes*. To optimize the synchronization, the change set should be kept to a minimum, and obsolete changes should not be applied to the destination replica. While adding a change to a change set, the Sync Framework compares the changed version against the destination replica's knowledge and excludes the change if it is already contained in the destination replica's knowledge.

The provider writer can also remove obsolete changes by using the Contains method of the SyncKnowledge class. In particular, the source provider checks whether the destination knowledge contains the local version of the item. If it does, the destination already knows about that item version, and the source provider does not need to send it. If the destination knowledge does not contain the item versions, the source provider sends them to a destination in the form of a change set.

Conflict Handling

Conflict detection and handling happens at the destination provider. The provider writer needs to implement conflict detection and conflict resolution.

Conflict Detection

As shown in Figure 3-5, the source provider sends its knowledge and change set to the destination provider. The destination provider retrieves the local version from the destination replica for each item changed in the change set. The destination provider checks whether the local version is contained in the source knowledge. If the local version is contained in the source knowledge, the source replica knew about the destination version when the change was made. However, if the local version is contained in the source knowledge, it means that the two changes were made without knowledge of each other. This is a conflict, which is detected when two changes (one at the source replica and the other at the destination replica) happen to the same item at the same time.

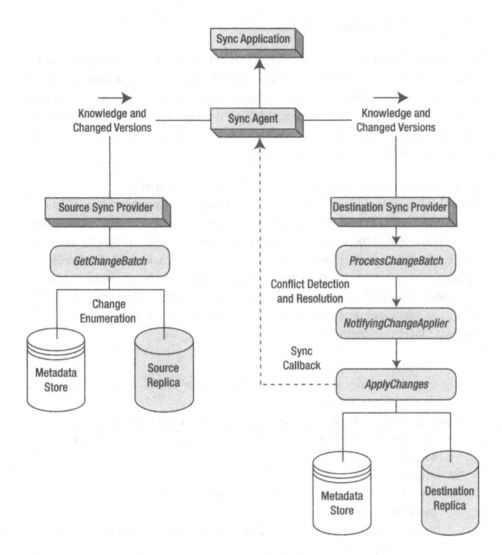

Figure 3-5. *Handling conflicts*

Conflicts are divided into two categories:

- *Constraint conflicts*: Detection of constraint conflicts depends on the type of under-lying replica. For example, if the replica is a file store or folder, a constraint conflict can be detected when there are two files with the same name in the same folder; that is, a file with same name was created at the same time in both source and destination folder (replica). So by definition, constraint conflicts are detected when constraints that are put on items in the replica are violated.

- *Concurrency conflicts*: Concurrency conflicts are detected by the NotifyingChangeApplier object of the Sync Framework. Concurrency conflicts are detected when a combination of update-delete or update-update was applied on the same item at the same time in the two replicas involved in synchronization. For example, if an item is deleted from the source replica, and the destination replica updates at the same time, the destination replica's change is not contained in the source replica's knowledge, so a conflict is detected. To understand how NotifyingChangeApplier detects concurrency conflicts, see the following ProcessChangeBatch method:

```
/// <summary>
/// Sync framework calls the ProcessChangeBatch method
    on the destination provider
/// Destination provider receives the changed versions and source
    knowledge in the form of two input parameters sourceChanges and
    changeDataRetriever.
/// </summary>
/// <param name="resolutionPolicy">Defines the way conflicts are
    handled</param>
/// <param name="sourceChanges">Chnage batch from the source
    provider</param>
/// <param name="changeDataRetriever">IChangeDataRetriever passed
    From the source</param>
/// <param name="syncCallback">Sync call abck for raising events
    to sync agent</param>
/// <param name="sessionStatistics">statistics about the sync
    session.</param>
public override void ProcessChangeBatch(ConflictResolutionPolicy
resolutionPolicy, ChangeBatch sourceChanges,
object changeDataRetriever, SyncCallbacks
syncCallback,SyncSessionStatistics sessionStatistics)
{
```

```
    IEnumerable<ItemChange> localChanges =
    _metadata.GetLocalVersions(sourceChanges);
     NotifyingChangeApplier changeApplier = new
     NotifyingChangeApplier(_idFormats);
     changeApplier.ApplyChanges(resolutionPolicy,
        sourceChanges,changeDataRetriever as
        IChangeDataRetriever,localChanges,_metadata.GetKnowledge(),
        metadata.GetForgottenKnowledge(), this,
        currentSessionContext,syncCallback);
 }
```

The destination provider does the following tasks to detect and handle conflicts:

1. It retrieves the list of local item changes from the destination replica for the change set supplied from the source provider.

2. It calls the ApplyChanges method on the change applier object passing it the list of local changes. It is here when the change applier determines whether the local version sent from the destination provider is contained in the source knowledge or not. If the source knowledge does not contain the local destination item version, the item is said to be in conflict. The change applier detects the conflict and then calls back to the sync agent (synchronizing application) using sync callbacks for conflict resolution policy. The change applier then calls methods on the providers to save the changes and knowledge as required.

Resolving Conflicts

Conflicts can be resolved in the following two ways:

- *Handle all conflicts for the entire sync session*: This can be done by setting the ConflictResolutionPolicy of the destination provider, which is an enum available in the Sync Framework. As discussed earlier in this chapter, this enum has following three values:

```
public enum ConflictResolutionPolicy
 {
  ApplicationDefined = 0,
  DestinationWins = 1,
  SourceWins = 2,       }
```

If the ConflictResolutionPolicy is set to ApplicationDefined, the provider leaves the handling of the conflict to the synchronizing application.

If you set the value of the ConflictResolutionPolicy to DestinationWins, the changes made by the destination replica overwrite the changes made by the source replica. In other words, no changes are made to the destination item.

If you set the value of the ConflictResolutionPolicy to SourceWins, the changes made by the source replica overwrite the changes made by the destination replica. In other words, no changes are made to the source item.

- *Handle each conflict individually.* Provider writers can also handle the conflict at the individual conflict level by using sync callbacks. The most common way to do it is to set the value of ConflictResolutionPolicy to the application defined and use the OnItemConflicting method of the SyncCallbacks class to raise the ItemConflicting event in the synchronizing application. The following code snippet shows you exactly how to do that:

```
//Define the conflict resolution policy
        providerA.Configuration.ConflictResolutionPolicy =
ConflictResolutionPolicy.ApplicationDefined;
        //Raise the event to handle conflicts
        providerA.DestinationCallbacks.ItemConflicting += new EventHandler
<ItemConflictingEventArgs>(DestinationCallbacks_ItemConflicting);
        static void DestinationCallbacks_ItemConflicting(object
        sender, ItemConflictingEventArgs e)


        {
    e.SetResolutionAction(ConflictResolutionAction.Merge);
        }
```

Let's explore the ConflictResolutionAction enum in more detail.

```
public enum ConflictResolutionAction
{
  SkipChange = 0,
  DestinationWins = 1,
  SourceWins = 2,
  Merge = 3,
  SaveConflict = 4,
}
```

- SkipChange: If ConflictResolutionAction is set to SkipChange, the conflicts are deferred. After detecting a conflict, the change applier simply ignores the conflict.

- DestinationWins: If ConflictResolutionAction is set to DestinationWins, the destination replica is always selected as winner in case a conflict is detected. This means that changes made at the source replica are ignored. However, unlike the SkipChange action, the change applier passes the conflicting change to the SaveItemChange method of the destination provider. No change is applied to the item in the destination replica, but the item metadata is updated with the new version.

- SourceWins: If ConflictResolutionAction is set to SourceWins, the source replica is always selected as the winner in case a conflict is detected. This means that changes made at the destination replica are ignored. The change applier passes the conflicting change to the SaveItemChange method of the destination provider. The destination provider updates the destination replica and metadata as if there were no conflict.

- Merge: If ConflictResolutionAction is set to SourceWins, the item from the source replica is merged with the item from the destination replica in case a conflict is detected. The change applier passes the conflicting change to the SaveItemChange method of the destination provider. The destination provider updates the item in the destination replica with the merge result obtained by merging the item from the source replica and destination replica.

- SaveConflict: If ConflictResolutionAction is set to SaveConflict, the destination provider logs the conflict for handling it later on and does not make any changes to the destination replica. The change applier does not pass the conflicting change to the SaveItemChange method; instead it passes the change to the SaveConflict method:

```
void SaveConflict(ItemChange conflictingChange, object
    conflictingChangeData, SyncKnowledge conflictingChangeKnowledge);
```

The change applier passes the conflicting change, conflicting data, and the knowledge of the item in conflict. These conflicts are then resolved later by writing another application that enumerates the conflicts in log and applying them to the destination replica as a local change. Because the changes are applied as local changes, the conflict-resolving application also needs to update the knowledge in the destination replica's metadata.

This kind of conflict-resolving application is also responsible for cleaning and handling obsolete conflicts in the log. When the destination provider logs a new conflict, it must check that the conflict being logged is not obsolete.

Saving the Changes

The next step after conflict detection and resolution is to save the changes in the destination replica. The destination provider requests the source provider for changed items. The source provider retrieves those items from its replica and sends them to the destination provider.

Figure 3-6 shows the steps involved during the process of saving changes to the destination replica.

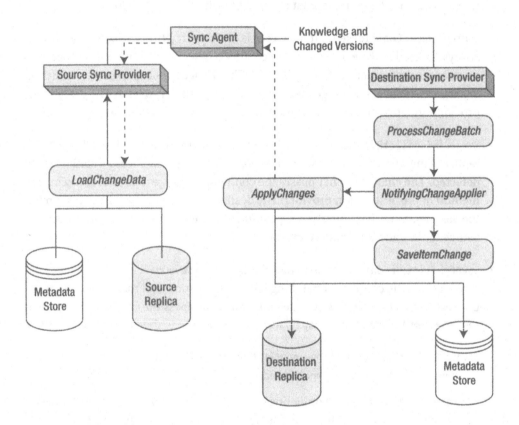

Figure 3-6. *Applying changes*

The destination provider detects and resolves the conflicts using the ApplyChanges method of the NotifyingChangeApplier object. The NotifyingChangeApplier object calls the LoadChangeData method on the source provider to obtain the changed items from the source replica. This method returns an object that represents the data transfer mechanism. The NotifyingChangeApplier object then calls the SaveItemChange method by passing it the saveChangeAction (which specifies what operation to perform—such as create/update or delete—on the destination replica), ItemChange (which contains the information about the change to an item), and SaveChangeContext (which contains the information about the change to an item). Remember that this method is called for each change in the change batch. Now the destination provider is ready to update the destination replica.

As a provider writer, your main two tasks in the SaveItemChange method are to update the destination replica with the changes sent by the source and update the metadata in the metadata store with the source knowledge. The knowledge of the source replica at the time when the change batch was made is called *made-with* knowledge. During the process of applying changes, NotifyingChangeApplier also updates the made-with knowledge to create learned knowledge as follows:

1. NotifyingChangeApplier also limits the learned knowledge to only those change sets that were applied without any error to the destination replica.

2. While building learned knowledge from made-with knowledge, NotifyingChangeApplier excludes the knowledge of the change that was not applied successfully to the destination replica because of some interruptions or cancellations.

Thankfully, provider writers do not have to perform the preceding two steps; the steps are taken care of by the NotifyingChangeApplier.

After the changes are applied to the destination replica, NotifyingChangeApplier combines the learned knowledge with the knowledge of destination replica and stores the result in the metadata store. To do this, provider writers should replace the knowledge of the destination replica atomically with the knowledge returned by calling the GetUpdatedDestinationKnowledge method of the SaveChangeContext class. To make this step atomic, it becomes very important to save the updated knowledge only one time per change batch. NotifyingChangeApplier does this by calling the StoreKnowledgeForScope method at the end of every batch. The following code snippet shows the most common implementation of the StoreKnowledgeForScope method:

```
public void StoreKnowledgeForScope(SyncKnowledge knowledge,
  ForgottenKnowledge forgottenKnowledge)

        _metadata.SetKnowledge(knowledge);
        _metadata.SetForgottenKnowledge(forgottenKnowledge);
        _metadata.SaveReplicaMetadata();
}
```

Before we can wrap up our discussion of saving changes on the destination replica, it is very critical to understand the following two problems associated with replicas that are hierarchical in nature, such as directories containing folders that contain files or parent-child relationships in two tables in a database.

- *Hierarchical updates*: This problem arises because updates are made in hierarchical replicas. For example consider the scenario in which you are synchronizing files between two folders:

  1. A new folder is created inside the source directory. Then a new file is created inside the new folder.

  2. Suppose that while sending the changes to the destination folder, the source provider sends the information about the newly created file in the first change batch and then sends the information about the newly created folder in the second change batch.

  3. While applying changes to the destination folder, the destination provider needs to make a decision about which folder it should create the new file in because it is not aware that source replica has also created a new folder to hold this new file.

  The most common and simple way to avoid this problem is to ensure that the source provider sends the change batches in the order of global IDs. This ensures that the parent folder change is sent in the first batch, and the child file change is sent in the second batch.

  In case of out-of-order parent-child relationships, the destination provider can fix this in two ways:

  - The destination provider queues the child change and applies the change later after it receives the parent change.

  - The destination provider drops the change and makes a note of the exception in the knowledge.

The second approach makes much more sense because the size of the items might be large, and queuing them can slow down the performance and can use lot of memory.

- *Hierarchical deletes*: This problem arises because of deletes in a hierarchical replica. Consider the previous example of file synchronization and think what should happen in the following scenario:

  1. All the files inside a folder are deleted in the source replica. The container folder is also deleted.

  2. Assume that while sending the changes to the destination replica, the source provider sends the information about the parent folder in the first batch and then it sends the information about the deleted file in the second batch.

3. Now the destination provider can delete a folder only when all the files inside it are marked for deletion.

- In this case, the destination provider can fix it by using either of the following two ways:

  - The destination provider queues the parent delete and deletes the folder later after it receives the deletes for all child files.

  - The destination provider drops the delete and makes a note of the exception in the knowledge.

So now we know how to fix the hierarchical deletes. But wait! What if the source replica deletes the folder and all the files inside it, and at the same time the destination replica creates a new file inside the same folder at the destination? In this scenario, as soon as the child file is created, queued deletions are considered invalid.

Now that you know how the data flows between synchronization providers, what happens at each provider, and the different classes offered by Sync Framework for helping provider writers to write their own provider, let's create our own sync provider.

Sample Synchronization Provider for Synchronizing SQL Server Databases

In this example, we'll synchronize three different replicas (SQL Server databases) by creating our own sync provider. For storing metadata, we'll use the built-in SQL CE metadata store. You'll learn about using custom metadata stores in detail in Chapter 7.

■Note Make sure that you have installed the Sync Framework and Visual Studio 2008 before implementing the sample application! Please refer to Chapter 1 for more details on installing the Sync Framework.

The source code for the entire solution can be found in the ProSyncFramework\ Chapter III\Code\CustomProvider folder. The sample uses three SQL Server 2005 databases named ReplicaA, ReplicaB, and ReplicaC. The SQL script for creating these replicas is located in the CustomProvider\CustomProvider\Sql folder. Execute this script on your local SQL Server to create the replicas. Each has a table called Customer (Figure 3-7 shows the Customer table schema).

In the sample application we'll synchronize the Customer table in all three replicas. The Customer table contains four fields (note that the field called ID is the unique identifier). We will be using this field to create sync IDs to uniquely identify the item in the metadata store. This is another great feature offered by the Sync Framework. It allows provider writers to use their existing unique identifiers as sync IDs.

Table - dbo.Customer

Column Name	Data Type	Allow Nulls
ID	int	☐
Name	varchar(127)	☑
Designation	nvarchar(127)	☑
Age	int	☑

Figure 3-7. *Customer table*

Next, open the solution in Visual Studio 2008 by double-clicking on the Solution file located in the ProSyncFramework\Chapter III\Code\CustomProvider folder. The Solution structure should look like Figure 3-8.

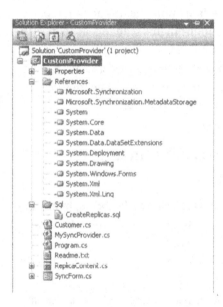

Figure 3-8. *Custom provider solution*

Let's examine the Solution structure in detail. To build our own customization provider, we need to add a reference to Microsoft.Synchronization. And because we're using the built-in SQL Server CE edition, we also need to add a reference to Microsoft. Synchronization.MetadataStorage.

To demonstrate how to create a custom synchronization provider to synchronize three SQL Server databases, we'll use the following steps:

1. Create three SQL Server databases, each containing a Customer table.

2. Create a class for manipulating and reading the records from the Customer table.

3. Create a user control for displaying the Customer table from each replica.

4. Create a generic custom sync provider for synchronizing the Customer table.

5. Create three instances of this custom sync provider and attach them to three replicas.

6. Synchronize the contents of one replica with another with the help of the sync agent and custom sync providers.

CreateReplica.Sql

As shown in the following code listing, the Createreplica.sql SQL file is used to create the ReplicaA, ReplicaB, and ReplicaC databases on the SQL server:

```
/****** Create Database ReplicaA ******/
USE master
GO
IF EXISTS (SELECT [name] FROM [master].[sys].[databases]
WHERE [name] = N'ReplicaA')
     BEGIN
   DROP DATABASE [ReplicaA]
     END
GO
CREATE DATABASE [ReplicaA]
GO
/****** Create Customer Table in ReplicaA ******/
USE [ReplicaA]
GO
IF  EXISTS (SELECT * FROM sys.objects WHERE object_id =
 OBJECT_ID(N'[dbo].[Customer]') AND type in (N'U'))
DROP TABLE [dbo].[Customer]
SET ANSI_NULLS ON
GO
SET QUOTED_IDENTIFIER ON
GO
CREATE TABLE [dbo].[Customer](
    [ID] [int] NOT NULL,
    [Name] [nvarchar](50) COLLATE SQL_Latin1_General_CP1_CI_AS
          NULL,
     [Designation] [nvarchar](50) COLLATE
           SQL_Latin1_General_CP1_CI_AS NULL,
          [Age] [int] NULL
) ON [PRIMARY]
Go
```

The preceding script contains code to create only ReplicaA, but similar logic can be used to create other replicas. The complete SQL script can be found in the `CustomProvider\CustomProvider\Sql\CreateReplicas.sql` folder.

Customer.cs

In a real-world scenario, the code to operate on replicas will be insulated in its own layer; for example, the data access layer (DAL). In this case, we'll be using the `Customer` class to do operations on each of the replicas.

Constructor

As shown in the following code listing, the `Constructor` class initializes the properties of the `Customer` object:

```
int m_ID;
string m_Name;
string m_Designation;
int m_Age;
string m_ReplicaCon;
string m_ReplicaName;

/// <summary>
/// Constructor
/// </summary>
/// <param name="ReplicaCon"></param>
/// <param name="ReplicaName"></param>
/// <param name="ID"></param>
/// <param name="Name"></param>
/// <param name="Designation"></param>
/// <param name="Age"></param>
public Customer(string ReplicaCon, string ReplicaName,
 int ID, string Name, string Designation, int Age)
    {
        m_ReplicaCon = ReplicaCon;
        m_ReplicaName = ReplicaName;
        m_ID = ID;
        m_Name = Name;
        m_Designation = Designation;
        m_Age = Age;
    }
```

Public Properties

The Customer class contains a property for each field available in the Customer table for changing or retrieving the value of the fields. There are two more properties: ReplicaCon, which holds the connection string for the replica (database), and ReplicaName, which specifies the replica name.

ID: Gets or sets the ID of the customer:

```
/// <summary>
/// ID
/// </summary>
public int ID
{
    get
    {
        return m_ID;
    }
    set
    {

        m_ID = value;
    }
}
```

Name: Gets or sets the name of the customer:

```
/// <summary>
/// Name
/// </summary>
public string Name
{
    get
    {
        return m_Name;
    }
    set
    {
        m_Name = value;
    }
}
```

Designation: Gets or sets the designation of the customer:

```
/// <summary>
/// Designation
/// </summary>
public string Designation
{
    get
    {
        return m_Designation;
    }
    set
    {
        m_Designation = value;
    }
}
```

Age: Gets or sets the age of the Customer:

```
/// <summary>
/// Age
/// </summary>
public int Age
{
    get
    {
        return m_Age;
    }
    set
    {
        m_Age = value;
    }
}
```

ReplicaCon: Gets or sets the connecting string for the replica to connect to the Customer table:

```
/// <summary>
/// ReplicaCon
/// </summary>
public string ReplicaCon
{
```

```
    get
    {
        return m_ReplicaCon;
    }
    set
    {
        m_ReplicaCon = value;
    }
}
```

ReplicaName. Gets or sets the name of the replica:

```
/// <summary>
/// ReplicaName
/// </summary>
public string ReplicaName
{
    get
    {
        return m_ReplicaName;
    }
    set
    {
        m_ReplicaName = value;
    }
}
```

Public Methods

The Customer class contains the CreateCustomer, Update, and Delete methods, which are used to create, update, or delete a customer record from the replica. To keep the sample application simple, we're using the hard-coded inline SQL statements (in a real-world application, you should try to avoid that, however).

```
/// <summary>
/// Creates a Customer in Database
/// </summary>
public void CreateCustomer()
{
    string insertQuery = "INSERT INTO dbo.Customer VALUES
({0}, '{1}', '{2}',{3})";
        ExecuteSQL(string.Format(insertQuery, ID, Name.TrimEnd(),
         Designation.Trim(), Age), ReplicaCon);
}
```

```
/// <summary>
/// Updates a Customer in Database
/// </summary>
public void Update()
{
    string updateQuery = "UPDATE dbo.Customer SET Name = \
'{0}',Designation ='{1}',Age = {2}
    Where ID = {3}";
    ExecuteSQL(string.Format(updateQuery, Name.TrimEnd(),
    Designation.Trim(), Age, ID),
    ReplicaCon);
}


/// <summary>
///  Deletes a Customer in Database
/// </summary>
public void Delete()
{
    string deleteQuery = "DELETE FROM dbo.Customer Where ID = {0}";
    ExecuteSQL(string.Format(deleteQuery, ID), ReplicaCon);
}
```

The Customer class also overrides the ToString method to return the properties of the Customer objects in a string format:

```
/// <summary>
/// Returns Customer Info
/// </summary>
/// <returns></returns>
public override string ToString()
{
    StringBuilder s = new StringBuilder("Customer Information : ");
    s.Append(Environment.NewLine);
    s.Append("Replica name = {0} ; Replica Connection = {1} ; ");
    s.Append(Environment.NewLine);
    s.Append(" Customer => ID = {2} ; Name = {3} ; Designation
            = {4}; Age = {5} ");

    return string.Format(s.ToString(), ReplicaName,
                        ReplicaCon,
                ID.ToString(), Name, Designation,
                    Age.ToString());
}
```

The GetCustomerById static method returns the customer from the replica specified by ReplicaName, ReplicaCon, and ID:

```
/// <summary>
/// Returns the customer specified by ID, ReplicaCon, and ReplicaName
/// </summary>
/// <param name="ID"></param>
/// <param name="ReplicaCon"></param>
/// <param name="ReplicaName"></param>
/// <returns></returns>
public static Customer GetCustomerById(int ID, string
ReplicaCon, string ReplicaName)
    {
        Customer customer = null;
        string sql = "SELECT ID,Name,Designation,Age FROM Customer
Where ID ={0}";
        sql = string.Format(sql, ID);
        using (SqlConnection con = new SqlConnection(ReplicaCon))
        using (SqlCommand cmd = new SqlCommand(sql, con))
        {
            con.Open();
            using (SqlDataReader dr = cmd.ExecuteReader())
            {
                if (dr.HasRows)
                {
                    dr.Read();
                    customer = new Customer(ReplicaCon,
                                ReplicaName, ID,dr["Name"].ToString(),

                                dr["Designation"].ToString(),

                            Int32.Parse(dr["Age"].ToString())));
                }
            }
        }
        return customer;

    }
```

Private Methods

The ExecuteSQL method executes the SQL query specified by the Query parameter on the replica specified by the ConnectionString parameter:

```
        private void ExecuteSQL(string Query, string ConnectionString)
        {
            using (SqlConnection con = new SqlConnection(ConnectionString))
            using (SqlCommand cmd = new SqlCommand(Query, con))
            {
                con.Open();
                cmd.ExecuteNonQuery();
            }
        }
```

ReplicaContent.cs

This is the user control that displays the content of each replica in a gridview. This control contains three gridviews to display records in the Customer table for each of the three replicas.

The following code snippet shows the content of the user control:

```
using System;
using System.Collections.Generic;
using System.ComponentModel;
using System.Drawing;
using System.Data;
using System.Linq;
using System.Text;
using System.Windows.Forms;
using System.Data.SqlClient;

namespace CustomProvider
{
    /// <summary>
    /// Displays the data from replica in gridview
    /// </summary>
    public partial class ReplicaContent : UserControl
    {

        #region Constructor
        /// <summary>
        /// Constructor
        /// </summary>
        public ReplicaContent()
        {
            InitializeComponent();
        }
```

```
#endregion
#region Public Methods
/// <summary>
/// Populates the data from the replicas
/// </summary>
/// <param name="providerA_ReplicaCon"></param>
/// <param name="providerB_ReplicaCon"></param>
/// <param name="providerC_ReplicaCon"></param>
/// <param name="query"></param>
public void Refresh(string providerA_ReplicaCon, string
                    providerB_ReplicaCon,
                    string providerC_ReplicaCon, string
                    query)
{
    BindDataGridView(providerA_ReplicaCon, query, grdViewA);
    BindDataGridView(providerB_ReplicaCon, query, grdViewB);
    BindDataGridView(providerC_ReplicaCon, query, grdViewC);
}

#endregion
#region Private helper methods
private void BindDataGridView(string conString,string
        query,DataGridView dgv )
{
    using (SqlConnection con = new SqlConnection(conString))
    using (SqlDataAdapter adr = new SqlDataAdapter(query, con))
    using (DataSet ds = new DataSet())
    {
        adr.Fill(ds);
        dgv.DataSource = ds.Tables[0];
    }
}
#endregion
    }
}
```

The code is self-explanatory. The ReplicaContent user control contains a refresh method that takes the SQL query and connection strings for each replica as input and uses BindDataGridView method to bind the data to the grids. We'll be using this control to show the contents of the replica before and after each synchronization.

MySyncProvider.cs

This is our custom provider class. We'll use three instances of this class as three providers attached to three replicas.

The following code snippet shows the declaration of this class:

```csharp
using System;
using System.Collections.Generic;
using System.Linq;
using System.Text;
using System.IO;
using System.Data;
using System.Data.SqlClient;
using Microsoft.Synchronization;
using Microsoft.Synchronization.MetadataStorage;

namespace CustomProvider
{
    /// <summary>
    /// Custom Synchronization Provider
    /// </summary>
    public class MySyncProvider : KnowledgeSyncProvider,
                                  IChangeDataRetriever,
                                  InotifyingChangeApplierTarget,
                                  IDisposable
    {

    }
```

Recall that provider writers usually start writing their own providers by deriving from KnowledgeSyncProvider, IChangeDataRetriever, and INotifyingChangeApplierTarget classes. These classes are available in the Microsoft.Synchronization namespace, so we need to add a reference to that namespace.

We're also inheriting the custom sync provider class from the IDisposable interface. This design allows us to dispose of the resources used by the sync provider after synchronization is finished.

In this sample, we'll be using the built-in SQL Server CE metadata store for storing sync metadata. So we also need to add a reference to the Microsoft.Synchronization. MetadataStorage namespace because it contains the classes required for implementing metadata storage.

Constructor

The code for Constructor and local variables of the class is shown in the following code snippet:

```
#region Local variables

//Built in SQL CE metadata store provided by MSF.In this sample
//we are going to use the metadata store provided by MSF
SqlMetadataStore _metadataStore = null;
ReplicaMetadata _metadata = null;
SyncId _replicaID = null;
SyncIdFormatGroup _idFormats = null;
SyncSessionContext _currentSessionContext = null;

string _replicaName;
//Connection string for the replica which is used by the
//provider to talk to the replica
string _replicaCon;
#endregion

#region Constructor
/// <summary>
/// Creates or opens the existing metadata store.
/// Initializes the Replica Id and replica connection
/// </summary>
/// <param name="replicaName"></param>
/// <param name="replicaCon"></param>
/// <param name="fileName"></param>
public MySyncProvider(string replicaName, string replicaCon,
 string fileName)
{
    _replicaName = replicaName;
    _replicaID = new SyncId(replicaName);
    _replicaCon = replicaCon;
    _idFormats = new SyncIdFormatGroup();
    _idFormats.ItemIdFormat.IsVariableLength = true;
    _idFormats.ItemIdFormat.Length = 500;
    _idFormats.ReplicaIdFormat.IsVariableLength = true;
    _idFormats.ReplicaIdFormat.Length = 500;
```

```
//Create or open the metadata store, initializing it with
//the flexible id formats we'll use to reference our items
//and endpoints
if (!File.Exists(fileName))
{
    _metadataStore = SqlMetadataStore.CreateStore(fileName);
    _metadata =
     _metadataStore.InitializeReplicaMetadata(_idFormats,
     _replicaID, null, null);
}
else
{
    _metadataStore = SqlMetadataStore.OpenStore(fileName);
    _metadata =
         _metadataStore.GetReplicaMetadata(_idFormats,
         replicaID);
}
_metadata.SetForgottenKnowledge(new
 ForgottenKnowledge(_idFormats,
 metadata.GetKnowledge()));
}

#endregion
```

As you can see from the code, the constructor initializes the provider with the replica it is attached to.

For each provider, we set the replica connection holding the connection string for the database, replica name, and file in which we will store the replica metadata. In our example, because we're using the built-in SQL CE metadata store, we'll be storing the replica metadata inside the bin folder in a file.

To create the unique replica ID, the sample uses the replica name itself. The constructor initializes ItemIDFormat and ReplicaIdFormat. If the metadata file already exists, the constructor opens the metadata store and gets the metadata for the replica using the GetReplicaMetadata method. If the metadata file does not exist, the constructor creates the metadata store by calling CreateStore on the SqlMetadataStore.

As discussed earlier in this chapter, provider writers' main tasks involve change enumeration, change tracking, conflict handling, and change saving. Now let's explore how the custom provider implements all these tasks.

Change Tracking

In this example, we're using inline change tracking. The valid operations are discussed in the following sections.

Creating a New Item

The CreateNewItem method of the class creates a new record in the Customer table and updates the metadata for the replica. The code for this method is the following: .

```
/// <summary>
/// Creates a new customer and updates the metadata
/// </summary>
/// <param name="customer"></param>
public void CreateNewItem(Customer customer)
{

        //Creates the Customer
        customer.CreateCustomer();

        //Creates new item metadata by using the
        //1. sync id [Created from ID field of Customer]
        //2. sync version which has replica Id [0] and the tick
count which a logical sync clock
        ItemMetadata item = _metadata.CreateItemMetadata(new
SyncId(customer.ID.ToString()), new SyncVersion(0,
_metadata.GetNextTickCount()));
        //sets the changed version to created version
        item.ChangeVersion = item.CreationVersion;
        //saves the item in metadata store
        _metadata.SaveItemMetadata(item);


    }
```

The CreateNewItem method first calls the CreateCustomer method on the Customer object to create the customer record in the database. At the same time, it needs to update the metadata. Updating the metadata store for the newly created item involves the following three tasks:

1. First, we need to create the new ItemMetadata method, which can be created by passing the sync ID and the sync version to the CreateItemMetadata method of the ReplicaMetadata class:

```
ItemMetadata item = _metadata.CreateItemMetadata(new

                SyncId(customer.ID.ToString()), new SyncVersion(0,
                 _metadata.GetNextTickCount()));
```

We use the ID of the customer record as the sync ID. The sync version is made of the replica key and tick count. Because this is a local change (the one not caused by synchronization), we pass the reply key as 0. If it were a remote change, we could pass the replica key as 1.The tick count is obtained by calling the GetNextTickCount method on the ReplicaMetadata class.

2. After creating the item metadata, the next task is to assign the changed version with the following statement:

```
item.ChangeVersion = item.CreationVersion;
```

3. Then we simply save this item in metadata by calling the SaveItemMetadata method of the ReplicaMetadata class.

■Note If you aren't using the built-in metadata store, you need to write your own code in the third step to save the metadata in the custom metadata store.

Updating an Item

The UpdateItem method of the class updates an existing record in the Customer table and updates the metadata for the replica. The code for this method is the following:

```
/// <summary>
/// Updates a customer and the metadata
/// </summary>
/// <param name="customer"></param>
public void UpdateItem(Customer customer)
{

    customer.Update();
    ItemMetadata item = null;

    //retrieve item's metadata by sync id
    item = _metadata.FindItemMetadataById(new
     SyncId(customer.ID.ToString()));
    if (null == item)
    {
        return;
    }
```

```
//sets the changed version by incrementing the tick count
item.ChangeVersion = new SyncVersion(0, _metadata.GetNextTickCount());

_metadata.SaveItemMetadata(item);
}
```

When updating an item, we need to find the item that is being updated in the metadata store. Then we have to update the changed version and save the item in the metadata store. As shown in the UpdateItem method, we first update Customer and then save the item metadata.

Deleting an Item

The DeleteItem method of the class deletes an existing record in the Customer table and updates the metadata for the replica. The code for this method is the following:

```
/// <summary>
/// Deletes a customer and updates the metadata
/// </summary>
/// <param name="customer"></param>
public void DeleteItem(Customer customer)
{

    customer.Delete();
    ItemMetadata item = _metadata.FindItemMetadataById(new
      SyncId(customer.ID.ToString()));
    if (null == item)
    {
        return;
    }
    item.ChangeVersion = new SyncVersion(0,
      _metadata.GetNextTickCount());
    item.MarkAsDeleted(item.ChangeVersion);
    _metadata.SaveItemMetadata(item);
}
```

When deleting an item, we need to find the item that is being deleted from the replica in the metadata store, update the changed version, mark it as deleted, and then save the item in the metadata store. As shown in the DeleteItem method, we first update the Customer and then save the item metadata in the metadata store.

Implementing Transactions

Transactions are implemented by BeginUpdates and EndUpdates methods, as shown in the following code listing:

```
/// <summary>
/// BeginUpdates() begins a transaction for the replica. Using
    BeginUpdates and EndUpdates the operations on the replica
    can be made transactional.
/// </summary>
public void BeginUpdates()
{
    _metadataStore.BeginTransaction();
}


/// <summary>
/// EndUpdates ends a transaction for the replica
/// </summary>
public void EndUpdates()
{
    _metadataStore.CommitTransaction();
}
```

It is good practice to make the changes to the replica and metadata store within a transaction. The built-in metadata store (SqlMetadataStore) has two methods to help us: BeginTransaction and CommitTransaction. The MySyncProvider class has two methods that wrap the preceding two methods: BeginUpdates and EndUpdates. These methods can then be called on the provider to make sure that metadata and the replica content are updated in a single transaction. You can also use the RollbackTransaction method of the SqlMetadataStore class to roll back the transaction on the metadata store in case of any error.

Overriding Provider Methods

The next task is to implement the methods of the KnowledgeSyncProvider, IChangeDataRetriever, and INotifyingChangeApplierTarget classes.

Before the sync session can begin, the IdFormats property of the provider is initialized to get the schema for ID format for the provider, as shown in the following code listing:

```
public override SyncIdFormatGroup IdFormats
{
    get { return _idFormats; }
}
```

As shown in the following code listing, the BeginSession and EndSession methods of the KnowledgeSyncProvider class are overridden in the custom sync provider:

```
public override void BeginSession(SyncProviderPosition
  position, SyncSessionContext syncSessionContext)
{
    _currentSessionContext = syncSessionContext;
}

public override void EndSession(SyncSessionContext syncSessionContext)
{

}
```

BeginSession is the first method that is called on a sync provider when it joins the sync session, and EndSession indicates that the sync session is completed.

The BeginSession method also saves the syncSessionContext into a local variable, currentSessionContext, which is then used by the ProcessChangebatch method later on. (To keep the example simple, some of the methods, such as EndSession, are not implemented.)

After BeginSession, the GetSyncBatchParameters method is called on the destination provider. The code for GetSyncBatchParameters is shown in the following code listing:

```
/// <summary>
/// Sync framework calls GetSyncBatchParameters method on the
   destination provider
/// </summary>
/// <param name="batchSize">an integer which returns the batch size </param>
/// <param name="knowledge">returns the knowledge of the destination</param>
public override void GetSyncBatchParameters(out uint
  batchSize, out SyncKnowledge knowledge)
{
    batchSize = 10;
    knowledge = _metadata.GetKnowledge();
}
```

GetSyncBatchParameters sets the batch size for a sync session. *Batch size* indicates the maximum number of changes that can be transferred within one batch from one provider to another. The GetSyncBatchParameters method also retrieves the knowledge of the destination replica and returns this knowledge in the form of an out parameter to the source provider.

The source provider receives the knowledge provided by the destination provider and compares this knowledge with its local item versions. The Sync Framework calls the GetChangeBatch method on the source provider. The code for the GetChangebatch method is shown in the following code listing:

```
/// <summary>
/// Sync framework calls the GetChangeBatch method on the source provider.
/// This method receives the batch size and the knowledge of
 the destination as two input parameters.
/// After comparing this with local item versions, source sync
  provider sends the summary of changed versions
/// and knowledge to the destination provider in form of the
  changeDataRetriever object.
/// </summary>
/// <param name="batchSize"></param>
/// <param name="destinationKnowledge"></param>
/// <param name="changeDataRetriever"></param>
/// <returns></returns>
public override ChangeBatch GetChangeBatch(uint batchSize,
 SyncKnowledge destinationKnowledge, out object
 changeDataRetriever)
{
    ChangeBatch batch = _metadata.GetChangeBatch(batchSize,
     destinationKnowledge);
    changeDataRetriever = this;
    return batch;
}
```

As you can see, this method receives the batch size and the knowledge of the destination as two input parameters. After comparing this with local item versions, the source sync provider sends the summary of changed versions and knowledge to the destination provider in the form of the changeDataRetriever object.

Because we're using inline change tracking, all the changes to data and metadata are made by calling methods on the provider. Sync metadata is always updated because changes to metadata are made immediately after the data changes.

■Tip In the next chapter, we'll create a sample sync provider using asynchronous change tracking, in which we need to update the metadata at this step.

Batch size parameters set by the destination provider are inputs to this method and determine the maximum number of changes that can be sent in one batch to the destination provider. What this means is that if the number of changes that have to be sent to the destination provider is greater than the batch size, the Sync Framework makes multiple calls to this method until all changes have been sent.

After receiving the changed version and knowledge from the source provider, the destination provider first retrieves its own local versions for the items that were changed at the source. The destination provider also detects and resolves or defers conflicts. To do this, the Sync Framework calls the ProcessChangeBatch method on the destination provider whose code is the following:

```
/// <summary>
/// Sync framework calls the ProcessChangeBatch method on the
    destination provider
/// Destination provider receives the changed versions and
    source knowledge in the form of two input parameters
    sourceChanges and changeDataRetriever.
/// </summary>
/// <param name="resolutionPolicy">Defines the way conflicts
    are handled</param>
/// <param name="sourceChanges">Chnage batch from the source
    provider</param>
/// <param name="changeDataRetriever">IChangeDataRetriever
    passed from the source</param>
/// <param name="syncCallback">Sync call back for raising
    events to sync agent</param>
/// <param name="sessionStatistics">statistics about the sync
    session.</param>
public override void
ProcessChangeBatch(ConflictResolutionPolicy resolutionPolicy,
    ChangeBatch sourceChanges,
    object changeDataRetriever, SyncCallbacks syncCallback,
    SyncSessionStatistics sessionStatistics)
{
    BeginUpdates();
    IEnumerable<ItemChange> localChanges =
    _metadata.GetLocalVersions(sourceChanges);
    NotifyingChangeApplier changeApplier = new
    NotifyingChangeApplier(_idFormats);
    changeApplier.ApplyChanges(resolutionPolicy,
    sourceChanges, changeDataRetriever as
    IChangeDataRetriever, localChanges,
    _metadata.GetKnowledge(),
     metadata.GetForgottenKnowledge(), this,
    _currentSessionContext, syncCallback);
    EndUpdates();
}
```

The destination provider receives the changed versions and source knowledge in the form of two input parameters: sourceChanges and changeDataRetriever.

The destination provider also receives a parameter called resolutionPolicy of the type ConflictResolutionPolicy. This parameter defines the way conflicts are handled.

The Sync Framework provides supports for callbacks. The destination provider receives an object of the SyncCallbacks class.

The last parameter in the ProcessChangeBatch method is sessionStatistics, which is of the type SyncSessionStatistics. As the name suggests, SyncSessionStatistics class represents the statistics about the sync session. The ChangesApplied property gets or sets the total number of changes applied successfully during a sync session. The ChangesFailed property gets or sets the total number of changes not applied or failed during a sync session.

After receiving the request for changed items from the destination provider, the source provider retrieves those items from its replica and sends them to the destination provider. In this case, changed items are represented by Customer objects. To achieve this, the Sync Framework calls the LoadChangeData method, as shown in the following code listing:

```
/// <summary>
/// Sync framework calls the LoadChangeData method on the source provider.
/// source provider retrieves the items requested by
    destination provider from its replica and sends them to
    the destination provider
/// </summary>
/// <param name="loadChangeContext"></param>
/// <returns></returns>
 public object LoadChangeData(LoadChangeContext loadChangeContext)
 {
     string ID = loadChangeContext.ItemChange.ItemId.GetStringId();
     return Customer.GetCustomerById(int.Parse(ID),
     _replicaCon, _replicaName);
 }
```

The destination provider receives the items from the source provider, applies them to its local replica, and updates the destination knowledge with the source knowledge. The destination provider can also handle any failures; in such cases, the destination provider marks the items as exceptions so that they can be handled during the next sync session.

The Sync Framework calls the SaveItemChange method that the destination provider needs to implement. This is the reason why we have derived our provider from the INotifyingChangeApplierTarget interface.

The code for the SaveItemChange is as follows:

```
/// <summary>
/// Saves the item and metadata in destination replica
/// </summary>
/// <param name="saveChangeAction">specifies what operation to
```

```
        perform on destination replica like create/update or
        delete</param>
/// <param name="change">contains the information about the
        change to an item</param>
/// <param name="context">represents information about a
        change to be saved to the item store</param>
public void SaveItemChange(SaveChangeAction saveChangeAction,
        ItemChange change, SaveChangeContext context)
{
    ItemMetadata item = null;
    switch (saveChangeAction)
    {
        case SaveChangeAction.Create:
            //Save the Change
            Customer customer = (Customer)context.ChangeData;
            customer.ReplicaCon = _replicaCon;
            customer.ReplicaName = _replicaName;
            customer.CreateCustomer();
            //Save the metadata
            item = _metadata.CreateItemMetadata(change.ItemId,
                    change.CreationVersion);
            item.ChangeVersion = change.ChangeVersion;
            _metadata.SaveItemMetadata(item);
            break;

        case SaveChangeAction.UpdateVersionAndData:
            {
                item = _metadata.FindItemMetadataById(change.ItemId);
                if (null == item)
                {
                    throw new Exception("Record is not present in replica");
                }

                item.ChangeVersion = change.ChangeVersion;
                Customer destCustomer =
Customer.GetCustomerById(Int32.Parse(item.GlobalId.GetStringId()),
                    _replicaCon, _replicaName);
                Customer SrcCustomer = (Customer)context.ChangeData;
                destCustomer.Name = SrcCustomer.Name;
                destCustomer.Designation = SrcCustomer.Designation;
                destCustomer.Age = SrcCustomer.Age;
                destCustomer.ReplicaCon = _replicaCon;
                destCustomer.ReplicaName = _replicaName;
```

```
                destCustomer.Update();
                _metadata.SaveItemMetadata(item);
            }
            break;
    case SaveChangeAction.UpdateVersionOnly:
        {
            item = _metadata.FindItemMetadataById(change.ItemId);
            if (null == item)
            {
                throw new Exception("Record is not present in replica");
            }

            item.ChangeVersion = change.ChangeVersion;
            _metadata.SaveItemMetadata(item);
        }
        break;


    case SaveChangeAction.DeleteAndStoreTombstone:
        item = _metadata.FindItemMetadataById(change.ItemId);
        if (null == item)
        {
            item =
                _metadata.CreateItemMetadata(change.ItemId,
                change.CreationVersion);
        }

        if (change.ChangeKind == ChangeKind.Deleted)
        {
            item.MarkAsDeleted(change.ChangeVersion);
        }
        else
        {
            throw new Exception("Invalid changeType");
        }

        item.ChangeVersion = change.ChangeVersion;
        Customer customerDelete =
Customer.GetCustomerById(Int32.Parse(item.GlobalId.GetStringId()),
                _replicaCon, _replicaName);
        if (null!=customerDelete) customerDelete.Delete();
        _metadata.SaveItemMetadata(item);
        break;
```

```
            case SaveChangeAction.UpdateVersionAndMergeData:
                item = _metadata.FindItemMetadataById(change.ItemId);
                item.ChangeVersion = new SyncVersion(0,
                                _metadata.GetNextTickCount());
                int ID = Int32.Parse(item.GlobalId.GetStringId());
                Customer destCustomerMerge =
                        Customer.GetCustomerById(ID, _replicaCon,
                                            _replicaName);
                Customer SrcCustomerMerge = (Customer)context.ChangeData;
                destCustomerMerge.Name += SrcCustomerMerge.Name;
                destCustomerMerge.Designation += SrcCustomerMerge.Designation;
                destCustomerMerge.Age += SrcCustomerMerge.Age;
                destCustomerMerge.ReplicaCon = _replicaCon;
                destCustomerMerge.ReplicaName = _replicaName;

                destCustomerMerge.Update();
                _metadata.SaveItemMetadata(item);
                break;
        }
    }
```

The LoadChangeData and SaveItemChange methods are called for each change in the change batch. So the Sync Framework makes multiple calls to these methods until all changes have been read from the source provider and applied to the destination provider.

The last step before ending the sync session is to save the knowledge that is done in the StoreKnowledgeForScope method, as shown in the following code listing:

```
/// <summary>
/// We also need to save the knowledge after each sync.
/// We just save the knowledge and forgotten Knowledge in the
    Replica metadata store.
/// </summary>
/// <param name="knowledge"></param>
/// <param name="forgottenKnowledge"></param>
public void StoreKnowledgeForScope(SyncKnowledge knowledge,
                ForgottenKnowledge forgottenKnowledge)
{
    _metadata.SetKnowledge(knowledge);
    _metadata.SetForgottenKnowledge(forgottenKnowledge);
    _metadata.SaveReplicaMetadata();
}
```

Not-Implemented Methods

To keep the example short, the following methods were not implemented for the sample application:

```
public override FullEnumerationChangeBatch
GetFullEnumerationChangeBatch(uint batchSize, SyncId
lowerEnumerationBound, SyncKnowledge
knowledgeForDataRetrieval, out object changeDataRetriever)

{
    throw new NotImplementedException();
}
public override void
ProcessFullEnumerationChangeBatch(ConflictResolutionPolicy
 resolutionPolicy, FullEnumerationChangeBatch sourceChanges,
 object changeDataRetriever, SyncCallbacks syncCallback,
 SyncSessionStatistics sessionStatistics)
{
    throw new NotImplementedException();
}

public void SaveChangeWithChangeUnits(ItemChange change,
    SaveChangeWithChangeUnitsContext context)
{
    throw new NotImplementedException();
}
public void SaveConflict(ItemChange conflictingChange, object
    conflictingChangeData, SyncKnowledge
    conflictingChangeKnowledge)
{
    throw new NotImplementedException();
}
```

The GetFullEnumerationChangeBatch and ProcessFullEnumerationChangeBatch methods are used when an out-of-date synchronization destination is detected. The SaveChangeWithChangeUnits is used to implement change units. The SaveConflict method is used when you want to save the conflicts using the SaveConflict option in its conflict detection event handler.

Releasing the Resources

It is very important to release the resources used for synchronization after the synchronization finishes. This is done by implementing a formalized dispose pattern as follows:

```
~MySyncProvider()
{
    CleanUp(false);
}

private bool disposed = false;
public void Dispose()
{
    CleanUp(true);
    GC.SuppressFinalize(this);
}

private void CleanUp(bool disposing)
{
    if (!this.disposed)
    {
        if (disposing)
        {
            // Dispose managed resources.
            _metadataStore.Dispose();
        }
        // Clean up unmanaged resources here.
    }
    disposed = true;
}
```

SyncForm.cs

This is the form that initiates the synchronization between three replicas (SQL Server databases) and displays the result of synchronization using the ReplicaContent user control.

This form creates three providers from the MySyncProvider class and hooks them to the three replicas. It also demonstrates how the Sync Framework detects and handles conflicts.

As shown in the following code listing, the SyncForm_Load event does the following:

- Creates files for storing sync metadata

- Creates a custom sync provider for each replica

- Sets the conflict resolution policy to ApplicationDefined

- Registers events to handle conflicts

- Creates a new instance of the sync agent

- Creates a new instance of the Random class to generate IDs for customer records

```
private void SyncForm_Load(object sender, EventArgs e)
{
    //Create provider and metadata for replica A
    providerA_ReplicaCon = string.Format(connection, replicaA);
    providerAMetadata = Environment.CurrentDirectory + "\\" + replicaA ➥
+ " .Metadata";
    if (File.Exists(providerAMetadata))
    {
        File.Delete(providerAMetadata);
    }
    providerA = new MySyncProvider(replicaA, providerA_ReplicaCon, ➥
providerAMetadata);
    //Create provider and metadata for replica B
    providerB_ReplicaCon = string.Format(connection, replicaB);
    providerBMetadata = Environment.CurrentDirectory + "\\" + replicaB ➥
+ " .Metadata";
    if (File.Exists(providerBMetadata))
    {
        File.Delete(providerBMetadata);
    }
    providerB = new MySyncProvider(replicaB, providerB_ReplicaCon, ➥
 providerBMetadata);
    //Create provider and metadata for replica C
    providerC_ReplicaCon = string.Format(connection, replicaC);
providerCMetadata = Environment.CurrentDirectory + "\\" + replicaC ➥
    + " .Metadata";
    if (File.Exists(providerCMetadata))
    {
        File.Delete(providerCMetadata);
    }
    providerC = new MySyncProvider(replicaC, providerC_ReplicaCon, ➥
providerCMetadata);
    //Define the conflict resolution policy
    providerA.Configuration.ConflictResolutionPolicy = ➥
ConflictResolutionPolicy.ApplicationDefined;
    providerB.Configuration.ConflictResolutionPolicy = ➥
ConflictResolutionPolicy.ApplicationDefined;
    providerC.Configuration.ConflictResolutionPolicy = ➥
 ConflictResolutionPolicy.ApplicationDefined;
```

```
            //Raise the event to handle conflicts
            providerA.DestinationCallbacks.ItemConflicting += new ➥
EventHandler<ItemConflictingEventArgs>(DestinationCallbacks_ItemConflicting);
            providerB.DestinationCallbacks.ItemConflicting += new ➥
EventHandler<ItemConflictingEventArgs>(DestinationCallbacks_ItemConflicting);
            providerC.DestinationCallbacks.ItemConflicting += new ➥
EventHandler<ItemConflictingEventArgs>(DestinationCallbacks_ItemConflicting);

            //create new instance of sync agent
            agent = new SyncOrchestrator();
            //Random class to generate Id for the records
            random = new Random(1);
        }
```

Creating New Customer Records

As shown in the following code listing, new customer records can be created in each of the
replicas by clicking the Create button:

```
        private void btnCreate_Click(object sender, EventArgs e)
        {

            //Begin transactions
            providerA.BeginUpdates();
            providerB.BeginUpdates();
            providerC.BeginUpdates();

            c1 = new Customer(providerA_ReplicaCon, replicaA, random.Next(1000), ➥
"A_TestName1", "A_TestDesig1", 10);
            providerA.CreateNewItem(c1);
            c2 = new Customer(providerA_ReplicaCon, replicaA, random.Next(1000), ➥
"A_TestName2", "A_TestDesig2", 20);
            providerA.CreateNewItem(c2);

            c3 = new Customer(providerB_ReplicaCon, replicaB, random.Next(1000), ➥
"B_TestName1", "B_TestDesig1", 30);
            providerB.CreateNewItem(c3);
            c4 = new Customer(providerB_ReplicaCon, replicaB, random.Next(1000), ➥
"B_TestName2", "B_TestDesig2", 40);
            providerB.CreateNewItem(c4);
```

```
            c5 = new Customer(providerC_ReplicaCon, replicaC, random.Next(1000), ➥
    "C_TestName1", "C_TestDesig1", 50);
            providerC.CreateNewItem(c5);
            c6 = new Customer(providerC_ReplicaCon, replicaC, random.Next(1000), ➥
    "C_TestName2", "C_TestDesig2", 60);
            providerC.CreateNewItem(c6);

            //End transactions
            providerA.EndUpdates();
            providerB.EndUpdates();
            providerC.EndUpdates();
        replicaContentIntial.Refresh(providerA_ReplicaCon, providerB_ReplicaCon, ➥
    providerC_ReplicaCon, query);
            btnCreate.Enabled = false;
        }
```

In the code listing, the btnCreate_Click event creates two customer records in each replica by calling the CreateNewItem method on the custom sync provider. This ensures that metadata for the Customer table is also updated in the metadata store.

The code for creating conflicts and handling deletes is very straightforward. To keep the example short, they are not included here. However, you can examine the code of SyncForm.cs to examine them in more detail.

Synchronizing Replicas

Replicas are synchronized by calling the private helper method Synchronize, as shown in this code listing:

```
        private void Synchronize(MySyncProvider sourceProvider,MySyncProvider
    destProvider)
        {
            agent.Direction = SyncDirectionOrder.DownloadAndUpload;
            agent.LocalProvider = sourceProvider;
            agent.RemoteProvider = destProvider;
            stats = agent.Synchronize();
        }
```

The Synchronize method accepts two instances of custom sync provider as input and sets them as local and remote providers for the sync agent. It also sets the sync direction as DownloadAndUpload, meaning that both the replicas will be synchronizing data with each other.

Finally it calls the Synchronize method on the sync agent to begin synchronization.

That's it; we have created our first custom synchronization provider. In the next two chapters of this book we will create more-complex providers using the Sync Framework.

Running the Sample Application

You can launch the application from Visual Studio by pressing F5 or Ctrl+F5 while the solution is open.

You can also double-click on CustomProvider.exe, located in the bin folder of the application to launch it.

After launching the application, the sync form is displayed, as shown in Figure 3-9.

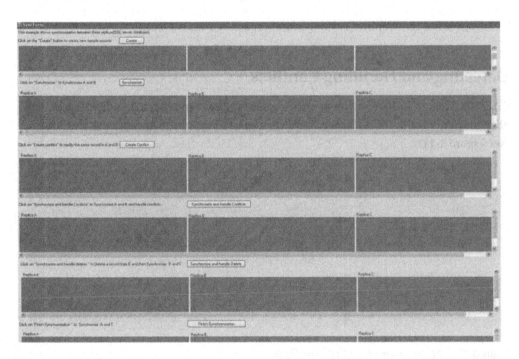

Figure 3-9. *Sync form*

You can exercise different options, such as creating records in a Customer table, synchronizing the replicas, and handling conflicts using the sync form.

Synchronizing New Records

Click the Create button to create a new record in each of the three databases. Now click the Synchronize button to synchronize replicas A and B (see Figure 3-10).

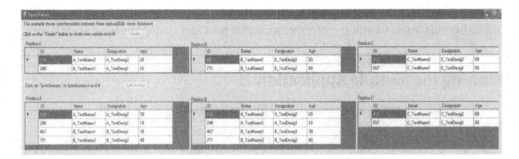

Figure 3-10. *Synchronizing new records*

Observe that now replica A and B contain records from each other as well.

Detecting and Handling Conflicts

Click the Create Conflict button to create conflicts between replica A and replica B. Now click the Synchronize And Handle Conflicts button to synchronize replica A and B again (see Figure 3-11).

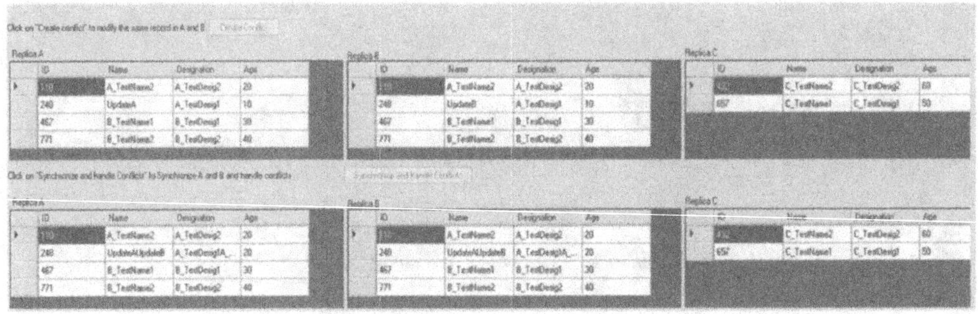

Figure 3-11. *Detecting and handling conflicts*

The name of the record with an ID of 248 is merged in both replica A and B because we have set the conflict resolution action to Merge.

Synchronize Deleted Records

Click the Synchronize And Delete button to delete records from replica B and then synchronize replicas B and C (see Figure 3-12).

Figure 3-12. *Synchronizing deleted records*

Finishing Synchronization

Click the Finish Synchronization button to synchronize replicas A and C (see Figure 3-13).

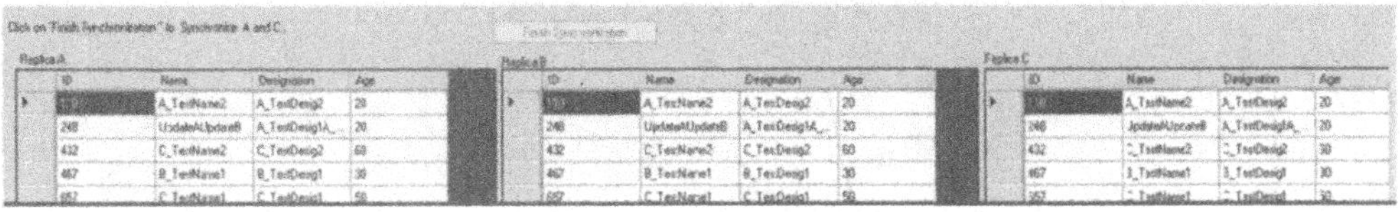

Figure 3-13. *Finishing the synchronization*

Summary

In this chapter, you learned about the synchronization provider. The Sync Framework ships with the built-in providers for the file system, ADO.NET data services, and simple sharing extensions (SSEs). You should always try to use them wherever possible.

Using the built-in provider is very straightforward: we just need to create a provider attached to each replica and then call the Synchronize method on the sync agent. If the built-in provider doesn't fit the need, we can also create our own custom provider.

When creating the custom sync provider, the main tasks are to implement change enumeration, track changes, detect and handle conflicts, and save changes.

The Sync Framework also provides the built-in metadata store built on the top of the SQL Server CE to simplify metadata manipulation.

In the next chapters, you'll learn in detail about built-in sync providers and how to build your own custom metadata store.

■ ■ ■

CHAPTER 4

Working with Synchronization Providers: Part 2

In the previous chapter, you learned a great deal about how to build a custom sync provider to synchronize the content of two replicas. In this chapter, you will learn how to fine-tune the custom sync provider to suit your synchronization scenario. You will learn about different patterns and practices for creating an efficient sync provider. The sync provider example in the previous chapter was very basic to get you started on different tasks that provider writers need to implement. In this chapter we will modify the same sync provider to handle advanced and more real-time synchronization scenarios such as the following:

- Creating sync providers that implement change units that allow better control over change tracking to reduce conflicts

- Creating custom sync providers that use asynchronous change tracking

- Creating extensible sync providers that allow code reuse and adding multiple sync providers into the existing synchronization scenario

By the time you complete this chapter, you'll have a solid understanding of how to create a custom sync provider that can handle complex scenarios with better performance, extensibility, and efficiency.

Change Units

Change units are used to represent an item change at more-granular level. To better understand the concept of change units, let's consider a scenario in which you have to build an application that synchronizes the data between two SQL Server databases. The first task is implementing change tracking. In this case, the decision a provider writer needs to make is to define what qualifies as an item in the replica.

This decision of defining an item within a replica is usually governed by the synchronization scenario. When synchronizing two SQL Server databases, an item can be a record or a column in a table in the database. After defining an item, a provider writer has to implement change tracking to determine the changes made to that item. Change units help compact subitem changes to be represented and enable more-granular change tracking. In our case, we can define an item as a record in a table in the database, and change units can be defined as columns in the record.

■**Note** All changes must occur at least at the level of the items.

If we consider our previous example of synchronizing a Customer table whose schema is shown in Figure 4-1, the item is the customer record, and change units can be the individual columns in the Customer table.

Table - dbo.Customer

Column Name	Data Type	Allow Nulls
ID	int	☐
Name	varchar(127)	☑
Designation	nvarchar(127)	☑
Age	int	☑

Figure 4-1. *Customer table*

The change unit set for the Customer table can be represented as follows:

Change Unit [0] = Name

Change Unit [1] = Designation

Change Unit [2] = Age

Typically, the ID would not be considered for the change unit because it is the primary key in the table. As discussed in the previous chapter, we can use the ID field to create an item ID, which is used to uniquely identify an item during the synchronization process.

The order in which the change units are added to the change unit set is determined by the replicas participating in the synchronization. The set of ordered change units can effectively form a schema.

Knowing the advantages and disadvantages of change units helps the provider writer determine whether to implement change tracking with change units or without change units. Change units provide the following three benefits:

- They provide better and efficient change tracking at more-granular level.

- They reduce the amount of data that has to be sent from one replica to another during synchronization.

- They reduce the number of conflicts during the synchronization process.

To understand these advantages, let's go back to the example of synchronizing the Customer table in the two replicas or databases. If we decide not to implement change unit synchronization and implement all change tracking at the level of the items, a change in value of any column will be treated as an item change. Now what happens if the name of the customer is changed in one replica and the age of the customer is changed in another replica? In this case, the Sync Framework will treat it as an item change, and the entire customer row will have to be transferred. During synchronization, the Sync Framework will also detect that the same item was modified in both replicas, so a conflict is detected. But if we decide to implement more-granular change tracking at the level of change units, the Sync Framework will detect that change unit [0] name was modified in one replica and change unit [2] was modified in another replica, so there is no conflict. It needs to transfer only the change units, not the whole item.

The only drawback of implementing more-granular change tracking at the level of the item is that it increases the amount of change tracking information that the provider writer needs to store.

The provider writer decides whether to implement change unit synchronization by examining the problem and the schema or structure of the replica to determine what level of granularity is needed.

Provider writers should also keep the following in mind when deciding whether to implement change tracking at the item level or at the change unit level:

- You can easily create as many change units as you want if the replica has not started participating in any synchronization; that is, before the replica metadata has ever been stored in the metadata store. But the addition of change units after a replica has already participated in the synchronization is based on an out-of-band schema change. To allow the addition of change units at a later stage, change units must have a default or null value. When a change unit is added to the set of already existing change units, its updated version is set to the creation version of the actual item. This makes the added change units appear as if they existed in the change unit set from the beginning.

- After you have defined the change units for an item, they can't be deleted like regular change items. Change units are actually treated as properties of the item and they exist as long as the item exists. Once the item is deleted, change units for that item are no longer available.

Creating Sync Providers with Change Units

While creating a custom sync provider that implements change units, you can make use of the SaveChangeWithChangeUnits method of the INotifyingChangeApplierTarget interface.

You need to override the SaveChangeWithChangeUnits method in the custom sync provider class, which should inherit from the INotifyingChangeApplierTarget interface. The signature of the method is shown in the following code snippet:

```
void SaveChangeWithChangeUnits(ItemChange change,
    SaveChangeWithChangeUnitsContext context);
```

This method has two parameters. The first parameter, Change, contains the item change; the second parameter, Context, contains information about the change to be applied. This method saves the change that has change unit revisions to the replica.

Creating Providers That Use Asynchronous Change Tracking

In Chapter 3, we created a custom sync provider that makes use of inline change tracking. In this section, you will learn how to create custom sync providers that make use of asynchronous change tracking.

Before digging deeply into the code for the provider that makes use of asynchronous change tracking, let's recall our discussion of change tracking from Chapter 3.

Change tracking happens before a sync session begins. To implement change tracking, the sync provider needs to update the sync versions for the changed items whenever changes happen in the replica. When creating custom sync providers before source sync providers begin to enumerate changes, we need to ensure that changes made locally to the source replica should also be reflected in its knowledge. This process, change tracking, can be implemented by using either of the following two methods:

- *Inline tracking:* Knowledge of the replica for an item is updated when a local change is made to the replica. Inline tracking is used when it is easy to plug in the logic for updating a replica's knowledge into the methods that change the content of the replica. For example, it can be a good idea to use inline tracking when synchronizing databases. We can use the triggers on the database to update the knowledge of the replica as soon as a record is modified.

- *Asynchronous tracking:* Knowledge of the replica is not updated as soon as the local changes happen in the replica. Instead, an external service or process is called on the replica to scan the changes and update the knowledge of the replica before the source provider begins to enumerate the changes. The tracking can be made a part of a scheduled process, but it needs to be executed before the sync session begins. Asynchronous tracking is used in scenarios in which it is difficult to plug in the logic for updating the replica's knowledge into the methods that change the content of the replica. The simplest way to implement asynchronous tracking is to store the state of an item after each sync session and then compare it with the state of that item before doing synchronization. For example, it might be a good idea to use asynchronous tracking to synchronize files between two folders. The easiest way to do this is to store the date modified and the file size after each sync session. Before beginning the new sync session, check these parameters to determine whether a change was made.

Now let's get into the code sample. We will be extending the example of synchronizing two databases from Chapter 3. We will make this sample to use asynchronous change tracking instead of inline change tracking.

The entire source code for the example using asynchronous change tracking is located in Sync\Chapter IV\Code\CustomProviderWithAsyncTracking. The solution structure of this project is shown in Figure 4-2.

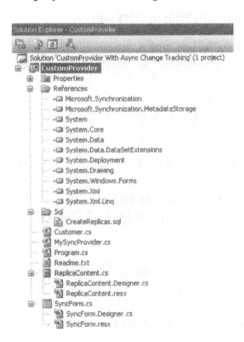

Figure 4-2. *Custom provider with async change tracking*

As you can see in the figure, there is no change in the solution structure except that the name of the solution is changed to CustomProvider With Async Change Tracking because we are using the same example of synchronizing two databases (as discussed in detail in Chapter 3). To use asynchronous change tracking, we need to make the following changes to the existing project:

1. Change the replicas or databases to add the DateModified and DateCreated fields in the Customer table, as shown in the following SQL script:

```
CREATE TABLE [dbo].[Customer](
       [ID] [int] NOT NULL,
       [Name] [nvarchar](1000) COLLATE
       SQL_Latin1_General_CP1_CI_AS NULL,
       [Designation] [nvarchar](1000) COLLATE
       SQL_Latin1_General_CP1_CI_AS NULL,
       [Age] [int] NULL,
       [DateModified] [datetime] NOT NULL CONSTRAINT
       [DF_Customer_DateModified]  DEFAULT (getdate()),
       [DateCreated] [datetime] NOT NULL CONSTRAINT
       [DF_Customer_DateCreated]  DEFAULT (getdate())
) ON [PRIMARY]
```

CreateReplicas.sql is modified to add these two fields in every replica.

These fields find changes to the replica since the last time it was modified. In later sections of this chapter, we will explore how to use these two fields to find updates made to the Customer table.

2. Change the custom sync provider (MySyncProvider.cs) to include methods that detect changes in the replica.

3. Change the custom sync provider to remove inline change tracking.

4. Change the Customer.cs class to include properties for DateModified and DateCreated. Include methods for retrieving the records modified since the last synchronization.

5. Change the synchronizing application (SyncForm.cs) to remove dependency on the provider to make changes to the Customer table.

Besides the preceding changes, the rest of the code in the existing project remains the same.

We have already seen the changes made to CreateReplicas.sql; now let's examine the changes made to the sync provider represented by the MySyncProvider.cs class.

MySyncProvider.cs

Changes to the MySyncProvider.cs class can be divided into following three categories:

- Removing inline tracking

- Implementing methods for asynchronous change tracking

- Changing the overridden provider methods to use these methods

Removing Inline Tracking

In the inline tracking project in Chapter 3, we updated the sync metadata as soon as any changes were made to the replica. This forced a limitation on us to combine the logic of creating/modifying/deleting an item (customer record), and to update the item metadata in a single method and have the synchronizing application (SyncForm.cs) call this method to modify contents of the replica. In a real-life problem, custom sync providers should also have the capability to update the metadata asynchronously because most of the applications have their own logic to update their replicas and they may not support the injection of custom logic to update the metadata.

So the replica operation methods such as create, update, and delete are removed from the sync provider, and the SyncForm creates/modifies/deletes the record within the Sync-Form itself. This removes the dependency between the SyncForm and the sync provider.

Implementing Asynchronous Change Tracking

The MySyncProvider.cs class includes the following three methods to implement asynchronous change tracking.

- GetLastSyncTime()

- SaveLastSyncTime()

- UpdateMetadataStoreWithChanges()

The first two methods are used to save the last synchronization time to a file and retrieve the last synchronization time from the same file.

As shown in the following code listing, the GetLastSyncTime() method retrieves the last synchronization time from a file on the system. The method determines whether the replicas are synchronized for the first time by checking whether the file that is used to save the sync time exists on the local system. If the file does not exist, the file is created, and the minimum value of the DateTime object is saved. If the file exists, the saved DateTime object is returned.

```
private DateTime GetLastSyncTime()
{
    string LastSyncTimeFilePath = Path.Combine(Environment.CurrentDirectory,
_replicaName + @".LastSyncTime");
    if (!File.Exists(LastSyncTimeFilePath))
    {
        DateTime dt = DateTime.MinValue;
        SaveLastSyncTime(dt);
        return dt;
    }
    else
    {
        using (FileStream fs = File.Open(LastSyncTimeFilePath,
         FileMode.Open, FileAccess.ReadWrite, FileShare.None))
        {
            // Read the LastSyncTime from the file.
            fs.Seek(0, SeekOrigin.Begin);
            BinaryReader br = new BinaryReader(fs);
            return new DateTime(br.ReadInt64());
        }
    }
}
```

As shown in the following code listing, the SaveLastSyncTime() method saves the last synchronization time to a file on the system:

```
private void SaveLastSyncTime(DateTime dt)
{
    using (FileStream fs =
    File.Open(Path.Combine(Environment.CurrentDirectory,
    replicaName + @".LastSyncTime"), FileMode.OpenOrCreate,
    FileAccess.ReadWrite, FileShare.None))
    {
        // Write the LastSyncTime to the file.
        fs.SetLength(0);
        BinaryWriter bw = new BinaryWriter(fs);
        bw.Write(dt.Ticks);
    }
}
```

The UpdateMetadataStoreWithChanges() method detects the changes made to the replica and updates the metadata store to reflect these changes.

If you examine the code in the UpdateMetadataStoreWithChanges() method in the
MySyncProvider.cs class, you notice that the UpdateMetadataStoreWithChanges() method
updates the metadata within a single transaction by wrapping the code within the
BeginTransaction() and CommitTransaction() methods of the built-in SQL Server CE
metadata store:

```
_metadataStore.BeginTransaction();
//Code to update Metadata
  _metadataStore.CommitTransaction();
```

The Sync Framework makes it mandatory to use these methods while updating the
metadata store. If you try to update the metadata store without the transaction, you will
get the following exception:

```
An unhandled exception of type
'Microsoft.Synchronization.MetadataStorage.ExplicitTransactionRequired
Exception' occurred in CustomProvider.exe
Additional information: An active transaction is required before any
change can be committed to the store.
```

After beginning the metadata store transaction, the
UpdateMetadataStoreWithChanges() method calls the GetUpdatedCustomersId() method
of the Customer class to retrieve a dictionary of the entire item's IDs and last modified date.
We will explore this method in more detail in a later section; right now just understand
that the GetUpdatedCustomersId() method takes the connection string for the database as
input and returns a dictionary of all customer IDs and the last time the customer record
was modified:

```
          _customersId = Customer.GetUpdatedCustomersId(_replicaCon);
```

_customersId is a local dictionary variable that holds this data. As shown in the following
code listing, this dictionary—along with the GetLastSyncTime() method—finds the following:

- Newly added customers

- Updated customers

- Deleted customers

```
          _metadata.DeleteDetector.MarkAllItemsUnreported();
          foreach (KeyValuePair<string, DateTime> customerId in _customersId)
          {
              SyncId syncId = new SyncId(customerId.Key);
              ItemMetadata existingItem = _metadata.FindItemMetadataById(syncId);
```

```
        if (existingItem == null)
        {
            existingItem =
            _metadata.CreateItemMetadata(syncId, new
              SyncVersion(0, _metadata.GetNextTickCount()));
            existingItem.ChangeVersion = existingItem.CreationVersion;
            //saves the item in metadata store
            _metadata.SaveItemMetadata(existingItem);
        }
        else
        {
            if (customerId.Value.CompareTo(GetLastSyncTime()) > 0)
            {
                existingItem.ChangeVersion = new
                  SyncVersion(0,
                  _metadata.GetNextTickCount());
                  _metadata.SaveItemMetadata(existingItem);
            }
            else
            {
                _metadata.DeleteDetector.ReportLiveItemById(syncId);
            }
        }
    }
    foreach (ItemMetadata item in
    _metadata.DeleteDetector.FindUnreportedItems())
    {
        item.ChangeVersion = new SyncVersion(0,
        _metadata.GetNextTickCount());
        item.MarkAsDeleted(item.ChangeVersion);
        _metadata.SaveItemMetadata(item);
    }
```

Finding a newly added or updated customer record is very straightforward. The UpdateMetadataStoreWithChanges() method loops through each customer ID in the dictionary and checks whether the metadata store contains an entry for that item. Searching the metadata store by customer ID is made possible because we are storing the customer ID as the sync ID to uniquely identify the item metadata in the metadata store.

If the item is not found in the metadata store, it's considered a newly added item, and the metadata for that item is created and stored in the metadata store (as shown in the previous code snippet). It's important to understand that not finding the item in the metadata store always means that there was a new record added that has not yet been synchronized.

Now what if the customer record was deleted from the table? In that case, although the customer record is deleted from the Customer table, the metadata for the item is not deleted from the metadata store.

If the item is found in the metadata store, and the customer record was modified after the last synchronization, it's considered an update.

The item metadata is located by using the customer ID, and the change version for the item is updated. Finally, the item metadata is saved in the metadata store.

The algorithm for finding deleted items is a little more complex and can be explained by the following steps:

1. Mark all items as unreported for the replica before beginning to enumerate the metadata store, as shown in this code:

   ```
   _metadataStore.BeginTransaction();
   ```

2. For a newly created or updated customer record, we're creating or updating the metadata in the metadata store; that is, we are already enumerating that item metadata in the metadata store. This is enough for the Sync Framework to assume that the customer record corresponding to the item data being created or updated in the item metadata store is not deleted from the database.

3. If the record was not updated since the last synchronization but is present in the metadata store, mark its existence by reporting it as a live item in the metadata store:

   ```
   __metadata.DeleteDetector.ReportLiveItemById(syncId);
   ```

4. After all three steps are completed, you can find the deleted items in the replica by calling _metadata.DeleteDetector.FindUnreportedItems(). Now loop through all items in _metadata.DeleteDetector.FindUnreportedItems()and mark them as deleted in the metadata store.

Changing Overridden Provider Methods to Use Asynchronous Change Tracking Methods

Now that you know how to implement asynchronous change tracking, let's examine when and where to call the methods.

Only two methods from the overridden provider region need to be changed:

- GetChangeBatch(): We need to call the UpdateMetadataStoreWithChanges() method inside the GetChangeBatch() method to update the metadata store with any changes in the replica and before the source provider begins to enumerate the changes in the replica:

```
public override ChangeBatch GetChangeBatch(uint batchSize,
    SyncKnowledge destinationKnowledge, out object
    changeDataRetriever)
    {
    //Make sure that Metadata store is updated with local
        changes in the replica.
    UpdateMetadataStoreWithChanges();
    ChangeBatch batch =
            _metadata.GetChangeBatch(batchSize,
            destinationKnowledge);
        changeDataRetriever = this;
        return batch;
    }
```

- EndSession(): After the sync session is finished, we need to save the time of the last synchronization to a file on the system. This is done by calling the SaveLastSyncTime() method inside the EndSession() method:

```
public override void EndSession(SyncSessionContext syncSessionContext)
{
    string filePath =
     Path.Combine(Environment.CurrentDirectory, _replicaName);
    if (File.Exists(filePath))
    {
        File.Delete(filePath);
    }
    SaveLastSyncTime(DateTime.Now);
}
```

Changing the Customer.cs Class

As shown in the following code listing, the Customer class is modified to include the following properties, which store the DateTime of creating and updating the record:

```csharp
/// <summary>
/// DateModified
/// </summary>
public DateTime DateModified
{
    get
    {
        return m_DateModified;
    }
    set
    {
        m_DateModified = value;
    }
}

/// <summary>
/// DateCreated
/// </summary>
public DateTime DateCreated
{
    get
    {
        return m_DateCreated;
    }
    set
    {
        m_DateCreated = value;
    }
}
```

Create; update, delete, and other methods are also modified to accommodate these newly added properties.

A new method, GetUpdatedCustomersId(), is added to the customer class. As shown in the following code listing, this method retrieves the customer IDs and their last modified date and returns them in dictionary form:

```
public static Dictionary<string, DateTime>
  GetUpdatedCustomersId(string ReplicaCon)
{
    Dictionary<string, DateTime> customersID = new
      Dictionary<string, DateTime>();
    string sql = "SELECT ID,DateModified FROM Customer";
    using (SqlConnection con = new SqlConnection(ReplicaCon))
    using (SqlDataAdapter adr = new SqlDataAdapter(sql, con))
    {
        DataSet ds = new DataSet();
        adr.Fill(ds);
        foreach (DataRow dr in ds.Tables[0].Rows)
        {
            customersID.Add(dr[0].ToString(), (DateTime)dr[1]);
        }
    }
    return customersID;
}
```

This dictionary is then used to determine the changes made to the Customer table since the last synchronization.

Changes in the Synchronizing Application

Because we removed the logic of manipulating customer records from the provider, the synchronizing application (the SyncForm) is changed to call the methods of the Customer class directly to create, update, and delete customer records.

ReplicaContent.cs

This is our user control, which displays the content of each replica in a gridview. This control contains three gridviews to display records in the Customer table for each of the three replicas. (This user control is similar to ReplicaContent.cs, which we used in the synchronous change tracking example in Chapter 3.)

There are no other changes to the SyncForm. The application's user interface remains the same as discussed in Chapter 3.

Running the Sample Application

You can launch the application by pressing F5 or Ctrl+F5 while the solution is open in Visual Studio.

You can also launch the application by double-clicking `CustomProvider.exe`, which is located in the `bin` folder of the application.

After launching the application, SyncForm is displayed, as shown in Figure 4-3.

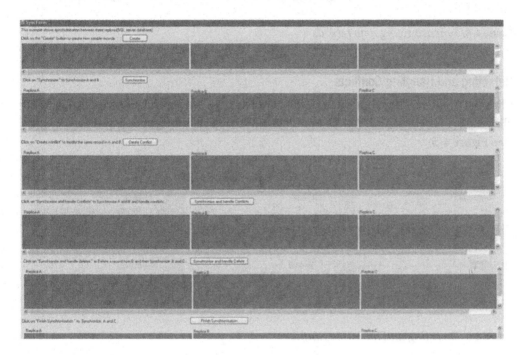

Figure 4-3. *SyncForm*

As shown in the figure, you can exercise different options, such as creating records in the Customer table, synchronizing the replicas, and handling conflicts using the SyncForm.

Synchronizing New Records

Click the Create button to make a new record in each of the three databases. Then click the Synchronize button to synchronize replicas A and B (see Figure 4-4).

Observe that replicas A and B now contain records from each other.

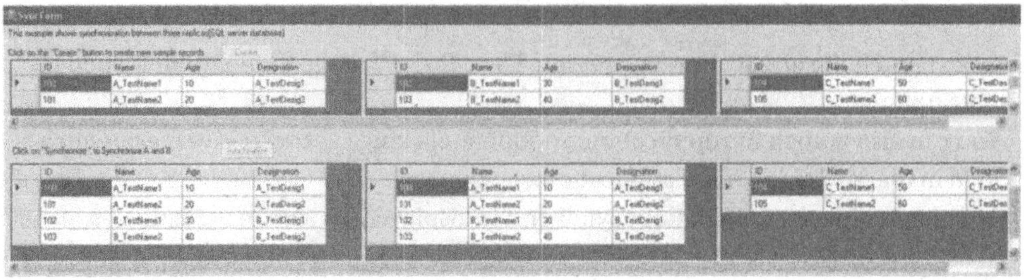

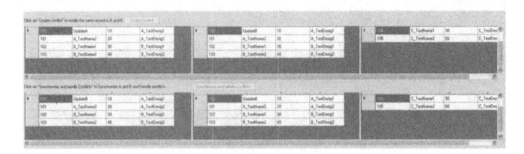

Figure 4-4. *Synchronizing new records*

Detecting and Handling Conflicts

Click the Create Conflict button to create conflicts between replica A and replica B. Then click the Synchronize And Handle Conflicts button to synchronize replicas A and B again (see Figure 4-5).

Figure 4-5. *Detecting and handling conflicts*

The name of the record having an ID of 100 is merged in both replicas A and B because we have set the conflict resolution action to Source Wins.

Synchronizing Deleted Records

Click the Synchronize And Handle Delete button to delete records from replica B and then synchronize replicas B and C (see Figure 4-6).

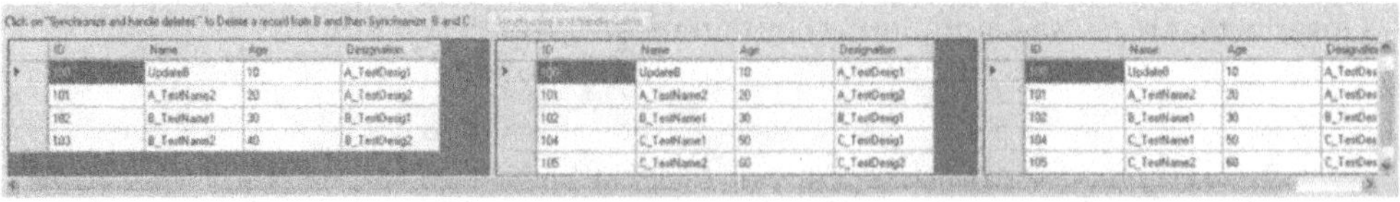

Figure 4-6. *Synchronizing deleted records*

Finishing Synchronization

Click the Finish Synchronization button to synchronize replicas A and C (see Figure 4-7).

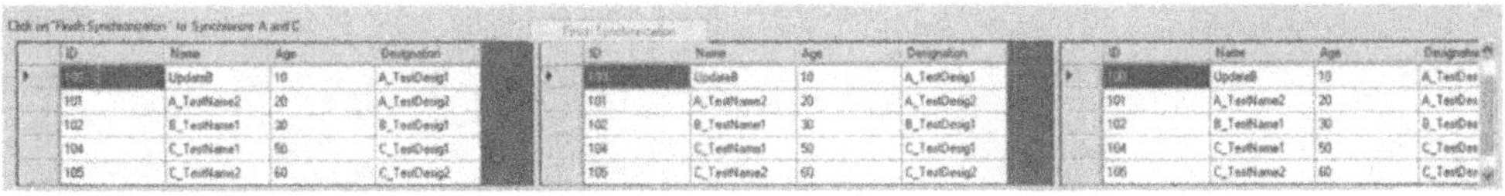

Figure 4-7. *Finishing the synchronization*

So far, you have learned how to create a custom sync provider using inline change tracking and asynchronous change tracking. Now let's create a generic sync provider that can be used as a base for adding future sync providers.

Creating a Generic Sync Provider

This section extends the previous example of synchronizing two databases to use a new DBSyncProvider that inherits from a generic sync provider class. This generic sync provider class is created by factoring out the replica-specific code from overridden provider methods and other common code such as methods to implement asynchronous change tracking. This common code can then be used by any future providers that inherit from the base sync provider. This facilitates code reuse and makes it easier to add new providers.

As shown in Figure 4-8, the solution structure for the generic sync provider contains three projects:

- BaseSyncProvider: In this project, we'll refactor the MySyncProvider.cs class used in a previous example to be generic so it can serve as the base class for adding new providers.

- CustomDBProvider: In this project, we'll create a new DBSyncProvider that will inherit from the MyBaseSyncProvider.cs class created in the previous project and synchronize SQL Server databases.

- CustomFileProvider: In this project, we'll create a new CustomFileProvider that will inherit from the MyBaseSyncProvider.cs class created in the previous project and will synchronize files between two folders.

The entire source code for the asynchronous change tracking example is located here: Sync\Chapter IV\Code\CustomProviderExtended.

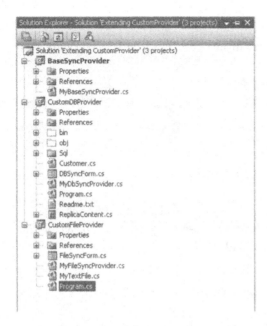

Figure 4-8. *Solution structure*

BaseSyncProvider

This project consists of the MyBaseSyncProvider.cs class, which can be derived to create new providers from it. The declaration of the MyBaseSyncProvider.cs class is the following:

```
public abstract class MyBaseSyncProvider<TransferClass> :
KnowledgeSyncProvider, IChangeDataRetriever,
INotifyingChangeApplierTarget, IDisposable
    {
            //Code goes here
    }
```

The MyBaseSyncProvider.cs class makes use of the Transfer class to determine the type of data the derived provider will synchronize. In our example, the Transfer class can be related to the Customer class. A new sync provider can be created by deriving this class, as shown in the following code:

```
    public class MyDbSyncProvider:
                                    MyBaseSyncProvider<Customer>
    public class MyFileSyncProvider:
                                    MyBaseSyncProvider<MyTextFile>
```

As stated earlier, we can create the MyBaseSyncProvider.cs class by refactoring the replica-specific code from the code that is common to sync providers. This refactoring is achieved by providing the following abstract method in the class, which will be overridden in the derived class:

```
public abstract void CreateItemData(TransferClass itemData);
public abstract void UpdateItemData(TransferClass itemData);
public abstract void DeleteItemData(TransferClass itemData);
public abstract void
    UpdateItemDataWithDestination(TransferClass sourceItemData,
    TransferClass destItemData);
public abstract void MergeItemData(TransferClass
    sourceItemData, TransferClass destItemData);
public abstract TransferClass GetItemData(string itemDataId,
    string replicaName);
public abstract Dictionary<string, DateTime> ItemDataIds { get; }
```

When these abstract methods are overridden in the derived sync provider, they help implement the replica-specific methods such as creating, deleting, updating, or retrieving an item in the replica.

The other methods remain unchanged in the MyBaseSyncProvider.cs class—which is the refactored version of the MySyncProvider.cs class used in the previous example—except the following two methods that require manipulating the item in the actual replica:

- LoadChangeData()

- SaveItemChange()

In these two methods, we remove the call to the actual Customer class to manipulate the customer record. Instead, these two methods now make use of abstract methods.

Extending the Generic Sync Provider Class

In the solution we will extend the generic sync provider MyBaseSyncProvider.cs class to create the following two new providers:

- CustomDBProvider synchronizes SQL Server databases

- CustomFileProvider synchronizes text files

To leverage the MyBaseSyncProvider.cs class, we need to add a reference to the BaseSyncProvider project. To do this, right-click on the project and click Add A Reference from the menu. Select the BaseSyncProvider project from the Projects tab, as shown in Figure 4-9.

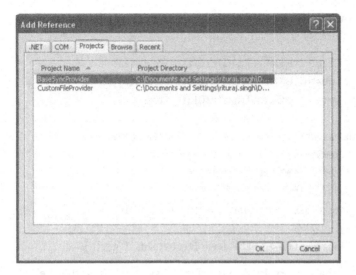

Figure 4-9. *Add Reference dialog box*

CustomDBProvider

This project contains the new custom database sync provider derived from the base sync provider.

The other files in this project are similar to those in the synchronizing databases example.

MyDbSyncProvider.cs

This class, which is derived from the MyBaseSyncProvider.cs class, implements the abstract method from the base class. Again, the implementation of these methods is very similar to the synchronizing databases example.

The MyDbSyncProvider.cs class makes calls to the Customer class to implement the abstract replica methods:

```
public  override void CreateItemData(Customer itemData)
{
    itemData.ReplicaCon = _replicaCon;
    itemData.Create();
}
public override void UpdateItemData(Customer itemData)
{
    itemData.ReplicaCon = _replicaCon;
    itemData.Update();
}
```

```
public override void DeleteItemData(Customer itemData)
{
    itemData.ReplicaCon = _replicaCon;
    itemData.Delete();
}
public override void UpdateItemDataWithDestination(Customer
 sourceItemData, Customer destItemData)
{
    destItemData.Name = sourceItemData.Name;
    destItemData.Designation = sourceItemData.Designation;
    destItemData.Age = sourceItemData.Age;
    destItemData.ReplicaCon = _replicaCon;
    destItemData.Update();
}
public override void MergeItemData(Customer sourceItemData,
 Customer destItemData)
{
    destItemData.Name += sourceItemData.Name;
    destItemData.Designation += sourceItemData.Designation;
    destItemData.Age += sourceItemData.Age;
    destItemData.ReplicaCon = _replicaCon;
    destItemData.Update();
}
public override Customer GetItemData(string itemDataId, string replicaName)
{
    return Customer.GetCustomerById(int.Parse(itemDataId),
    _replicaCon, replicaName);
}
public override Dictionary<string, DateTime> ItemDataIds
{
    get
    {
        return Customer.GetUpdatedCustomersId(_replicaCon);
    }
}
}
```

Customer.cs

This class is similar to the Customer.cs class from the previous code sample. In this case, we'll use the Customer class to perform create/read/update/delete (CRUD) operations on each of the replicas. The Customer class contains a property for each field available in the Customer table for changing or retrieving the value of the fields.

ReplicaContent.cs

This class is the user control that displays the content of each replica in a gridview. This control contains three gridviews to display records in the Customer table for each of the three replicas. This user control is similar to the user control ReplicaContent.cs used in the previous example.

Running the Sample Application

There are no changes to the SyncForm; it is the same (and the user interface of the application is the same) as the previous example.

CustomFileProvider

This project, which contains the new custom text file provider derived from the base sync provider, contains the following files:

- MyFileSyncProvider.cs

- MyTextFile.cs

- FileSyncForm.cs

MyFileSyncProvider.cs

This class is derived from the MyBaseSyncProvider.cs class:

```
public class MyFileSyncProvider : MyBaseSyncProvider<MyTextFile>
```

It uses the MyTextFile.cs class to create, update, delete, and retrieve files from the folders:

```
public override void CreateItemData(MyTextFile itemData)
{
    itemData.FolderPath = _folderPath;
    itemData.Create();
}
public override void UpdateItemData(MyTextFile itemData)
{
    itemData.FolderPath = _folderPath;
    itemData.Update();
}
public override void DeleteItemData(MyTextFile itemData)
{
    itemData.FolderPath = _folderPath;
    itemData.Delete();
}
```

```
public override void UpdateItemDataWithDestination(MyTextFile
  sourceItemData, MyTextFile destItemData)
{
    destItemData.Text = sourceItemData.Text;
    destItemData.FolderPath = _folderPath;
    destItemData.Update();
}
public override void MergeItemData(MyTextFile sourceItemData,
  MyTextFile destItemData)
{
    destItemData.Text += sourceItemData.Text;
    destItemData.FolderPath = _folderPath;
    destItemData.Update();
}
public override MyTextFile GetItemData(string itemDataId,
  string replicaName)
{
    return MyTextFile.GetFileByFileName(itemDataId, _folderPath);
}
public override Dictionary<string, DateTime> ItemDataIds
{
    get
    {
        return MyTextFile.GetUpdatedFileNames(_folderPath);
    }
}
}
```

MyTextFile.cs

As shown in the following code listing, this class contains properties to hold the name of the text file, the text in the file, and the path of folder in which the file is saved:

```
public string FileName
{
    get
    {
        return m_fileName;
    }
    set
    {
        m_fileName = value;
    }
}
```

```
public string Text
{
    get
    {
        return m_text;
    }
    set
    {
        m_text = value;
    }
}
public string FolderPath
{
    get
    {
        return m_folderPath;
    }
    set
    {
        m_folderPath = value;
    }
}
```

The class also contains the following methods to create, update, delete, and retrieve files from the folder:

```
public void Create()
{
    using (FileStream fs1 = File.Open(Path.Combine(FolderPath,
      FileName), FileMode.Create))
    {
        BinaryFormatter bf = new BinaryFormatter();
        bf.Serialize(fs1, Text);
        fs1.Flush();
    }
}
public void Update()
{
    Delete();
    Create();
}
```

```
public void Delete()
{
    File.Delete(Path.Combine(FolderPath, FileName));
}
public static MyTextFile GetFileByFileName(string fileName,
  string folderName)
{
    string _text = string.Empty;
    using (TextReader tr = new
      StreamReader(Path.Combine(folderName, fileName)))
    {
        _text = tr.ReadToEnd();
    }
    return new MyTextFile(fileName, _text, folderName);
}
public static Dictionary<string, DateTime>
  GetUpdatedFileNames(string folderName)
{
    Dictionary<string, DateTime> fileNames = new
      Dictionary<string, DateTime>();

    DirectoryInfo df = new DirectoryInfo(folderName);

    foreach (FileInfo  fi in df.GetFiles())
    {
        fileNames.Add(fi.Name, fi.LastWriteTime);
    }
    return fileNames;
}
```

You can relate the MyTextFile.cs class to the Customer.cs class created earlier.

FileSyncForm.cs

This form works as the synchronizing application. The form contains two text boxes to accept the source and destination folder locations and initiates the synchronization between the source and destination folders.

The form initializes two instances of the MyFileSyncProvider.cs class and hooks them to two folder locations. Folder locations are specified by the two text boxes present on the form, as shown in the following code:

```
private void btnSync_Click(object sender, EventArgs e)
{
    btnSync.Enabled = false;
    string sourceFolderPath = txtSource.Text;
    string destFolderPath = txtDestination.Text;

    if (string.IsNullOrEmpty(sourceFolderPath))
    {
        MessageBox.Show("Please Enter a value for Source folder");
        return;
    }
    if (string.IsNullOrEmpty(destFolderPath))
    {
        MessageBox.Show("Please Enter a value for Destination folder");
        return;
    }
    sourceProvider = new MyFileSyncProvider(sourceReplicaName,
        sourceFolderPath, sourceProviderMetadataPath);
    destinationProvider = new
        MyFileSyncProvider(destinationReplicaName,
        destFolderPath, destinationMetadataPath);
    Synchronize();
    btnSync.Enabled = true;
}
```

The Synchronize() method is a helper method that sets the local and remote provider on the sync agent and then calls the Synchronize() method to synchronize files in the folders:

```
private void Synchronize()
{
    try
    {
        agent.Direction = SyncDirectionOrder.DownloadAndUpload;
        agent.LocalProvider = sourceProvider;
        agent.RemoteProvider = destinationProvider;
        stats = agent.Synchronize();

        MessageBox.Show("Synchronization Finished");
    }
    catch (Exception ex)
    {
        throw ex;
        //TODO : Exception handling
    }
```

```
        finally
        {
            sourceProvider.Dispose();
            destinationProvider.Dispose();
        }
    }
```

You can run the application by right-clicking the project in the solution explorer in Visual Studio and then selecting Debug and Start New Instance from the menu.

Running the application will launch a form, as shown in Figure 4-10.

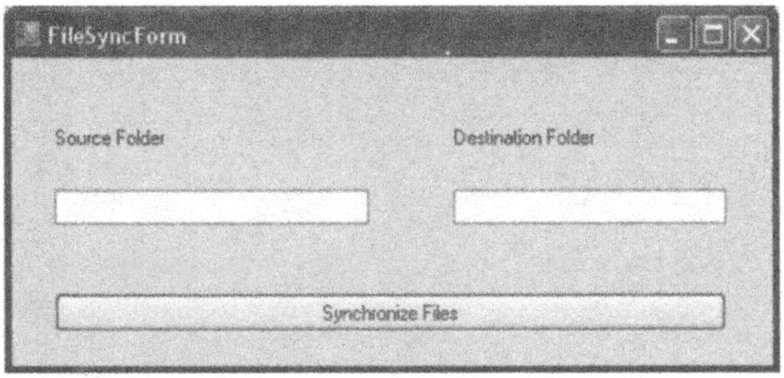

Figure 4-10. *FileSync form*

Enter values in the two text boxes and then click Synchronize Files. After the synchronization finishes, a message stating that synchronization is complete will display.

Summary

In this chapter, you learned advanced concepts of building custom sync providers. The Sync Framework offers great flexibility to developers by providing very nice features such as synchronizing change units that allow better control over change tracking and filtered synchronization that allows developers to easily create filters on the type of data that needs to be synchronized.

We also learned a great deal about implementing custom providers with asynchronous change tracking. Finally, we created a generic sync provider that enables the easy addition of future sync providers into the existing synchronization system. All these examples used the built-in SQL Server CE metadata storage.

In the next chapter, you'll learn about creating a custom sync provider that can make use of the custom metadata store.

CHAPTER 5

■ ■ ■

Working with File Synchronization Providers

The Microsoft Sync Framework is a comprehensive framework for synchronizing offline data with its online counterpart. It is independent of the protocol used and the data store that contains the data to be synchronized and can be used to implement applications that can synchronize data seamlessly.

This chapter explores how we can use managed and unmanaged code to synchronize files and folders in our system. But first, let's have a quick look at the core components of the Sync Framework.

Sync Framework Core Components

In its simplest form, synchronization can be described as the process of bringing together two endpoints or data stores. When the contents of the two data stores are the same, they are known to be in sync with each other. The core components of the Sync Framework comprise the following:

- Providers

- Metadata storage services

- Application

- Error codes

File Sync Provider

A provider in the Sync Framework can be defined as a component that enables a data source to participate in a synchronization process to facilitate offline collaboration of applications, data, and services.

The basic objective of the file sync provider is to synchronize files and folders on your system and enable you to synchronize files and folders in the same system or across systems in your network. You can use it to maintain a backup copy of your files and folders from one system to another.

The Microsoft white paper, "Introducing Microsoft Sync Framework: Sync Services for File Systems." states the following: "The file system provider is designed to be a generic, reusable component that can be used for synchronizing files and folders between any NTFS or FAT formatted file volumes. It uses the Sync Framework's powerful metadata model to enable peer-to-peer sync of file data with support for arbitrary topologies (client/server, full-mesh, P2P), including support for removable media such as flash drives, USB thumb drives, etc. It enables third parties to build file synchronization and roaming scenarios into their end-to-end sync solutions without having to worry about directly interacting with the file system." (See msdn.microsoft.com/en-us/sync/bb887623.aspx.)

File Sync Provider Features

The file sync provider provides a number of features:

- Support for incremental synchronization

- Support for synchronization in preview and nonpreview modes of operation

- Support for detecting file changes

- Conflict detection

- Support for filtering the files that will participate in the synchronization process

Sync Services Components for File Systems

Sync Services for file systems is actually a component that is provided as part of the Sync Framework and includes the file sync provider that can be used to synchronize files and folders in systems with NT file system (NTFS), file allocation table (FAT), or Server Message Block (SMB) file systems. This section lists the components of Sync Services for file systems.

Enumerations

Here is a list of the enumerations:

- SYNC_SAVE_ACTION

- CONFLICT_RESOLUTION_POLICY

- SYNC_FULL_ENUMERATION_ACTION

This is what the SYNC_SAVE_ACTION enumeration looks like:

```
typedef enum
{
  SSA_CREATE,
  SSA_UPDATE_VERSION_ONLY,
  SSA_UPDATE_VERSION_AND_DATA,
  SSA_UPDATE_VERSION_AND_MERGE_DATA,
  SSA_DELETE_AND_STORE_TOMBSTONE,
  SSA_DELETE_AND_REMOVE_TOMBSTONE
} SYNC_SAVE_ACTION;
```

This is what the CONFLICT_RESOLUTION_POLICY enumeration looks like:

```
typedef enum
{
  CRP_NONE,
  CRP_DESTINATION_PROVIDER_WINS,
  CRP_SOURCE_PROVIDER_WINS,
  CRP_LAST,
} CONFLICT_RESOLUTION_POLICY;
```

And, this is what the SYNC_FULL_ENUMERATION_ACTION enumeration looks like:

```
typedef enum
{
  SFEA_FULL_ENUMERATION,
  SFEA_PARTIAL_SYNC,
  SFEA_ABORT,
} SYNC_FULL_ENUMERATION_ACTION;
```

Interfaces

And, here is a list of the interfaces:

- IKnowledgeSyncProvider

- ILoadChangeContext

- IProviderSyncServices

- IAsynchronousNotifyingChangeApplierTarget

- ISynchronousDataRetriever

- ISaveChangeContext

- IAsynchronousDataRetriever

- ISaveChangeWithChangeUnitsContext

- IAsynchronousNotifyingChangeApplier

- ISyncFilter

- IAsynchronousNotifyingChangeApplierTargetCallback

- ISynchronousNotifyingChangeApplier

- IDataRetrieverCallback

- ISynchronousNotifyingChangeApplierTarget

- IFileSyncProvider

Applications

An application uses some structures and interfaces to start and control synchronization among the synchronization providers. It uses the SYNC_SESSION_STATISTICS structure and the following interfaces:

- IApplicationSyncServices

- ISyncSession

- ISyncCallback

- IFilterSyncServices

- ISyncSessionState

You can use the FILESYNC_CHANGE_TYPE enumeration to specify the changes that can be applied to the destination replica. This enumeration is represented as follows:

```
typedef enum
{
    FILESYNC_CHANGE_TYPE_CREATE = 0,
    FILESYNC_CHANGE_TYPE_DELETE = 1,
      FILESYNC_CHANGE_TYPE_UPDATE = 2,
    FILESYNC_CHANGE_TYPE_RENAME = 3,
} FILESYNC_CHANGE_TYPE;
```

You can use the FILESYNC_INIT_FLAGS enumeration to control how the file sync provider works:

```
typedef enum
{
    FILESYNC_INIT_FLAGS_NONE = 0x00000000,
    FILESYNC_INIT_FLAG_USE_HASHING = 0x00000001,
    FILESYNC_INIT_FLAG_RECYCLE_DELETED_FILES = 0x00000002,
    FILESYNC_INIT_FLAG_RECYCLE_PREVIOUS_FILE_ON_UPDATES = 0x00000004,
        FILESYNC_INIT_FLAG_RECYCLE_CONFLICT_LOSER_FILES = 0x00000008,
    FILESYNC_INIT_FLAG_DISABLE_IMPLICIT_DETECT_CHANGES = 0x00000010,
} FILESYNC_INIT_FLAGS;
```

When a file or folder has been skipped during the synchronization process, you can use the FILESYNC_SKIP_REASON enumeration to determine the reason:

```
typedef enum
{
    FILESYNC_SKIP_REASON_UNKNOWN_ERROR = 0,
    FILESYNC_SKIP_REASON_APPLICATION_REQUEST = 1,
    FILESYNC_SKIP_REASON_SOURCE_CONCURRENCY_CHECK = 2,
    FILESYNC_SKIP_REASON_DESTINATION_CONCURRENCY_CHECK = 3,
    FILESYNC_SKIP_REASON_SOURCE_READ_ERROR = 4,
    FILESYNC_SKIP_REASON_DESTINATION_WRITE_ERROR = 5,
        FILESYNC_SKIP_REASON_FILE_TYPE_NOT_SUPPORTED = 6,
        FILESYNC_SKIP_REASON_CONFLICT_LOSER_FILE_WRITE_ERROR = 7
} FILESYNC_SKIP_REASON;
```

Synchronizing Files and Folders Using Unmanaged Code

You can use the Sync Framework to synchronize files and directories in your system. This section discusses how we can use unmanaged code to synchronize files and directories.

To synchronize files and folders in your system, follow these steps:

1. Create and initialize a file synchronization provider to represent files and folders in your system that will participate in the synchronization process.

2. Next, pass two sync providers to the synchronization session instance—for the source and destination providers, respectively.

3. Finally, start the synchronization session.

Creating the File Sync Provider

To create a file sync provider, you can use a pointer to IFileSyncProvider and the
CoCreateInstance() method:

```
IFileSyncProvider* ptrFileSync = NULL;
hr = CoCreateInstance(CLSID_FileSyncProvider, NULL,
CLSCTX_INPROC_SERVER, __uuidof(ptrFileSynchronization),
(void**)&ptrFileSynchronization);
```

Initializing the File Sync Provider

Before you use the provider, you can initialize it with the Initialize() method:

```
hr = ptrFileSynchronization->Initialize(*ptrGuidReplicaSource,
ptrStrFolderSource->GetString(),
ptrStrMetadataSource->GetString(), NULL,
FILESYNC_INIT_FLAGS_NONE, ptrFilter, NULL, NULL);
```

Creating the Filter

You need to create a filter using the IFileSyncProvider::CreateNewScopeFilter() method.
This code illustrates how to create the filter:

```
IFileSyncScopeFilter* ptrFilter = NULL;
hr = ptrProviderSource->CreateNewScopeFilter(&ptrFilter);

if (SUCCEEDED(hr))
{
    hr = ptrFilter->SetFilenameExcludes(m_strFilenameExc.GetString());

    if (SUCCEEDED(hr))
    {
        hr = ptrFilter->SetSubDirectoryExcludes(m_strDirExc.GetString());
    }

    if (SUCCEEDED(hr))
    {
        DWORD dwMask = wcstoul(m_strAttrExc.GetString(), NULL, 16);
        hr = pFilter->SetFileAttributeExcludeMask(dwMask);
    }
```

```
    if (SUCCEEDED(hr))
    {
        if (!m_strFilenameInc.IsEmpty())
        {
            hr = ptrFilter->SetFilenameIncludes(m_strFilenameInc.GetString());
        }
    }
}
```

Note To exclude file(s) from the synchronization process using unmanaged code, use the following code:

```
IFileSyncScopeFilter* ptrFilter = NULL;
hr = pProvSrc->CreateNewScopeFilter(&ptrFilter);
if (SUCCEEDED(hr))
{
    hr = pFilter->SetFilenameExcludes(m_strFilenameExc.GetString());
}
```

Starting the Synchronization Process

As a last step, you need to start the synchronization process. Here's how to start:

```
IApplicationSyncServices* ptrSvc = NULL;
hr = CoCreateInstance(CLSID_SyncServices, NULL, CLSCTX_INPROC_SERVER,
IID_IApplicationSyncServices, (void**)&ptrSvc);

if (SUCCEEDED(hr))
{
    ISyncSession* ptrSession = NULL;
    hr = ptrSvc->CreateSyncSession(ptrProviderDestination,
    ptrProviderSource, &ptrSession);

    if (SUCCEEDED(hr))
    {
        SYNC_SESSION_STATISTICS syncStats;
        hr = ptrSession->Start(CRP_DESTINATION_PROVIDER_WINS, &syncStats);
        ptrSession->Release();
    }

    ptrSvc->Release();
}
```

■**Note** To build the examples provided in this section, you need to include the following header files:

```
#include <synchronization.h>
#include <filesyncprovider.h>
```

Synchronizing Files and Folders Using Managed Code

There are three sync providers available:

- *Sync provider for ADO.NET*: Synchronizes data sources that are supported by ADO.NET

- *Sync provider for file systems*: Provides synchronization of files and folders in your system

- *Sync provider for RSS feeds*: Synchronizes data retrieved through Really Simple Syndication (RSS) feeds

■**Note** A file system is the organization that an operating system follows for the purpose of storage of files and folders in a system. The sync provider for file systems supports NTFS, FAT, and SMB file systems only.

The file system provider in the Sync Framework is a reusable component that can be used to synchronize files and folders in your system using the metadata model of the Sync Framework. Literally, *metadata* means "data about the data." The Sync Framework relies on the common metadata model to solve various common synchronization problems such as conflict detection, network failures, and storage and application errors. It is the sync metadata that makes synchronization using the Sync Framework independent of network topology, data store type, data type, or transfer protocol type.

Metadata storage service (MSS) provides the necessary infrastructure to store the sync metadata. Sync metadata is used by the Sync Framework runtime during the synchronization. The Sync Framework uses an MSS that is used to store the synchronization metadata in a file. Further, this metadata file can be stored along with the files and the folders participating in the synchronization process, or even in a separate location. If the location is separate, you need to specify it when you create and initialize the file sync provider.

Metadata in the Sync Framework is of two types: replica metadata and item metadata. (For more information on sync metadata, refer to Chapter 2.)

To perform synchronization using the file sync provider, you need to do the following:

1. Create and initialize an instance of the FileSyncProvider class.

2. Pass this instance to a sync agent.

3. Start the synchronization process.

The attributes supported by the file sync provider are the following:

- FILE_ATTRIBUTE_SYSTEM

- FILE_ATTRIBUTE_READONLY

- FILE_ATTRIBUTE_TEMPORARY

- FILE_ATTRIBUTE_HIDDEN

- FILE_ATTRIBUTE_DIRECTORY

You can use the FileSyncOptions enumeration to configure how the file sync provider works. This enumeration comprises the following members:

- CompareFileStreams

- ExplicitDetectChanges

- RecycleConflictLoserFiles

- RecycleDeletedFiles

- RecyclePreviousFileOnUpdates

To do a bitwise combination of these members, this enumeration also provides a FlagsAttribute.

Skipping the Files and Folders to Synchronize

You can dynamically skip files during the synchronization process. Here's how:

1. Register a handler to the ApplyingChange event.

2. Set the SkipChange property to true in this event handler. You can now write your custom code in the OnAppliedChange event handler.

Here's how to implement the OnAppliedChange event handler:

```
FileSyncProvider fileSyncProvider;
fileSyncProvider.AppliedChange += new EventHandler (OnAppliedChange);
destinationProvider.SkippedChange += new EventHandler (OnSkippedChange);

public static void OnAppliedChange(object sender, AppliedChangeEventArgs args)
{
 switch (args.ChangeType)
 {
 case ChangeType.Create:
   Console.WriteLine("Applied Create for the file named" + args.NewFilePath);
   break;
 case ChangeType.Delete:
   Console.WriteLine("Applied Delete for the file named" + args.OldFilePath);
   break;
 case ChangeType.Overwrite:
   Console.WriteLine("Applied Overwrite for the file named" + args.OldFilePath);
   break;
 default:
   break;
 }
}
```

Here's how to implement the OnSkippedChange event handler to discover why a particular file has been skipped during the synchronization process:

```
public static void OnSkippedChange(object sender, SkippedChangeEventArgs args)
{
 if (args.Exception != null)
 Console.WriteLine("Error occured: "+args.Exception.Message);
}
```

Controlling Files and Folders to Synchronize

Note that the following files are automatically excluded from the synchronization process:

- Desktop.ini with system and hidden attributes

- Thumbs.db with system and hidden attributes

- Metadata files

You can also use the FileSyncScopeFilter to let the Sync Provider know about the files and folders that you need to synchronize.

Applying Static Filters

You can apply static filters to control files and folders that you want to participate in the synchronization process. You can apply these filters to exclude files and folders from the synchronization process using wildcards and filters.

To use static filters, do the following:

1. Create an instance of the FileSyncScopeFilter class and specify the exclusion or inclusion filters to its constructor.

2. Pass this instance to the constructor of the FileSyncProvider class when creating an instance of the FileSyncProvider class.

Microsoft.Synchronization.Files Namespace

The Microsoft.Synchronization.Files namespace contains the classes and enumerations required to synchronize files and folders in your system using the file sync provider. The following are the major classes in the Microsoft.Synchronization.Files namespace:

- FileSyncProvider

- FileSyncScopeFilter

- AppliedChangeEventArgs

- ApplyingChangeEventArgs

- DetectedChangesEventArgs

- DetectingChangesEventArgs

- SkippedChangeEventArgs

- SkippedFileDetectEventArgs

Following are the enumerations:

- ChangeType

- FileSyncOptions

- SkipReason

In the sections that follow, we will take a look at two of the most important classes of this namespace: FileSyncProvider and FileSyncScopeFilter.

FileSyncProvider Class

The FileSyncProvider class extends the UnManagedSyncProvider class and implements the IDisposable interface:

```
public class FileSyncProvider : UnmanagedSyncProviderWrapper, IDisposable
{
  //members of the FileSyncProvider class
}
```

Table 5-1 lists the important properties of the FileSyncProvider class.

Table 5-1. *FileSyncProvider Properties*

Property	Purpose
FileSyncOptions	Specifies how the FileSyncProvider will behave during the synchronization process.
PreviewMode	Gets or sets the preview mode of the FileSyncProvider.
ReplicaId	Returns the replica ID of the FileSyncProvider.
ScopeFilter	Returns the names of the files and directories in the current scope.
RootDirectoryPath	Returns the absolute path of the folder that contains the files and directories that will participate in the synchronization process.
TempDirectoryPath	Returns the location where the temporary files created during the synchronization process will be stored.
MetadataFileName	Returns the name of the metadata storage file.
MetadataDirectoryPath	Returns the location of the metadata storage file.

Table 5-2 lists the important methods and events of the FileSyncProvider class.

Table 5-2. *FileSyncProvider Class Methods and Events*

Method/Event	Purpose
DetectChanges	This method can be used to get to know the changes to the file(s) that participated in the synchronization process.
ApplyingChange	This event is fired when a particular file participating in the synchronization process is about to change.
AppliedChange	This event is fired after a change is applied to a file participating in the synchronization process.

Table 5-2. *FileSyncProvider Class Methods and Events (Continued)*

Method/Event	Purpose
CopyingFile	This event is fired periodically to see the progress of copying a particular file.
SkippedChange	This event is fired when a particular file participating in the synchronization process has been skipped.

FileSyncScopeFilter Class

The FileSyncScopeFilter class is used to include or exclude files and folders that will be participating in the synchronization process:

```
public class FileSyncScopeFilter
{
 //members of the FileSyncScopeFilter class
}
```

Table 5-3 lists the important members of the FileSyncScopeFilter class.

Table 5-3. *FileSyncScopeFilter Class Properties*

Property	Purpose
FileNameExcludes	Public property used to get the collection of the names of the files that will be excluded from the synchronization process.
FileNameIncludes	Public property used to get the collection of the names of the files that will be included in the synchronization process.
SubdirectoryExcludes	Public property used to get the collection of all the relative paths of the directories that will be excluded from the synchronization process.
AttributeExcludeMask	Gets or sets attributes that exclude files and folders in the synchronization process.

Detecting the Changes

The file sync provider enables you to detect file changes on the file system. It does this by detecting the changes in the replica since the last synchronization. Each time a new synchronization session is started, the changes are detected.

Note A file system is the organization that an operating system follows for the purpose of storage and retrieval of data. As an example, the file system used by MS DOS is FAT, the one used by Windows 98 is VFAT, the one used by Windows NT/XP/Vista is NTFS, and the one used for Unix OS is UFS.

The trick to detecting the changes to the files and folders is in the sync metadata, which contains information about files and folders that participate in the synchronization process. You can have two types of metadata: replica metadata and item metadata. The file sync provider stores the metadata that describes the time and location of the changes of every folder that participated in the synchronization process. It identifies the changes by comparing file size, attributes, and times when the file was last modified. It also checks the hash contents (if the feature is turned on). In order to detect the changes in the folders participating in the synchronization process, it checks the attributes and the name of the folders.

In essence, there can be two ways in which the changes can be detected:

- Using the built-in change detection algorithm

- Using the changes to the hash value of the file

Using the Built-in Change Detection Algorithm

In this case, the changes are reported when any of the following changes:

- The name of the file or folder

- The size or modification time of the file

- Any file attributes that the file sync provider handles

- The hash value (if hashing is enabled)

Using Changes to the Hash Value

In this case, you need to specify the CompareFileStreams flag when you are creating and initializing the file sync provider. In doing so, the file sync provider will compute a hash value for each file participating in the synchronization process. This value will then be compared to detect the changes that happen to files and folders participating in the synchronization process.

Reporting Progress

You can make use of the preview mode synchronization to understand the changes and the progress when synchronization happens when the preview mode is not set. Note that when the synchronization is executed in preview mode, there won't be any changes in your file system. When synchronization is run in a nonpreview mode, the progress reporting notifications would be sent for the changes that happen. You can make use of this to detect the changes that happen when synchronization is run in these two modes. To report the progress during the synchronization process, follow these steps:

1. Register a handler for the ApplyingChange event.

2. Set the PreviewMode property of the file sync provider to true to enable preview mode.

3. Set a counter and increase its value depending on the number of times the ApplyingChange event is fired.

4. Start the synchronization process.

5. Disable the PreviewMode property of the file sync provider by setting its value to false.

6. Start synchronization again. You can easily inspect the changes between synchronization in the preview and nonpreview modes of operation.

Implementing a Sample Application

Before we delve into implementing the sample application to synchronize files and folders in our system, let's recall how synchronization works.

To implement the sample application provided in this chapter, we need to create two synchronization providers: one for the source and the other for the destination. After you create these two synchronization providers, you need to create a sync agent and attach these two providers to it. What is this sync agent? It is responsible for establishing and managing the sync session. Sync providers can receive and apply the changes to the replicas.

After being invoked by a sync agent, the destination sync provider sends its knowledge to the source sync provider. The source provider uses this knowledge to determine the changes and sends its knowledge back to the destination. The destination provider compares its knowledge with the source, resolves the conflicts, and then sends the request to the source provider for changed data. The source provider sends the changes to the destination provider, and the destination provider applies the changes to the destination replica.

Let's implement a sample application that will be used to synchronize files between a source and destination folder. Follow these steps:

1. Create a new console application project in Visual Studio.

2. Right-click References and add the following assemblies to the project:

   Microsoft.Synchronization

   Microsoft.Synchronization.Files

3. Create two folders in your system with the following names:

   C:\Apress\SyncFramework\SourceFolder

   C:\Apress\SyncFramework\DestinationFolder

4. Set the source and destination replica path:

```
String sourceReplicaPath = "C:\\Apress\\SyncFramework\\SourceFolder";
String destinationReplicaPath = "C:\\Apress\\SyncFramework\\DestinationFolder";
```

5. Get the source and destination replica IDs:

```
SyncId sourceReplicaID = GetReplicaID(sourceReplicaPath +"\\MySyncFile.ID");
SyncId destinationReplicaID = GetReplicaID(destinationReplicaPath
+"\\ MySyncFile.ID");
```

■**Note** *Replica* refers to the actual data store. For example, if you synchronize two databases, each of them is known as a replica. Replicas also contain items.

---

6. Create and initialize the source and destination providers:

```
FileSyncProvider fileSyncProviderSource = new FileSyncProvider(
sourceReplicaID, sourceReplicaPath, fileSyncScopeFilter, fileSyncOptions);

FileSyncProvider fileSyncProviderDestination = new FileSyncProvider(
destinationReplicaID, destinationReplicaPath, fileSyncScopeFilter, ➥
fileSyncOptions);
```

■**Note** You might want to delete some file(s) in your source folder. If you do, the destination folder should also have those file(s) deleted. To ensure that the deleted files are thrown into the Recycle Bin, you can use the FileSyncOptions.RecycleDeletes option when you are creating the destination sync provider instance:

```
FileSyncProvider destinationProvider = new FileSyncProvider(destinationReplicaID
"C:\\Apress\\Sync\\DestinationFolder\\", filter, FileSyncOptions.RecycleDeletes);
```

You can also ensure that after each change or delete, a file should be thrown to the Recycle Bin. To do so, you need to specify the following at the time when you are creating the destination provider:

```
FileSyncProvider destinationProvider = new FileSyncProvider(destinationReplicaID,
 "C:\\Apress\\Sync\\DestinationFolder\\", filter, FileSyncOptions.RecycleDeletes |
FileSyncOptions.RecycleOverwrites);
```

---

7. Create and initialize the agent that will perform the actual synchronization:

```
SyncAgent syncAgent = new SyncAgent();
syncAgent.LocalProvider = sourceReplicaID;
syncAgent.RemoteProvider = destinationReplicaID;
```

8. Set the synchronization destination:

```
syncAgent.Direction = SyncDirection.Upload;
```

9. Start the synchronization process by making a call to the Synchronize() method:

```
syncAgent.Synchronize();
```

Here is the source code of the GetReplicaID() method that is responsible for returning the replica ID to be used in the synchronization process:

```
private static SyncId GetReplicaID(String syncFileName)
{
    Guid guid = null;
    SyncId replicaID = null;
    StreamWriter streamWriter = null;
    FileStream fileStream = null;
    StreamReader streamReader = null;
    bool fileExists = File.Exists(syncFilePath);
    //If the sync file does not exist, a new sync id will be created,
    //else, the existing sync id will be used.
    if (!fileExists)
    {
        guid = Guid.NewGuid();
        replicaID = new SyncId(guid);
        fileStream = File.Open(syncFilePath, FileMode.Create);
        streamWriter = new StreamWriter(fileStream );
        streamWriter.WriteLine(guid.ToString());
        streamWriter.Close();
        fileStream.Close();
    }
    else
    {
        fileStream = File.Open(syncFilePath, FileMode.Open);
        streamReader = new StreamReader(fs);
        String guidString = streamReader.ReadLine();
        guid = Guid.NewGuid(guidString);
        replicaID = new SyncId(guid);
```

```
        streamReader.Close();
        fileStream.Close();
    }
    return replicaID;
}
}
```

Note You can set the direction of synchronization using `SyncDirection`. Its value can be one of the following:

SyncDirection.Upload

SyncDirection.Download

SyncDirection.UploadAndDownload

SyncDirection.DownloadAndUpload

Complete Source Code

Here is the complete source code for your reference:

```
using System;
using System.IO;
using Microsoft.Synchronization;
using Microsoft.Synchronization.Files;

public class SyncFiles
{

public void Main(String[] args)
{

String sourceReplicaPath = "C:\\Apress\\SyncFramework\\SourceFolder";
String destinationReplicaPath = "C:\\Apress\\SyncFramework\\DestinationFolder";

SyncId sourceReplicaID = GetReplicaID("C:\\Apress\\SyncFramework\\
SourceFolder\\ MySyncFile.ID ");
SyncId destinationReplicaID = GetReplicaID("C:\\Apress\\SyncFramework\\
DestinationFolder\\
MySyncFile.ID ");
```

```
FileSyncProvider fileSyncProviderSource = new FileSyncProvider(
sourceReplicaID, sourceReplicaPath, fileSyncScopeFilter, fileSyncOptions);

FileSyncProvider fileSyncProviderDestination = new FileSyncProvider(
destinationReplicaID, destinationReplicaPath, fileSyncScopeFilter, fileSyncOptions);

FileSyncProvider fileSyncProvider;
fileSyncProvider.AppliedChange += new EventHandler (OnAppliedChange);
destinationProvider.SkippedChange += new EventHandler (OnSkippedChange);

SyncAgent syncAgent = new SyncAgent();
syncAgent.LocalProvider = sourceReplicaID;
syncAgent.RemoteProvider = destinationReplicaID;

syncAgent.Direction = SyncDirection.Upload;

syncAgent.Synchronize();

}


private static SyncId GetReplicaID(String syncFileName)
{

    Guid guid = null;
    SyncId replicaID = null;
    StreamWriter streamWriter = null;
    FileStream fileStream = null;
    StreamReader streamReader = null;

    bool fileExists = File.Exists(syncFilePath);
    //If the sync file does not exist, a new sync id will be created,
    //else, the existing sync id will be used.

    if (!fileExists)
    {

        guid = Guid.NewGuid();

        replicaID = new SyncId(guid);
```

```
            fileStream  = File.Open(syncFilePath, FileMode.Create);

            streamWriter = new StreamWriter(fileStream );

            streamWriter.WriteLine(guid.ToString());

            streamWriter.Close();

            fileStream.Close();

        }

        else

        {

            fileStream = File.Open(syncFilePath, FileMode.Open);

            streamReader = new StreamReader(fs);

            String guidString = streamReader.ReadLine();

            guid = Guid.NewGuid(guidString);

            replicaID = new SyncId(guid);

            streamReader.Close();

            fileStream.Close();

        }

        return replicaID;

    }

}
```

Summary

This chapter looked at synchronization providers for file systems. We discussed how to work with unmanaged and managed file providers to synchronize files and folders in systems with NTFS, FAT, or SMB file systems installed. We also implemented a sample application to illustrate how to use the managed file synchronization provider to synchronize files and folders in our systems.

■ ■ ■

CHAPTER 6

Microsoft Sync Framework Metadata Storage Service

The Microsoft Sync Framework provides a comprehensive synchronization platform that enables offline and collaborative services for applications, stores, and devices without agreeing on the type of the data to be synchronized, the data store or transfer protocols, or even the network topology. What makes this possible is the common metadata model. The Sync Framework allows developers to create custom providers for their synchronization needs with complete freedom (except that the custom providers have to store the sync metadata using a common metadata model).

The Sync Framework metadata storage service (MSS) makes the job of implementing a common metadata model a lot easier by providing application programming interface (API) methods to create, update, and access sync metadata for a provider. The Sync Framework ships with a built-in implementation of the MSS. This built-in metadata store uses the SQL Server Compact Edition (CE) to store synchronization metadata for a provider.

This chapter will explore the design goals of the MSS and the built-in SQL Server CE metadata store. We will also explore the different scenarios that help you decide whether to choose the built-in SQL Server CE metadata store or implement a custom metadata store. Finally, we will explore in detail how to implement the custom metadata store.

Metadata Storage Service

The MSS helps provider writers (developers responsible for creating custom providers) implement a common metadata model.

The MSS has two main goals:

- It is designed to handle most of the details of storing, retrieving, and manipulating sync metadata. This design allows provider writers to focus on the synchronization problem without worrying too much about the complicated task of storing and retrieving the sync metadata.

- It provides a clear separation between the data store used for storing sync metadata and interfaces, and methods that are used to access the sync metadata from the metadata store. This design helps change the type of data store used to store the metadata in the future with little or no change to the custom sync provider. For example, suppose that you built a custom sync provider that uses a custom metadata store to store the sync metadata on the file system. Then you decide to change the metadata store to use a SQL Server database. This task of changing the type of sync metadata store can be easily implemented with minimal changes to the provider because of the separation provided by the MSS.

The MSS APIs can be implemented using both managed and unmanaged code. In this chapter we will be using the managed code, but there is little difference between the functionality provided by the managed and unmanaged implementation of the MSS APIs.

Built-in SQL Server CE Metadata Store

The Sync Framework also ships with an implementation of the APIs of the MSS. This implementation is built on top of the SQL Server CE. The built-in SQL Server CE metadata store is a ready-to-use component for storing sync metadata such as version and change detection information. This store greatly simplifies the development of custom providers that do not have a natural place to store metadata.

The SQL Server CE built-in metadata store has the following salient features:

- It is lightweight and compact.

- It provides reliability, performance, and security like a SQL Server database, while using compact data types so that it can be easily used for building client applications with less data storage capacity.

- It provides methods to create a new store or open the existing metadata store, initialize and load the metadata for a replica, and access and save the metadata in the store.

- It provides support for tick count management. (Tick count is used by providers to create or update the sync versions.)

- It provides support for implementing implicit and explicit implementing transactions.

- It is extensible because it provides the option to easily add a custom field to the metadata store.

Using a SQL Server CE Metadata Store vs. a Custom Metadata Store

So when should we use the built-in SQL Server CE metadata store and when should we create our own implementation of the metadata store? The answer is very simple: if the actual replica or data store you are synchronizing can be extended to store the sync metadata, you should try to create your own implementation of the metadata store because it provides unified access. For example if you are synchronizing the contents of two databases and you have the flexibility to extend or change the schema, consider creating your own implementation of the metadata store. In this scenario, you would usually extend the replica's schema to include additional fields to store the sync metadata.

On the other hand, if you're synchronizing two replicas that don't have a data store of their own or the flexibility of changing the schema, you might want to use the built-in SQL Server CE metadata store to store metadata while creating custom sync providers. An example of this scenario is synchronizing line of business (LOB) applications such as Microsoft CRM. In this case, you don't have the flexibility of changing the schema because it can have an adverse effect on the application.

Besides these two scenarios, there might be a situation in which both options can work for you. For example, you might want to synchronize two files on a file system. In this case, you can use the built-in SQL Server CE metadata store or a custom metadata store. Usually the built-in SQL Server CE metadata store gets the higher priority because the built-in SQL Server CE is a ready-to-use component, and you don't need to reinvent the whole wheel again.

Locating the Metadata Store

The Sync Framework can enable offline and collaboration for any type of application, store, and device. In this section, you will learn how to select the location of a metadata store with different devices and the role played by the MSS for storing metadata on different devices.

After selecting an implementation approach for storing the sync metadata, provider writers need to determine the location of the metadata store. This decision is governed by the type of participants involved in the synchronization. (A *participant* refers to the location from which the data to be synchronized is retrieved.)

Participants can be one of the following three types:

- *Full participants*: Full participants are devices that can create the new data stores and execute applications on the device itself. Examples of full participants are laptops, tablet PCs, and smart phones. Full participants can also store the sync metadata required for synchronization.

Consider the example of synchronizing files between two folders on a file system. In this case, we need to store the sync metadata as well as the necessary information for change tracking—such as when and where a file was last modified, the file name and its attributes, and so on. The MSS can be used to efficiently store all this information.

With full participants, the metadata store can be created on any of the devices that contain replicas participating in the synchronization. For example, for synchronizing files between two folders in two different laptops, the metadata store can be created on each laptop or both laptops. Provider writers can also choose to create one metadata store on each of the laptops for each of the replicas or folders.

For synchronizing files between a smart phone and laptop, you might want to store the metadata on the laptop and not on the smart phone device because of the amount of the data that can be stored on a smart phone.

- *Partial participants:* Like full participants, partial participants can create new data stores and store sync metadata, but they can't create or execute new applications. Thumb drives are a good example of partial participants because they can store the data but can't execute an application. Partial participants can synchronize with full participants, but they can synchronize directly with partial participants.

  The MSS store can be created on one or both of the partial participants. However, because the code of retrieving and manipulating the metadata can't be executed on partial participants, it's better to store the metadata on full participants such as laptops, which synchronize data with partial participants such as thumb drives. Storing the metadata on full participants makes the metadata local to the application manipulating the metadata and hence yields better performance.

- *Simple participants:* Simple participants are devices that can't store the new data or execute any application; they can just provide the information if requested. Some of the examples of simple participants include Really Simple Syndication (RSS) feeds and third-party web services such as those offered by Amazon or Google. Simple participants can synchronize only with full participants because they require sync metadata to be stored on full participants.

Interacting with Provider

In this section, you'll learn how sync providers use the MSS store to retrieve and manipulate the sync metadata. Figure 6-1 represents the interaction between the Sync Framework runtime, sync providers, and the MSS store by describing the components involved and different methods used to provide the interaction between them.

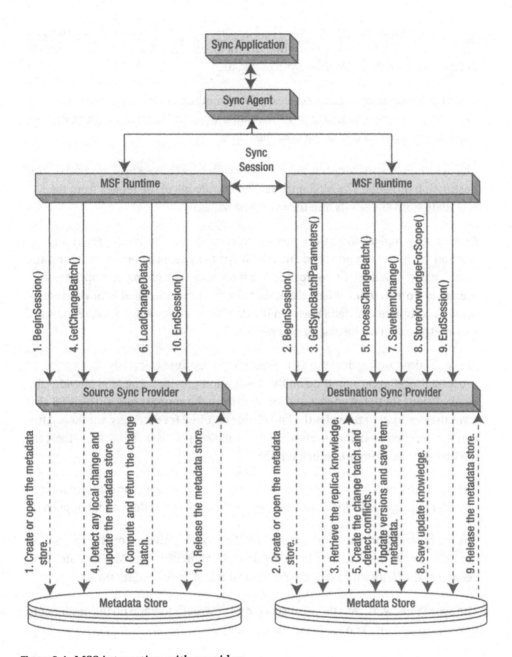

Figure 6-1. *MSS interaction with providers*

As shown in Figure 6-1, you need one sync provider for each replica for the replica to synchronize its data with other replicas. A replica synchronizes its data with another replica by establishing a sync session. The synchronizing application calls the Synchronize() method on the sync agent to start the synchronization process between two replicas.

The following steps describe the sync metadata flow in a typical sync session:

1. The Sync Framework runtime calls the BeginSession() method on the source provider. The MSS data store ensures that the metadata store for the source replica is created and initialized with the sync metadata.

2. The Sync Framework calls the BeginSession() method on the destination provider. The MSS data store ensures that the metadata store for the destination replica is created and initialized with the sync metadata.

3. The Sync Framework runtime calls the GetSyncBatchParameters() method on the destination provider. The MSS retrieves the knowledge of the replica from the metadata store and sends it to the source provider.

4. At the source replica, the Sync Framework runtime calls the GetChangeBatch() method on the source provider. The MSS helps the sync provider by detecting any local changes made to the source replica; if there are any changes, it updates the metadata store to reflect these changes. After this process, called *change enumeration*, is complete, the delta between the destination knowledge and the source knowledge is sent to the destination replica.

5. At the destination replica, the Sync Framework runtime calls the ProcessChangeBatch() method on the destination provider. The MSS provides the local versions for the change items received from the source replica. The MSS also gives the destination provider the knowledge required for detecting conflicts. After conflicts are detected and resolved, the destination provider sends the request for the actual items from the source replica.

6. The Sync Framework runtime calls the LoadChangeData() method on the source provider to retrieve the local item and sends the item to the destination replica.

7. The Sync Framework runtime calls the SaveItemChange() method on the destination provider to save the actual items to the destination replica. The MSS updates the version of the items and saves the item metadata in the metadata store.

8. The Sync Framework calls the StoreKnowledgeForScope() method on the destination provider to save the knowledge in the metadata.

9. The Sync Framework calls the EndSession() method on the destination provider to release the metadata store.

10. Finally, the EndSession() method is called on the source provider to release the metadata store for the source replica.

You can also choose to implement the same metadata store for both providers. In this case, the metadata for the source replica and destination replica will be saved in the common metadata store.

Implementing the Custom Metadata Store

We have already covered an example of creating a custom synchronization provider with the built-in SQL Server CE metadata store in Chapter 3. In this section, you'll learn how to create a custom synchronization provider with a custom metadata store.

We will use the same example discussed in Chapter 3. Recall that the sample custom sync provider is used to synchronize the data between three SQL Server databases. We will create a custom implementation of MSS and change the code of the sync provider to use the custom metadata store.

We will convert the example from Chapter 3 to use the custom metadata store to do the following:

1. Create a custom metadata store.

2. Change the custom sync provider to use the custom metadata store.

3. Change the application to use the changed custom sync provider.

The entire source code for the example using the custom metadata store is located here: Sync\Chapter VI\Code\CustomProvider.

Creating a Custom Metadata Store

The custom metadata store is created by starting a new class library project, as shown in Figure 6-2.

The dialog box shown in Figure 6-2 can be launched by clicking New Project in the Visual Studio IDE.

Creating a custom metadata store involves two tasks:

1. Create a class for holding the required metadata for an item.

2. Create a class that implements MSS APIs and contains methods for manipulating item metadata and replica metadata.

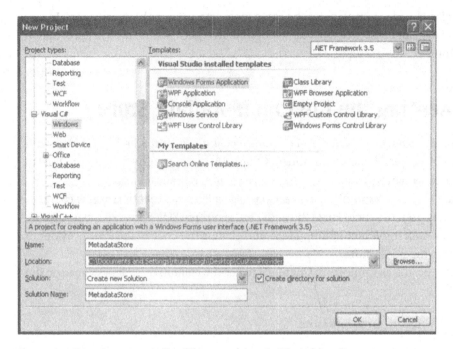

Figure 6-2. *Creating a new class library project in Visual Studio*

To implement these tasks, the MetadataStore project contains the following two class files.

- CustomItemMetadata.cs: This class file contains the properties that hold the required sync metadata for an item.

- CustomMetadataStore.cs: This class file contains the properties that hold the required metadata for a replica and implements the MSS by providing methods to retrieve and save the metadata. This class is also responsible for searching item metadata, providing support for tick count and knowledge management.

CustomItemMetadata.cs

We need to import the Microsoft.Synchronization namespace in the class file that contains the definition for SyncId and SyncVersion classes.

```
using Microsoft.Synchronization;
```

This class contains the following local private variables for getting and setting the properties of the class:

```
private SyncId itemId = null;
private SyncVersion creationVersion = null;
private SyncVersion changeVersion = null;
private string uri = null;
    private bool isTombstone = false;
```

The properties discussed in the next sections represent the required sync metadata for an item.

ItemId

ItemId is used to uniquely identify an item within a replica:

```
public SyncId ItemId
{
    get
    {
        if (itemId == null)
        {
            throw new InvalidOperationException("ItemId not
            yet set.");
        }
        return itemId;
    }
    set
    {
        if (value == null)
        {
            throw new ArgumentNullException("value", "ItemId
            cannot be null.");
        }
        itemId = value;
    }
}
```

CreationVersion

CreationVersion contains information about when and in which replica the item was created:

```
public SyncVersion CreationVersion
{
    get { return creationVersion; }
    set { creationVersion = value; }
}
```

ChangeVersion

ChangeVersion tracks when and where an item was last modified:

```
public SyncVersion ChangeVersion
{
    get { return changeVersion; }
    set { changeVersion = value; }
}
```

Uri

This property gets or sets the Uniform Resource Identifier (URI) of an item:

```
public string Uri
{
    get
    {
        if (uri == null)
        {
            throw new InvalidOperationException("Uri not yet set.");
        }
        return uri;
    }
    set
    {
        if (value == null)
            throw new ArgumentNullException("value", "Uri cannot be null.");
        uri = value;
    }
}
```

IsTombstone

This property tracks whether the item was deleted from the replica. If the value returned is true, it means the item contains information about a deleted item from the actual replica:

```
public bool IsTombstone
{
    get { return isTombstone; }
    set { isTombstone = value; }
}
```

The CustomItemMetadata.cs class also contains a method called Clone() that returns a new instance of CustomItemMetadata that is a member-by-member copy of the current CustomItemMetadata object:

```
    public CustomItemMetadata Clone()
    {
        return (CustomItemMetadata)this.MemberwiseClone();
    }
```

CustomMetadataStore.cs

This class file contains the properties that hold the required metadata for a replica and implements the MSS by providing methods to retrieve and save the metadata. This class is not only a full-fledged implementation of MSS but also contains properties and methods for manipulating the knowledge, replica ID, and the tick count.

This class stores the metadata, tick count, knowledge, and replica ID on the file system. For this purpose, it uses the FileStream object provided by the .NET Framework. As with the CustomItemMetadata class, this class also needs to import the Microsoft.Synchronization namespace:

```
    using Microsoft.Synchronization;
    using System.IO;
    using System.Runtime.Serialization.Formatters.Binary;
```

The CustomMetadataStore class inherits from the IEnumerable<CustomItemMetadata> and IDisposable interfaces:

```
public class CustomMetadataStore : IEnumerable<CustomItemMetadata>, IDisposable
```

Inheriting from the IEnumerable interface of the CustomItemMetadata type helps to enumerate the item metadata in the store by using the for-each loop.

Properties

In this section, we will go over each property of the CustomMetadataStore class in detail.

Metadata Directory

The metadata directory gets the parent directory in which all the metadata files are stored. Note that this directory holds all the files for storing metadata, tick count, knowledge, and replica ID. It is a read-only property because after you set the metadata directory, it can't be changed. This condition forces the sync provider to always refer to the same metadata. The default value of this property is set to C:\CustomMetadata. The application creates this directory if it does not exist already. This is done in the CreateMetadataStore() method of the CustomMetadataStore class:

```
private string __metadataDir = @"C:\CustomMetadata";
/// <summary>
/// Gets the Directory where metadata is stored
/// </summary>
 public virtual string MetadataDir
 {
   get { return __metadataDir; }
 }
```

ItemMetadataFilePath

This property gets or sets the file path that stores the required metadata for the items:

```
private string __itemMetadataFilePath;
/// <summary>
/// Gets or sets the file path of metadata
/// </summary>
public string ItemMetadataFilePath
{
    get { return _ _itemMetadataFilePath; }
    set
    {
        if (value == null)
        {
            throw new ArgumentNullException("value", "
            ItemMetadataFilePath cannot be null.");
        }
        if (value == String.Empty)
        {
            throw new ArgumentOutOfRangeException("value", "
            ItemMetadataFilePath cannot be the empty
             string.");
        }
        _ _itemMetadataFilePath = value;
    }
}
```

ReplicaIdFilePath

This property gets or sets the file path for storing and retrieving the replica ID:

```
private string _replicaIdFilePath;
/// <summary>
/// Gets or sets the file path which is used to store the replica ID
/// </summary>
public string ReplicaIdFilePath
{
    get { return _replicaIdFilePath; }
    set
    {
        if (value == null)
        {
            throw new ArgumentNullException("value",
            "ReplicaIdFilePath cannot be null.");
        }
        if (value == String.Empty)
        {
            throw new ArgumentOutOfRangeException("value",
            "ReplicaIdFilePath cannot be the empty string.");
        }
        _replicaIdFilePath = value;
    }
}
```

ReplicaId

This property gets or sets the replica ID from the metadata store. Replica ID is stored in the file whose location can be retrieved by combining ReplicaIdFilePath and _replicaIdFileName. The default value of replicaIdFileName is set to ReplicaId.msf:

```
            private const string _replicaIdFileName =
"ReplicaId.msf";
        private SyncId _replicaId = null;
    /// <summary>
/// Gets or sets the replica ID
/// </summary>
public SyncId ReplicaId
{
    get { return _replicaId; }
    set { _replicaId = value; }
}
```

TickCountFilePath

This property gets or sets the file path for storing and retrieving the tick count:

```
            private string __tickCountFilePath;
    /// <summary>
    /// Gets or sets the file path which is used to store the Tick Count
    /// </summary>
    public string TickCountFilePath
    {
        get { return __tickCountFilePath; }
        set
        {
            if (value == null)
            {
                throw new ArgumentNullException("value",
                "TickCountFilePath cannot be null.");
            }
            if (value == String.Empty)
            {
                throw new ArgumentOutOfRangeException("value",
                "TickCountFilePath cannot be the empty string.");
            }
            __tickCountFilePath = value;
        }
    }
```

TickCount

This property returns the current tick count for the replica. The default or initial value of tick count is set to 1 and it is incremented whenever an item metadata is updated or created in the metadata store:

```
    private ulong __tickCount = 1;
    /// <summary>
    /// Gets the Tick Count
    /// </summary>
    public ulong TickCount
    {
        get { return __tickCount; }
    }
```

KnowledgeFilePath

This property gets or sets the file path for storing and retrieving the knowledge of the replica:

```
private string __knowledgeFilePath;
/// <summary>
/// Gets or sets the file path which is used to store the Knowledge
/// </summary>
public string KnowledgeFilePath
{
    get { return __knowledgeFilePath; }
    set
    {
        if (value == null)
        {
            throw new ArgumentNullException("value",
              "KnowledgeFilePath cannot be null.");
        }
        if (value == String.Empty)
        {
            throw new ArgumentOutOfRangeException("value",
            "KnowledgeFilePath cannot be the empty string.");
        }
        __knowledgeFilePath = value;
    }
}
```

MyKnowledge

This property gets or sets the current knowledge of the replica:

```
private SyncKnowledge __myKnowledge;
/// <summary>
/// Current Knowledge
/// </summary>
public SyncKnowledge MyKnowledge
{
    get
    {
        return __myKnowledge;
    }
    set
    {
        __myKnowledge = value;
    }
}
```

MyForgottenKnowledge

This property gets or sets the forgotten knowledge of the replica. ForgottenKnowledge helps a replica find out the information about the deleted items in a replica that the other replica doesn't know about:

```
private ForgottenKnowledge __myForgottenKnowledge;
/// <summary>
/// Forgotten Knowledge
/// </summary>
public ForgottenKnowledge MyForgottenKnowledge
{
    get
    {
        return __myForgottenKnowledge;
    }
    set
    {
        __myForgottenKnowledge = value;
    }
}
```

RequestedBatchSize

This property gets or sets the batch size for a replica (the default value is set to 100):

```
//Default Batch Size
private uint __requestedBatchSize = 100;
        /// <summary>
/// Gets or sets the Batch size
/// </summary>
public uint RequestedBatchSize
{
    get { return __requestedBatchSize; }
    set { __requestedBatchSize = value; }
}
```

IdFormats

This property gets or sets the formats for the item ID and replica ID:

```
private SyncIdFormatGroup __idFormats = null;
/// <summary>
/// Gets or sets the Id format
/// </summary>
public SyncIdFormatGroup IdFormats
{
    get
    {
        return __idFormats;
    }
    set
    {
        __idFormats = value;
    }
}
```

Methods

The CustomMetadataStore class contains methods for creating the metadata store, initializing the store with sync metadata, managing replica metadata, and managing tick count.

While creating a custom metadata store, you need to implement the following tasks:

1. Create a metadata store.

2. Initialize the metadata store.

3. Provide methods for searching, manipulating, and saving item metadata.

4. Provide methods for manipulating and saving the replica ID.

5. Provide methods for manipulating and saving current knowledge as well as forgotten knowledge.

6. Provides methods for manipulating and saving a tick count.

7. Provides methods for releasing the metadata store at the end of the sync session.

Now let's examine the code of the CustomMetadataStore class to understand how it implements these tasks.

Creating a Metadata Store

The metadata store is created in the constructor of the class. The code of the constructor is shown in the following code listing:

```
/// <summary>
/// Creates and intializes the metadata store
/// </summary>
/// <param name="filename">Location of the Metadata</param>
/// <param name="replicaID">Id of the replica</param>
/// <param name="idFormats">ID formats for replica na ditem</param>
public CustomMetadataStore(string filename, SyncId replicaID,
SyncIdFormatGroup idFormats)
    {
        _replicaId = replicaID;
        _idFormats = idFormats;
        CreateMetadataStore(filename);
        IntializeSyncMetadata();
    }
```

The constructor has three input parameters. The filename parameter describes the location where the metadata store should be created. The replicaId uniquely identifies a replica. The idFormats parameter describes the format of the IDs used by the item and replica.

The constructor makes a call to the CreateMetadataStore() method to create the files and folders that will hold the item metadata. It determines the exact path for creating files that will store tick count, replica ID, and knowledge. The code for CreateMetadataStore() is shown in the following code listing:

```
/// <summary>
/// Intializes the metadata store.
/// </summary>
/// <param name="filename">Location for the metadata</param>
private void CreateMetadataStore(string filename)
    {

        //Create parent directory
        Directory.CreateDirectory(_metadataDir);
        //Create the directory for each replica
        _metadataDir = Path.Combine(_metadataDir, filename);
        //Clean up the Metadata Store
```

```
    if (Directory.Exists(_metadataDir))
    {
        Directory.Delete(_metadataDir, true);
    }
    Directory.CreateDirectory(_metadataDir);
    KnowledgeFilePath = Path.Combine(_metadataDir, _knowledgeFileName);
    ItemMetadataFilePath = Path.Combine(_metadataDir,
    _itemMetadataFileName);
    ReplicaIdFilePath = Path.Combine(_metadataDir, _replicaIdFileName);
    TickCountFilePath = Path.Combine(_metadataDir, _tickCountFileName);
}
```

Initializing the Metadata Store

After creating the metadata store, it's time to initialize the metadata store with sync metadata. To do this, the constructor calls the IntializeSyncMetadata() method:

```
/// <summary>
/// Intializes the Sync Metadata
/// </summary>
private void IntializeSyncMetadata()
{
    try
    {
        bool replicaIdFileAlreadyExists = File.Exists(ReplicaIdFilePath);
        _replicaIdFileStream = File.Open(ReplicaIdFilePath,
            FileMode.OpenOrCreate, FileAccess.ReadWrite,
            FileShare.None);
        if (replicaIdFileAlreadyExists)
        {
            LoadReplicaIDFile();
        }
        else
        {
            SaveReplicaIDFile();
        }
        bool itemMetadataFileAlreadyExists =
            File.Exists(ItemMetadataFilePath);
        _itemMetadataFileStream =
            File.Open(ItemMetadataFilePath,
            FileMode.OpenOrCreate, FileAccess.ReadWrite,
            FileShare.None);
```

```
            if (itemMetadataFileAlreadyExists)
            {
                // Exists so load.
                LoadItemMetadataFromStore ();
            }
            else
            {
                CreateItemMetadataInStore ();
            }
            bool tickCountFileAlreadyExists = File.Exists(TickCountFilePath);
            _tickCountFileStream = File.Open(TickCountFilePath,
                FileMode.OpenOrCreate, FileAccess.ReadWrite,
                FileShare.None);
            if (tickCountFileAlreadyExists)
            {
                LoadTickCountFile();
            }
            else
            {
              SaveTickCountFile();
            }
            bool knowledgeFileAlreadyExists = File.Exists(KnowledgeFilePath);
            _knowledgeFileStream = File.Open(KnowledgeFilePath,
                FileMode.OpenOrCreate, FileAccess.ReadWrite,
                FileShare.None);
            if (knowledgeFileAlreadyExists)
            {
                LoadKnowledgeFile();
            }
            else
            {
                CreateKnowledgeBlob();
            }
        }
        catch (IOException ex)
        {
            throw ex;
        }
    }
```

This method creates the files for storing item metadata, replica ID, tick count, and replica knowledge. It loads the item metadata, replica ID, knowledge, and tick count from the files if the file already exists. If the file does not exist, it creates the file and saves the default value to the file. The method uses objects of the FileStream class to create, open, and save the files. We will explore each of these methods in detail in the following sections.

Searching, Manipulating, and Saving Item Metadata

The CustomMetadataStore class provides a way to create item metadata in the store, load the list of item metadata from the store, search item metadata in the store by URI or ID, and save the item metadata to the store.

The CreateItemMetadataInStore() method creates a new list to hold the item metadata and writes the list to the file:

```
/// <summary>
/// Creates the Item metadata store
/// </summary>
private void CreateItemMetadataInStore()
{
    // Create data list
    __data = new List<CustomItemMetadata>();
    // Write out the new metadata store instance
    // Clear out any existing contents.
    __itemMetadataFileStream.SetLength(0);

    // Serialize the data into the file
    BinaryFormatter bf = new BinaryFormatter();
    bf.Serialize(__itemMetadataFileStream, __data);
    __itemMetadataFileStream.Flush();
}
```

The job of this method is to initialize the item metadata store. All throughout the CustomMetadataStore class a binary formatter is used to serialize the data to the FileStream and deserialize the data back from the FileStream.

This method is called only if the file containing the item metadata does not exist. This method is called by IntializeSyncMetadata() while initializing the item metadata store. If the file already exists, the IntializeSyncMetadata() method calls the LoadItemMetadataFromStore() method to load the item metadata from the disk.

The code for LoadItemMetadataFromStore() is shown in the following code listing:

```
/// <summary>
/// Loads a metadata store from disk
/// </summary>
private void LoadItemMetadataFromStore()
{
    // Reset stream to the beginning
    __itemMetadataFileStream.Seek(0, SeekOrigin.Begin);
    // Deserialize the data from the file
    BinaryFormatter bf = new BinaryFormatter();
    _data = bf.Deserialize(__itemMetadataFileStream) as
            List<CustomItemMetadata>;
}
```

The LoadItemMetadataFromStore() method loads the metadata from the file to a local list of item data represented by the variable _data. During the synchronization session, the metadata store uses this list to search and update the item metadata.

The CustomMetadataStore class uses SaveItemMetadata() to create and update the item metadata to disk:

```
/// <summary>
/// Saves the item metadata to disk.
/// </summary>
/// <param name="itemMetadata">Item to save</param>
public void SaveItemMetadata(CustomItemMetadata itemMetadata)
{
    int index = _data.FindIndex(delegate(CustomItemMetadata
     compareItem) { return (compareItem.ItemId ==
     itemMetadata.ItemId);      });
    if (index >= 0)
    {
        _data[index] = itemMetadata.Clone();
    }
    else
    {
        _data.Add(itemMetadata.Clone());
    }
    // Clear out any existing contents.
    __itemMetadataFileStream.SetLength(0);
    // Serialize the data into the file
    BinaryFormatter bf = new BinaryFormatter();
    bf.Serialize(__itemMetadataFileStream, _data);
    __itemMetadataFileStream.Flush();
}
```

SaveItemMetadata() first finds whether the item metadata to be saved already exists in the item metadata list represented by the _data variable. A predicate is used to search the item metadata in the list. If the item metadata to be saved already exists in the item metadata list, the item in the item metadata list is updated; otherwise, the item is added to the item metadata list. Finally, the item metadata list is serialized and saved to the disk using FileStream and BinaryFormatter.

CustomMetadataStore provides methods to search an item in the metadata store by using the item ID or URI of the item.

The TryGetItem() method is overloaded to provide searching based on the item ID or URI of the item:

```
/// <summary>
/// Gets the Item Metadata by URI of the item
/// </summary>
/// <param name="uri">URI of the Item </param>
/// <param name="item">Item Metadata</param>
/// <returns>True if found, else false</returns>
public bool TryGetItem(string uri, out CustomItemMetadata item)
{
    CustomItemMetadata im =
      data.Find(delegate(CustomItemMetadata compareItem) {
        return (compareItem.Uri == uri &&
        compareItem.IsTombstone == false); });
    if (im == null)
    {
        item = null;
        return false;
    }
    item = im.Clone();
    return true;
}


/// <summary>
/// Gets the Item Metadata by ID of the item
/// </summary>
/// <param name="id">ID of the Item </param>
/// <param name="item">Item Metadata</param>
/// <returns>True if found, else false</returns>
public bool TryGetItem(SyncId itemId, out CustomItemMetadata item)
{
    CustomItemMetadata im =
      _data.Find(delegate(CustomItemMetadata compareItem) {
        return (compareItem.ItemId == itemId); });
```

```
        if (im == null)
        {
            item = null;
            return false;
        }
        item = im.Clone();
        return true;
    }
```

Note that while retrieving an item's URI, a check is made to make sure that item was not deleted.

Manipulating and Saving the Replica ID

The CustomMetadataStore class contains the LoadReplicaIDFile() and SaveReplicaIDFile() methods for retrieving the replica ID from the file store and saving the replica ID to the file, respectively.

Following is the code for these two methods:

```
    /// <summary>
    /// Loads the Replica ID
    /// </summary>
    /// <param name="stream"></param>
    private void LoadReplicaIDFile()
    {
        // Deserialize the replicaId from the file.
        __replicaIdFileStream.Seek(0, SeekOrigin.Begin);
        BinaryFormatter bf = new BinaryFormatter();
        __replicaId = new
 SyncId((bf.Deserialize(__replicaIdFileStream).ToString()));
    }


    /// <summary>
    /// Saves the Replica ID
    /// </summary>
    /// <param name="stream"></param>
    private void SaveReplicaIDFile()
    {
        // Serialize replica Id to the file.
        BinaryFormatter bf = new BinaryFormatter();
        bf.Serialize(__replicaIdFileStream, __replicaId.ToString());
        __replicaIdFileStream.Flush();
    }
```

Manipulating and Saving Current and Forgotten Knowledge

CustomMetadataStore contains the methods for storing and retrieving the current and forgotten knowledge from the file store.

LoadKnowledgeFile() retrieves the current knowledge and forgotten knowledge from the file:

```
/// <summary>
/// Loads the knowledge
/// </summary>
private void LoadKnowledgeFile()
{
    // deserialize the knowledge from the file.
    __knowledgeFileStream.Seek(0, SeekOrigin.Begin);
    BinaryFormatter bf = new BinaryFormatter();
    __myKnowledge = (SyncKnowledge)bf.Deserialize(__knowledgeFileStream);

    // Check that knowledge should be for this replica.
    if (__myKnowledge.ReplicaId != __replicaId)
    {
        throw new Exception("Replica id of loaded knowledge
          doesn't match replica id provided in constructor.");
    }
    // Load the forgotten knowledge.
    __myForgottenKnowledge =
        (ForgottenKnowledge)bf.Deserialize
        (knowledgeFileStream);
    // Check that knowledge should be for this replica.
    if (__myForgottenKnowledge.ReplicaId != __replicaId)
    {
        throw new Exception("Replica id of loaded forgotten
          knowledge doesn't match replica id provided in
          constructor.");
    }
}
```

It's also a good practice to check whether the replica ID of the knowledge matches with the replica ID retrieved from the replica file store. This check helps to determine whether the knowledge of the correct replica is loaded.

For storing the knowledge back to the file, a combination of two methods—CreateKnowledgeBlob() and SaveKnowledgeFile()—is used:

```
/// <summary>
/// Creates the knowledge
/// </summary>
private void CreateKnowledgeBlob()
{
    __myKnowledge = new SyncKnowledge(__idFormats,
                    __replicaId,_tickCount);
    __myForgottenKnowledge = new ForgottenKnowledge(IdFormats,
                             __myKnowledge);
    SaveKnowledgeFile();
}

/// <summary>
/// Saves the knowledge
/// </summary>
public void SaveKnowledgeFile()
{
    // Serialize knowledge to the file.
    _knowledgeFileStream.SetLength(0);
    BinaryFormatter bf = new BinaryFormatter();
    bf.Serialize(_knowledgeFileStream, _myKnowledge);
    bf.Serialize(_knowledgeFileStream, _myForgottenKnowledge);
}
```

The CreateKnowledgeBlob() method is called by IntializeSyncMetadata() while initial-izing the custom metadata store. CreateKnowledgeBlob() is called only if the knowledge file does not exist. Current knowledge for the replica is created with a new instance of the SyncKnowledge class and passing replica ID, tick count, and ID formats as input parameters. Forgotten knowledge of the replica is created with a new instance of the ForgottenKnowledge class and passing it current knowledge and ID formats as input parameters. The method also initializes two local variables, _myKnowledge and _myForgottenKnowledge, which are serial-ized using BinaryFormatter and saved in the knowledge file.

Recall that current knowledge (represented by _myKnowledge) is the knowledge of the replica at a given stage in the synchronization process, and forgotten knowledge (repre-sented by _myForgottenKnowledge) contains the information about the deleted items in a replica that the other replica doesn't know about.

Note that the SaveKnowledgeFile() method is a public method because it will be called by custom sync providers to update the knowledge after synchronizing the data between the replicas.

Manipulating and Saving Tick Count

The CustomMetadataStore class provides the following methods for retrieving and saving the tick count to the tick count file:

```
/// <summary>
/// Loads the tick count
/// </summary>
private void LoadTickCountFile()
{
    // Read the tick count from the file.
    _tickCountFileStream.Seek(0, SeekOrigin.Begin);
    BinaryReader br = new BinaryReader(_tickCountFileStream);
    _tickCount = br.ReadUInt64();
}


/// <summary>
/// Saves the Tick count
/// </summary>
private void SaveTickCountFile()
{
    // Write the tick count to the file.
    _tickCountFileStream.SetLength(0);
    BinaryWriter bw = new BinaryWriter(_tickCountFileStream);
    bw.Write(_tickCount);
}
```

The CustomMetadataStore class also retrieves the next tick count. The GetNextTickCount() increments the local tick count by 1 and saves it to the tick count file:

```
/// <summary>
/// Gets the next tick count and store the tick count
/// </summary>
/// <returns></returns>
public ulong GetNextTickCount()
{
    _tickCount++;
    SaveTickCountFile();
    return _tickCount;
}
```

Releasing the Metadata Store at the End of the Sync Session

It's very important to release the metadata store after synchronization. The CustomMetadataStore class contains a method called ReleaseMetadataStore(), which releases all the FileStream objects:

```
/// <summary>
/// Releases the metadata store
/// </summary>
public void ReleaseMetadataStore()
{
    if (_replicaIdFileStream != null)
    {
        _replicaIdFileStream.Close();
        _replicaIdFileStream = null;
    }
    if (_itemMetadataFileStream != null)
    {
        _itemMetadataFileStream.Close();
        _itemMetadataFileStream = null;
    }
    if (_tickCountFileStream != null)
    {
        _tickCountFileStream.Close();
        _tickCountFileStream = null;
    }
    if (_knowledgeFileStream != null)
    {
        _knowledgeFileStream.Close();
        _knowledgeFileStream = null;
    }
}
```

The last piece that needs to be discussed in the CustomMetadataStore class is the default implementation of IEnumerable<CustomItemMetadata> Members:

```
public IEnumerator<CustomItemMetadata> GetEnumerator()
{
    return _data.GetEnumerator();
}
System.Collections.IEnumerator
    System.Collections.IEnumerable.GetEnumerator()
{
    return ((System.Collections.IEnumerable)_data).GetEnumerator();
}
```

That's it; we have created the custom metadata store that stores the metadata in the file system. Now let's see the changes that we need to make to the custom sync provider to use this metadata store.

Changing the Custom Sync Provider to Use the Custom Metadata Store

In order for custom sync providers to use the new custom metadata store, we need to add the MetadataStore project as a reference to the synchronizing application. The synchronizing application is represented by the CustomProvider project.

To add the MetadataStore project as a reference to the CustomProvider project, right-click on the CustomProvider project and click Add Reference Menu. In the Add Reference dialog box, select the Projects tab and choose the project named MetadataStore, as shown in Figure 6-3.

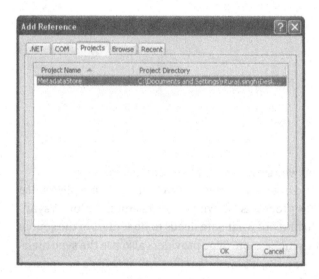

Figure 6-3. *Adding a project reference*

Let's add a new Windows form and a new class to the CustomProvider project to create a new sync provider that will use the custom metadata store. This will enable us to run the same synchronizing application with a custom sync provider using the built-in SQL Server CE metadata store and a custom provider that uses a custom metadata store.

To add a new class, right-click on the project, click Add and then click New Class. Name the class MySyncProviderWithCustomMetadataStore.cs. Copy the code from the MySyncProvider.cs to this class.

To add a new Windows form, right-click on the project, click Add and then click New Windows Form. Name the form SyncFormWithCustomMetadataStore.cs. Copy the code from the SyncForm.cs to this form (SyncFormWithCustomMetadataStore.cs). Later we will make changes to this form to use the new custom provider.

The rest of the files (for example, Customer.cs, Program.cs, ReplicaContent.cs, and SyncForm.cs) remain the same as the example from Chapter 3.

The solution should look similar to Figure 6-4.

Figure 6-4. *Solution structure*

Before making changes, let's recap why sync providers need metadata.

Sync providers use metadata to find out the changes that were made to a replica since the last time it was synchronized. This process is known as change enumeration. A sync provider also needs sync metadata to find out what data needs to be sent from the source replica to the destination replica in a sync session. Sync providers also use the sync metadata to detect conflicts. To achieve these tasks, it's important that sync metadata be updated when changes are made to a replica. This process is called change tracking.

To summarize, the sync metadata is retrieved to be modified by the sync providers under following two conditions

- During change tracking

- During sync sessions for change enumeration, conflict detection, and so on

Implementing Change Tracking with the Custom Metadata Store

Change tracking can be of two types:

- *Inline tracking*: In this method of tracking, replica knowledge for an item is updated when a local change is made to the replica.

- *Asynchronous tracking*: In this method of tracking, replica knowledge is not updated as soon as the local changes happen in a replica. Instead, an external service or process is called on the replica to scan the changes and update the replica knowledge before the source provider begins to enumerate the changes.

In this example, we are using inline tracking. The changes that need to made to the change-tracking process between the provider that uses the built-in SQL Server CE metadata store and the provider that uses the custom metadata store are very few because the metadata store implements the same MSS APIs.

Let's examine the CreateNewItem() method, in which the customer record is created and a new item metadata is generated and stored in the metadata store.

Code in the old custom sync provider using the built-in SQL Server CE metadata store is the following:

```
public void CreateNewItem(Customer customer)
{
    //Creates the Customer
    customer.CreateCustomer();
    ItemMetadata item = metadata.CreateItemMetadata(new
        SyncId(customer.ID.ToString()), new SyncVersion(0,
metadata.GetNextTickCount()));
    item.ChangeVersion = item.CreationVersion;
    //saves the item in metadata store
    _metadata.SaveItemMetadata(item);
}
```

Code in the new custom sync provider using the custom metadata store is the following:

```
Public void CreateNewItem (Customer customer)
{
    //Creates the Customer
    customer.CreateCustomer();
```

```
        ulong currentLocalTickCount = GetNextTickCount();
        CustomItemMetadata item = new CustomItemMetadata();
        item.Uri = customer.ID.ToString();
        item.IsTombstone = false; // Not a tombstone, since alive
        item.ItemId = new SyncId(customer.ID.ToString());
        item.CreationVersion = new SyncVersion(0, currentLocalTickCount);
        item.ChangeVersion = item.CreationVersion;
        _customMetadataStore.SaveItemMetadata(item);
    }
```

The only major change is using the new custom metadata store classes instead of the built-in SQL Server CE metadata store classes to create and save item metadata.

Similar logic is applied to the two methods involved in change tracking: UpdateItem() and DeleteItem(). We will not go in more detail about these two methods because there isn't much difference between the old provider and new provider. You can examine the code to study the use of the new metadata store classes. The entire code for the new sync provider with custom metadata store is located here: ProSyncFramework\ChapterVI\Code\CustomProvider.

Implementing Sync Session Methods with Custom Metadata Store

This section examines the changes that need to be made to different sync session methods for using the new custom metadata store.

The following methods need to be modified in the old sync provider using the built-in SQL Server CE metadata store to now use the new custom metadata store:

- GetNextTickCount()

- IdFormats()

- GetSyncBatchParameters()

- GetChangeBatch()

- ProcessChangeBatch()

- LoadChangeData()

- SaveItemChange()

- StoreKnowledgeForScope()

- CleanUp()

The only major change in these methods is to use the methods and properties in the new custom metadata store classes. Special attention must be given to the CleanUp() method in which the metadata store needs to be disposed and releases all managed and unmanaged resources, as shown in the following code listing:

```
private void CleanUp(bool disposing)
{
    if (!this.disposed)
    {
        if (disposing)
        {
            // Dispose managed resources.
            _customMetadataStore.ReleaseMetadataStore();
            _customMetadataStore.Dispose();

        }
        // Clean up unmanaged resources here.
    }
    disposed = true;
}
```

Changing the Application to Use the Changed Custom Sync Provider

The only change in the SyncFormWithCustomMetadataStore.cs application is the change in the way providers are created. This change is reflected in the Form_load event of the SyncFormWithCustomMetadataStore form:

```
private void SyncFormWithCustomMetadataStore_Load(object
 sender, EventArgs e)
{

    //In our example we are storing metadata in a file
    //Create provider for replica B
    providerA_ReplicaCon = string.Format(connection, replicaA);
    providerA = new
        MySyncProviderWithCustomMetadataStore(replicaA,
        providerA_ReplicaCon);
```

```
            //Create provider for replica B
            providerB_ReplicaCon = string.Format(connection, replicaB);
            providerB = new
                MySyncProviderWithCustomMetadataStore(replicaB,
                providerB_ReplicaCon);

            //Create provider for replica C
            providerC_ReplicaCon = string.Format(connection, replicaC);
            providerC = new
                MySyncProviderWithCustomMetadataStore(replicaC,
                providerC_ReplicaCon);

            //Define the conflict resolution policy
            providerA.Configuration.ConflictResolutionPolicy =
                ConflictResolutionPolicy.ApplicationDefined;
            providerB.Configuration.ConflictResolutionPolicy =
                ConflictResolutionPolicy.ApplicationDefined;
            providerC.Configuration.ConflictResolutionPolicy =
                ConflictResolutionPolicy.ApplicationDefined;

            //Raise the event to handle conflicts
            providerA.DestinationCallbacks.ItemConflicting += new
                EventHandler<ItemConflictingEventArgs>
                (DestinationCallbacks_ItemConflicting);
            providerB.DestinationCallbacks.ItemConflicting += new
                EventHandler<ItemConflictingEventArgs>
                (DestinationCallbacks_ItemConflicting);
            providerC.DestinationCallbacks.ItemConflicting += new
                EventHandler<ItemConflictingEventArgs>
                (DestinationCallbacks_ItemConflicting);

            //create new instance of sync agent
            agent = new SyncOrchestrator();

            //Random class to generate Id for the records
            random = new Random(1);
        }
```

We create the new instance of the provider by passing the replica name and connecting string for the replica.

Running the Application

You can launch the application from Visual Studio by pressing F5 or Ctrl+F5 while the solution is open in Visual Studio.

Make sure to update the connection string represented by the connection variable in the SyncFormWithCustomMetadataStore.cs inside the Local variables region.

You can also double-click the CustomProvider.exe file located in the bin folder of the application to launch the application. After launching the application, the SyncForm is displayed (see Figure 6-5).

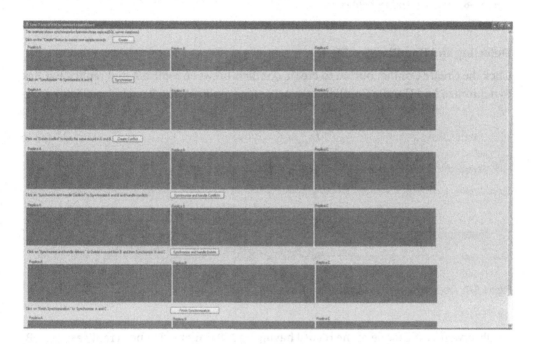

Figure 6-5. *SyncForm*

As shown in the figure, you can exercise different options, such as creating records in the Customer table, synchronizing the replicas, and handling conflicts using the SyncForm.

Synchronizing New Records

Click the Create button to create a new record in each of the three databases. Now click the Synchronize button to synchronize replicas A and B (see Figure 6-6).

Observe that replicas A and B now contain records from each other.

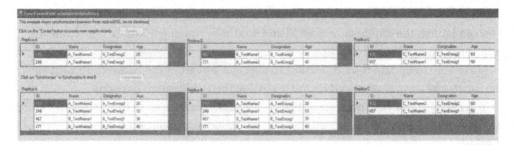

Figure 6-6. *Synchronizing new records*

Detecting and Handling Conflicts

Click the Create Conflict button to create conflicts between replica A and replica B. Click Synchronize And Handle Conflicts to synchronize replica A and B again (see Figure 6-7).

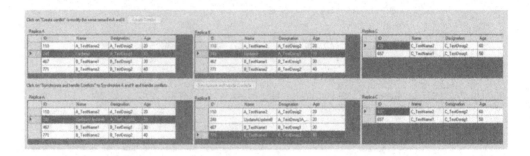

Figure 6-7. *Detecting and handling conflicts*

Observe that the name of the record having ID 248 is merged in both replicas A and B because we have set the conflict resolution action to merge.

Synchronize Deleted Records

Click the Synchronize And Handle Delete button to delete records from replica B and then synchronize replica B and C (see Figure 6-8).

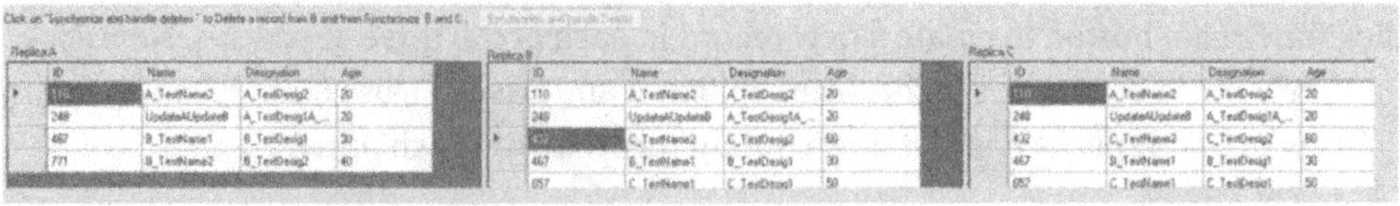

Figure 6-8. *Synchronizing deleted records*

Completing Synchronization

Click the Finish Synchronization button to synchronize replicas A and C (see Figure 6-9).

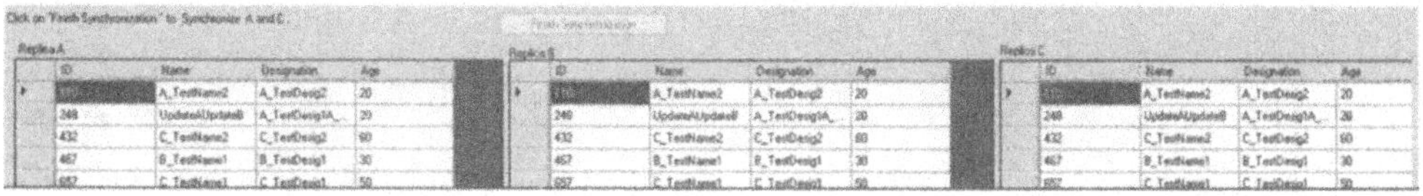

Figure 6-9. *Completing the synchronization*

Summary

The Microsoft Sync Framework relies heavily on the common metadata model to implement important synchronization tasks, such as change enumeration, change tracking, determination of changes since the last synchronization, conflict detection, and so on. To enable developers to rapidly create custom sync providers, the Sync Framework comes with a built-in metadata storage service (MSS). The Sync Framework also ships with a default implementation of built-in MSS. This default implementation is built on top of SQL Server CE and is a lightweight metadata store. Developers can choose to either use this built-in SQL Server CE metadata store or create a custom metadata store by implementing the MSS.

■ ■ ■

CHAPTER 7

Working with RSS Sync Feeds

The Microsoft Sync Framework, a comprehensive synchronization platform, is instrumental in synchronizing data—both offline and online—and provides support for any platform, data store, data type, and protocol.

Microsoft says this: "Microsoft Sync Framework is a comprehensive synchronization platform that enables collaboration and offline access for applications, services, and devices. It features technologies and tools that enable roaming, sharing, and taking data offline. Using Microsoft Sync Framework, developers can build sync ecosystems that integrate any application, with any data from any store using any protocol over any network."

The Sync Framework ships with built-in providers for synchronizing some very common end points such as files, simple sharing extensions such as Really Simple Syndication (RSS) and Atoms, and ADO.NET-compliant data sources. This chapter discusses how to use Sync Services for FeedSync, which provides a powerful support for producing and consuming RSS and Atom feeds from any sync provider.

Sync Services for FeedSync

FeedSync (formerly known as simple sharing extensions, or SSE) is the name given to the open and interoperable standard that is used to represent synchronization metadata in XML format. Sync Services for RSS feeds is particularly useful when you need to produce and consume your application's data as RSS or Atom feeds. Sync Services for FeedSync can be used to publish replica data to be consumed by subscribers as an RSS or Atom feed. The Sync Framework takes care of change detection, conflict detection, and applying changes to the feed. You need to only write your own methods that can convert IDs from the FeedSync format to the sync provider formats, and vice versa.

Microsoft.Synchronization.FeedSync Namespace

Before we proceed further, let's have a quick look at the classes of the `Microsoft.Synchronization.FeedSync` namespace.

Managed Code

Table 7-1 shows the classes in the `Microsoft.Synchronization.FeedSync` namespace.

Table 7-1. *Microsoft.Synchronization.FeedSync Classes*

Class Name	Purpose
EndpointState	This class is the FeedSync end point state.
FeedBuilder	Creates a FeedSync feed during a synchronization process.
FeedConsumer	Retrieves items from a FeedSync feed and passes them onto a sync provider.
FeedIdConverter	Can be overridden and then used to translate IDs in FeedSync format to the corresponding IDs in provider format.
FeedItemConverter	Can be overridden and then used to translate items in FeedSync format to corresponding items in provider format.
FeedItemHistory	Represents the history information of a FeedSync item.
FeedItemMetadata	Contains the FeedSync metadata information for an item.
FeedMetadata	Represents the metadata information for a FeedSync feed.
FeedSyncServices	Used as a service that can translate data from FeedSync XML to Sync Framework object format.
FeedProducer	Produces sync feeds based on data from a sync provider.

Out of the classes listed in the table, the following are the most important classes in the Sync Services for FeedSync library:

- FeedProducer

- FeedConsumer

- FeedItemConverter

- FeedIdConverter

- FeedItemHistory

- FeedItemMetadata

Although the FeedProducer class is responsible for producing sync feeds based on the data from a sync provider, the FeedConsumer class is responsible for consuming feeds and importing them to a sync provider. This is what the FeedProducer and the FeedConsumer classes look like:

```
public class FeedProducer
{
public FeedProducer(KnowledgeSyncProvider storeProvider,
FeedIdConverter idConverter, FeedItemConverter itemConverter);
public FeedIdConverter IdConverter { get; set; }
public EndpointState IncrementalFeedBaseline { get; set; }
public FeedItemConverter ItemConverter { get; set; }
public KnowledgeSyncProvider StoreProvider { get; set; }
public void ProduceFeed(Stream feedStream);
}
```

```
public class FeedConsumer
{
public FeedConsumer(KnowledgeSyncProvider storeProvider,
FeedIdConverter idConverter, FeedItemConverter itemConverter);
public FeedItemConverter FeedItemConverter { get; set; }
public FeedIdConverter IdConverter { get; set; }
public KnowledgeSyncProvider StoreProvider { get; set; }
public EndpointState ConsumeFeed(Stream feedStream);
}
```

The FeedItemConverter abstract class is responsible for translating items in FeedSync format to the corresponding items in the sync provider format. This is what the FeedItemConverter class looks like:

```
public abstract class FeedItemConverter
{
 protected FeedItemConverter();
 public abstract string ConvertItemDataToXmlText(object itemData);
 public abstract object ConvertXmlToItemData(string itemXml);
}
```

This is what the FeedIdConverter class looks like:

```
public abstract class FeedIdConverter
{
 protected FeedIdConverter();
 public abstract SyncIdFormatGroup IdFormats { get; }
 public abstract string ConvertItemIdToString(SyncId itemId);
 public abstract string ConvertReplicaIdToString(SyncId replicaId);
 public abstract SyncId ConvertStringToItemId(string value);
 public abstract SyncId ConvertStringToReplicaId(string value);
 public abstract SyncId GenerateAnonymousReplicaId(string when,
 uint sequence);
}
```

The FeedItemHistory class represents the item history for a particular item. This is what the FeedItemHistory class looks like:

```
public class FeedItemHistory
{
  public string By { get; }
  public uint Sequence { get; }
  public string When { get; }
}
```

The FeedItemMetadata class represents the metadata information for a FeedSync. This is what the FeedItemMetadata class looks like:

```
public class FeedItemMetadata
{
  public bool IsNoConflicts { get; }
  public bool IsTombstone { get; }
  public IEnumerable<FeedItemMetadata> ItemConflictCollection { get; }
  public string ItemData { get; }
  public IEnumerable<FeedItemHistory> ItemHistoryCollection { get; }
  public string ItemId { get; }
  public uint UpdateCount { get; }
}
```

You also have two important delegates: ItemDataMerger and ItemMetadataFilter. The former handles data merging when there is a change; the latter filters the items that are to be incorporated in a change batch during the synchronization process.

This is the syntax of the ItemDataMerger delegate:

```
public delegate string ItemDataMerger (
      string sourceItemData,
      string destinationItemData
)
```

This is the syntax of the ItemMetadataFilter delegate:

```
public delegate bool ItemMetadataFilter (
     string itemId,
     SyncVersion creationVersion,
     SyncVersion changeVersion
)
```

Unmanaged Code

Table 7-2 shows the interfaces of the Sync Services for FeedSync components for unmanaged code.

Table 7-2. *Sync Services Interfaces*

Interface Name	Purpose
IFeedProducer	Produces a FeedSync feed from the data that is retrieved from a sync provider.
IFeedConsumer	Consumes items from a FeedSync feed and then imports them to a sync provider.
IFeedItemConverter	Converts items between FeedSync and sync provider formats.
IFeedIdConverter	Converts IDs between FeedSync and sync provider formats.
IFeedItemConverterCallback	Contains callback methods that get executed when IFeedIdConverter methods get called.
IEndpointState	Represents history information of a FeedSync item.
IFeedIdConverterCallback	Contains FeedSync metadata information for an item.
IFeedProducerConsumerServices	Represents metadata information for a FeedSync feed.

Why Use FeedSync?

FeedSync is a specification that can be used to synchronize data (especially when there are asynchronous updates to data), regardless of the data source, topology, and protocol in use. It facilitates a two-way secure communication that can synchronize data over the Web. You can use FeedSync to publish or consume data as RSS or Atom feeds. The Sync Framework is independent of the underlying protocol on which a synchronization process would work. You can use FeedSync to design a calendar application that can synchronize the data among a group of users who might even enter the calendar entries in a disconnected mode.

How Does FeedSync Work?

FeedSync uses XML elements to attach synchronization information to the items present in either an RSS or Atom feed to facilitate a two-way communication of feeds. There are basically two end points: one can publish its feed, the other can subscribe to that feed. Note that as soon as there are any changes in one end, the changes are effected in the other end, too. FeedSync can automatically handle data conflicts. You have to determine the information that you need to expose. Let's assume that there is a Products database that's spread across geographical locations with the users entering data in offline mode. The application needs to synchronize this data. This is what typical product information would look like when represented as an RSS feed:

```
<Item>
  <title>Product Information</title>
  <description>This contains product information</description>
  <Product>
    <ID>P001</ID>
    <Name>Acer Laptop</Name>
    <Company>Acer</Company>
  </Product>
</Item>
```

The next step toward synchronization is to map this data with the RSS data. You can do this by implementing your own version of the FeedItemConverter class. Note that the FeedItemConverter class is responsible for translating the replica and item IDs to and fro between the FeedSync and the provider formats. Next, you should have your custom FeedIdConverter class that can convert the IDs in the FeedSync format into corresponding provider formats. Now that the FeedItem and FeedID converters are in place, the next step is to publish or consume feeds using the FeedProducer and FeedConsumer classes.

Conflict Detection and Resolution

This section discusses how conflicts are detected using the metadata information just before a merge operation is about to start. Suppose that two replicas, replica 1 and replica 2, contain the metadata information shown in Table 7-3.

Table 7-3. *Before Synchronization Session*

REPLICA 1	REPLICA 2
Item 1–Iteration 1	Item 3–Iteration 1
Item 2–Iteration 1	

Note that after each synchronization session, the iteration or sequence number will increase. We will represent the increment in the synchronization sequences or iterations by incrementing the iteration numbers as iteration 1, iteration 2, and so on.

After we synchronize these two end points the first time, the information in the two replicas looks as shown in Table 7-4.

Table 7-4. *After the First Synchronization Session*

REPLICA 1	REPLICA 2
Item 1–Iteration 1	Item 3–Iteration 1
Item 2–Iteration 1	Item 1–Iteration 1
Item 3–Iteration 1	Item 2–Iteration 1

Let's now assume that replica 2 changes the items item 1 and item 2. Table 7-5 shows how the metadata information of the two replicas looks like now.

Table 7-5. *After the Second Synchronization Session*

REPLICA 1	REPLICA 2
Item 1–Iteration 1	Item 3–Iteration 1
Item 2–Iteration 1	Item 1–Iteration 2
Item 3–Iteration 1	Item 2–Iteration 2

After another synchronization session, the resulting changes in the metadata information of the two replicas look as shown in Table 7-6.

Table 7-6. *After the Third Synchronization Session*

REPLICA 1	REPLICA 2
Item 1–Iteration 2	Item 3–Iteration 1
Item 2–Iteration 2	Item 1–Iteration 2
Item 3–Iteration 1	Item 2–Iteration 2

As shown in the table, item 1 and item 2 have been synchronized between the two replicas in this sequence. So when does a conflict occur?

Let's assume that both replicas change item 1 and item 2 before the synchronization session starts. This causes a conflict. Table 7-7 shows what the metadata information for the two replicas now looks like.

Table 7-7. *Conflict Detected!*

REPLICA 1	REPLICA 2
Item 1–Iteration 3	Item 3–Iteration 1
Item 2–Iteration 3	Item 1–Iteration 3
Item 3–Iteration 1	Item 2–Iteration 3

Producing RSS and Atom Feeds Using Managed and Unmanaged Code

The Sync Framework provides you an application programming interface (API) to produce or consume RSS or Atom feeds. This section discusses how to produce RSS and Atom feeds using Sync Services for FeedSync. You'll learn how to produce RSS and Atom feeds using both managed and unmanaged code.

Managed Code

Follow these steps to produce a feed using managed code:

1. Create an instance of the feed producer using the FeedProducer class and pass the following as parameters:

   - An instance of FeedIdConverter

   - An instance of FeedItemConverter

   - An instance of KnowledgeSyncProvider

2. Call the ProduceFeed method on the feed consumer instance and pass a Stream instance to it as well. This Stream instance will contain an empty RSS or Atom feed.

The following piece of code illustrates how to produce a sync feed:

```
FileSyncProvider provider = new FileSyncProvider
(replicaId, replicaRootPath, filter, options);
```

```
FeedProducer feedProducer = new FeedProducer(provider, new CustomSyncIdConverter
(provider.IdFormats),new CustomSyncItemConverter());

File.WriteAllText("C:\\test.xml", Resources.EmptyRSSFeed);

using (FileStream fileStream = new FileStream
("C:\\test.xml", FileMode.Open, FileAccess.ReadWrite, FileShare.None))
{

  feedProducer.ProduceFeed(fileStream);

}
```

You should add a reference to the Microsoft.Synchronization.FeedSync namespace. The CustomSyncIdConverter class should be inherited from the SyncIdConverter class of the Sync Framework library.

Unmanaged Code

To do the same using unmanaged code, follow these steps:

1. Create an instance of IFeedProducerConsumerServices.

2. Call the ProduceFeed method of IFeedProducer and pass the following as parameters:

   - An instance of FeedIdConverter

   - An instance of FeedItemConverter

   - An instance of ISyncProvider

   - An instance of IStream that will contain an empty RSS or Atom feed

Consuming RSS and Atom Feeds Using Managed and Unmanaged Code

This section discusses how to consume RSS and Atom feeds using Sync Services for FeedSync. You'll see how to consume RSS and Atom feeds using both managed and unmanaged code.

Managed Code

Follow these steps to consume a feed using managed code:

1. Create an instance of the feed consumer using the FeedConsumer class and pass the
   following as parameters:

   - An instance of FeedIdConverter

   - An instance of FeedItemConverter

   - An instance of KnowledgeSyncProvider

2. Call the ConsumeFeed method on the feed consumer instance and pass a Stream
   instance to it. This Stream instance will contain an empty RSS or Atom feed.

This code illustrates how to consume a sync feed:

```
FileSyncProvider provider = new FileSyncProvider
(replicaId, replicaRootPath, filter, options);

FeedConsumer consumer = new FeedConsumer(provider,
        new CustomSyncIdConverter(provider.IdFormats),
new CustomSyncItemConverter());

using (FileStream fileStream = new FileStream
("C:\\test.xml", FileMode.Open, FileAccess.Read,
FileShare.Read))
 {
        consumer.ConsumeFeed(fileStream);
 }
```

Note that you should add a reference to the Microsoft.Synchronization.FeedSync
namespace, and your CustomSyncIdConverter class should be inherited from the
SyncIdConverter class, as in the previous example.

Unmanaged Code

To use unmanaged code, follow these steps:

1. Create an instance of IFeedProducerConsumerServices.

2. Call the ConsumeFeed method of IFeedConsumer and pass the following as parameters:

- An instance of FeedIdConverter

- An instance of FeedItemConverter

- An instance of ISyncProvider

- An instance of IStream that will contain an empty RSS or Atom feed

Converting IDs and ItemData

Another important point to consider is how IDs and item data are converted to and fro between the FeedSync feed and the sync provider when the synchronization is taking place. Similar to what we have just discussed, you will learn how these take place in both managed and unmanaged code.

To convert IDs between the FeedSync feed and the sync provider, and vice versa, the application should implement the FeedIdConverter class in managed code and the IFeedIdConverter interface in unmanaged code. To convert item data between the FeedSync feed and the sync provider, and vice versa, the application should implement the FeedItemConverter class in managed code and the IFeedItemConverter interface in unmanaged code.

Summary

Microsoft's Sync Framework blog states the following: "FeedSync defines the minimum extensions necessary to enable loosely cooperating applications to use XML-based container formats such as Atom and RSS as the basis for item sharing. One of the guiding principles of FeedSync is to reinvent as little as possible—hence the use of Atom and RSS for exchanging FeedSync data. It is expected that there will be additional container format bindings for FeedSync in the future. FeedSync is useful in any scenario that uses Web protocols and data representations such as RSS and Atom to exchange information with the Web services and between peers where there are no inter-item dependencies and item can be synchronized as a whole entity."

This chapter discussed Sync Services for FeedSync and how it can be used to synchronize replica data of RSS and Atom feeds. You also learned how conflicts are detected using an in-built algorithm during a merge operation in the synchronization process.

CHAPTER 8

■■■

Sync Services for ADO.NET 2.0: Offline Scenarios

Sync Services for ADO.NET 2.0 is a part of the Microsoft Sync Framework for synchronizing ADO.NET-enabled databases. Sync Services for ADO.NET 2.0 exposes application programming interfaces (APIs) to support synchronization between the following data stores:

- Two SQL server databases

- SQL Server Compact Edition (CE) 3.5 sp1 as client and SQL Server database as server

- SQL Server CE 3.5 sp1 and any other database for which an ADO.NET provider is available

- Two ADO.NET-enabled databases

Sync Services for ADO.NET 2.0 is very developer-focused when compared with other tools (such as Merge replication or remote data access, which are available from Microsoft for synchronizing databases). Sync Services for ADO.NET 2.0 follows the ADO.NET provider model, so it's easy for developers to get started with Sync Services for ADO.NET 2.0. Sync Services for ADO.NET 2.0 is based on the Sync Framework and (just like the Sync Framework) it works with any network topology, such as the client-server or hub-spoke model. The basic design goal of the Sync Services for ADO.NET 2.0 is to provide support for Occasionally Connected Systems (OCS) to synchronize their data. Using Sync Services for ADO.NET 2.0, OCS can synchronize data in the following two ways:

- Client-server synchronization—also called *offline scenarios*

- Peer-to-peer synchronization—also called *collaboration scenarios*

This chapter explores how Sync Services for ADO.NET 2.0 can be used to support OCS in offline scenarios.

Later in the chapter we will discuss the architecture for client-server synchronization and how Sync Services for ADO.NET 2.0 compares with other technologies that support offline scenarios in OCS.

Occasionally Connected and Peer to Peer Systems

The core problem with distributed computing and connected systems is that the network is not a reliable element. OCS employ a publish-subscribe model between client and server, and updates are pushed to the server once connectivity is established. Note that only the updates that were done since the last change are pushed to the server. It is imperative that a full data refresh does not happen every time because it would not be scalable and would be a performance hit for transactional databases.

Figure 8-1 shows how offline scenarios work compared with connected scenarios. Client-server systems need to have the following elements to support an offline scenario:

- Smart clients with a local data store in which the transactional data will be persisted and can be pushed to a centralized data store in the form of change units. These smart clients can detect connectivity with the server for data synchronization.

- A centralized data store that can accept the data periodically from various smart clients installed at different locations.

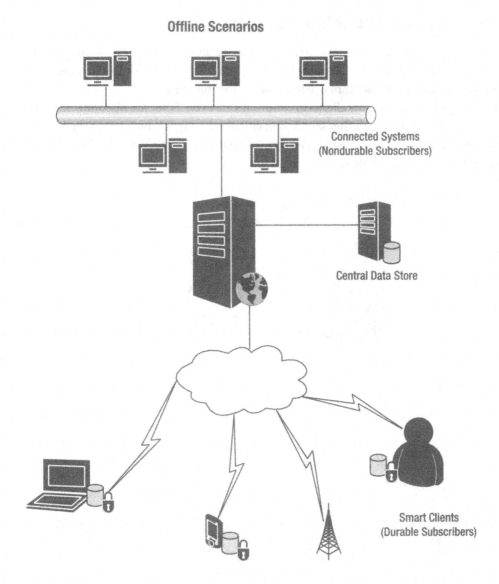

Figure 8-1. *Offline scenarios*

Smart Clients As Durable Subscribers

One of the important features of smart clients is that they behave as durable subscribers. In a durable subscription, the messages are saved for an inactive subscriber and the saved messages are pushed to the store when the subscriber reconnects.

Peer-to-peer systems allow clients to communicate even if they are disconnected from the central server. This is another scenario in client-server synchronization called collaboration scenarios. Figure 8-2 illustrates what collaboration scenarios look like. (Collaboration scenarios are discussed in more detail in Chapter 9.)

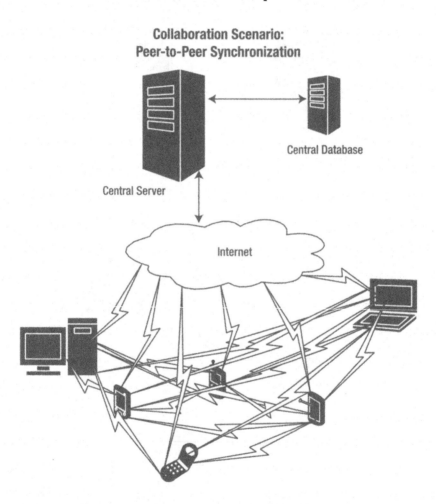

Figure 8-2. *Collaboration scenario: peer-to-peer synchronization*

Offline Scenarios Architecture

Sync Services for ADO.NET 2.0 supports the following architectures:

- Two-tier

- N-tier

- Service-based

Figure 8-3 illustrates these architectures. Sync Services for ADO.NET 2.0 uses models to synchronize changes between the client and the server. The N-tier and service-based architectures require a proxy and service to complete the transport layer. The difference between the N-tier and service-based model is that N-tier architecture has a server sync provider. For a service-based model, a custom proxy and service have to be written to communicate with a sync agent.

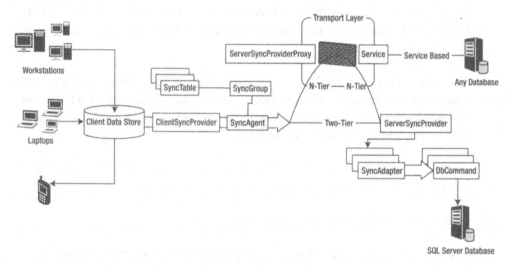

Figure 8-3. *Architecture of Sync Services for ADO.NET 2.0*

Sync Services for ADO.NET Components 2.0

As shown in Figure 8-3, the following components make up the architecture in Sync Services for ADO.NET 2.0:

- *Sync agent:* Exposed by `Microsoft.Synchronization.Data.dll`, it is responsible for the overall orchestration. It works with the client and server synchronization providers to apply changes to the client and server databases. It is also responsible for maintaining session-level information.

- *Sync table and group:* Exposed by `Microsoft.Synchronization.Data.dll`, a *sync table* is the smallest unit of work. Sync tables store metadata information for tables to be synchronized, such as the sync direction and creation option. The *sync group* acts as a transactional boundary for sync tables to ensure that all changes are consistent across tables in a group.

- *Client synchronization provider:* Exposed by `Microsoft.Synchronization.Data.SqlServerCe.dll`, it is responsible for communicating with the client and spares the sync agent of the detailed implementation of the client database. It is also responsible for conflict detection and applying incremental changes to the client database.

- *Server synchronization provider:* Exposed by `Microsoft.Synchronization.Data.Server.dll`, it is similar to that of a client synchronization provider except that it takes care of applying the retrieved changes to the server database. It works as an aggregate for sync adapters.

- *Sync adapter:* Exposed by `Microsoft.Synchronization.Data.Server.dll`, it exposes commands that are used to communicate with the server database. For synchronization between a client and a SQL Server database, the Sync Framework has exposed a `SqlSyncAdapterBuilder` that does the following:

  - Accepts the name of the table and a tombstone table. (A *tombstone table* is used to track delete operations, as discussed later in the chapter.)

  - Accepts the direction of synchronization.

  - Accepts the columns that will be used to track inserts, updates, and deletes.

- *Proxy:* In N-tier and service-based applications, the server components exposed by the Sync Services for ADO.NET 2.0 reside on an application server, which in turn communicates with the database server. The Sync Framework exposes a proxy for the clients, which is responsible for communicating with the sync provider.

- *Sync anchors:* Sync anchors act as a starting point for synchronizing the next sequence of changes. There are two types of sync anchors: a last receive anchor that identifies the last change that was downloaded from the server and a last sent anchor that identifies the last change that was published to the server.

- *Sync session*: Encapsulates the process of a single sync operation and is responsible for managing states and transactions.

- *Sync session statistics*: Provides trace and exception information for a sync operation.

Choosing Sync Services for ADO.NET 2.0 over ADO.NET Data Access

So why and when should you use Sync Services for ADO.NET 2.0 over vanilla ADO.NET? Figure 8-4 shows the differences between the two.

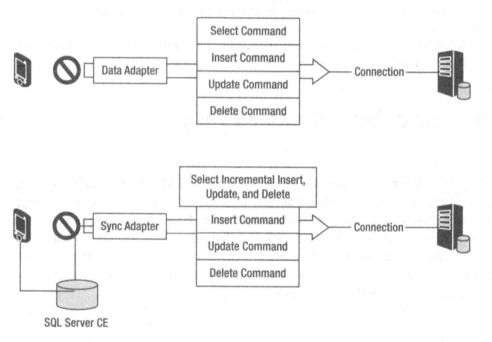

Figure 8-4. *Key differences between ADO.NET data access and Sync Services for ADO.NET 2.0*

As shown in Figure 8-4, one of the major differences is the availability of the network. Although ADO.NET data access is fragile to network instability, Sync Services for ADO.NET 2.0 makes applications resilient to network instability by providing local storage. One other disadvantage of ADO.NET data access is that all operations require round trips to the server, and there is minimal usage of client memory. This puts too much load on the server.

Synchronization Types for Occasionally Connected Systems

Sync Services for ADO.NET 2.0 provides four synchronization types:

- *Snapshot:* This synchronization type is a complete refresh of reference data. It is used in scenarios in which the database is incapable of handling incremental change units.

- *Download Only:* In this synchronization type, only the incremental changes made since last sync operation are downloaded. One of the important configurations for this type of synchronization is that change tracking should be built into the server. In most other scenarios, change tracking is a feature of the client.

- *Upload Only:* This synchronization type is used for insert operations.

- *Bidirectional:* This synchronization type is used for update operations. One of the important things it takes care of is conflict management.

Code Examples of Common Tasks

Note All code examples discussed in this section use SQL Server CE 3.5 sp1 as the client database, and SQL Server 2005 sp2 or SQL Server 2008 RC0 as the server database. SQL Server 2008 has built-in change-tracking capabilities, which are supported in Visual Studio 2008 sp1. In the following examples, the option to use built-in change tracking will be available only if you are configuring against a SQL Server 2008 database. Other synchronization options will be disabled if the built-in change-tracking feature is used. After the synchronization process is complete, the local data store is updated, not the dataset. Ensure that you explicitly reload the data objects with data from the local data store.

Exploring the Sync Services for ADO.NET 2.0 API

Until now we've discussed how the Sync Framework supports offline scenarios and the architecture of OCS. We now explore how to program the different components exposed by the Sync Services for ADO.NET 2.0 API.

To explore the API, let's assume a scenario of a corporation that manufactures valves and has sales representatives in several geographical locations. Some of these representatives use their PDAs to create quotes using the mobile version of the corporation's quoting engine, which has a central SQL Server 2005 sp2 database and is based on the OCS architecture.

The figures in the following section show how to use Visual Studio to quickly create OCS.

■Note The figures are screen captures with Sync Framework version 2.0 and they might change in later versions.

Local Database Cache Using Visual Studio 2008

Visual Studio 2008 comes with built-in data synchronization capabilities for Windows, Console, and Windows Presentation Foundation (WPF)–based applications. You will see shortly how to use Visual Studio to create a local database cache and explore how a wizard uses the different components of the API to synchronize data between clients and the Quote engine database.

Before we can start exploring the different components of the API, we have to prepare the Quote database for change tracking. Figure 8-5 shows what the Quote table looks like in the server database.

Figure 8-5. *Quote table*

Following is the script to create the Quote table:

```
SET ANSI_NULLS ON
GO


SET QUOTED_IDENTIFIER ON
GO
```

```
SET ANSI_PADDING ON
GO


CREATE TABLE [dbo].[Quote](
              [Quote_ID] [bigint] IDENTITY(1,1) NOT NULL,
              [QuoteNumber] [bigint] NOT NULL,
              [QuoteVersion] [bigint] NOT NULL,
              [SalesRepFName] [varchar](50) NOT NULL,
              [SalesRepLName] [varchar](50) NOT NULL,
              [CreatedDate] [datetime] NOT NULL,
              [LastEditDate] [datetime] NULL,
 CONSTRAINT [PK_Quote] PRIMARY KEY CLUSTERED
(
              [Quote_ID] ASC
)WITH (PAD_INDEX  = OFF, STATISTICS_NORECOMPUTE  = OFF, IGNORE_DUP_KEY = OFF,
 ALLOW_ROW_LOCKS  = ON, ALLOW_PAGE_LOCKS  = ON) ON [PRIMARY]
) ON [PRIMARY]

GO

SET ANSI_PADDING OFF
GO

ALTER TABLE [dbo].[Quote] ADD  CONSTRAINT [DF_Quote_CreatedDate]
DEFAULT (getdate()) FOR [CreatedDate]
```

Enabling Change Tracking in a Server Database

Let's create a Windows application named QuoteClient. To do this, open Visual Studio 2008 and click on the Windows forms application template under Visual C# projects. Name the project **QuoteClient** and create the project. Once the project is created, a simple Windows form will be added to the project.

After the project is created, right-click on the project and choose Add Item. As you can see in Figure 8-6, different items are available to be added to this project. Those that are of particular interest to us are the following:

- *Local Database*: An empty SQL Server CE database for local data.

- *Service-based Database*: An empty SQL Server database for service-based data access.

- *Local Database Cache*: A settings file for configuring a local database for client-server data synchronization.

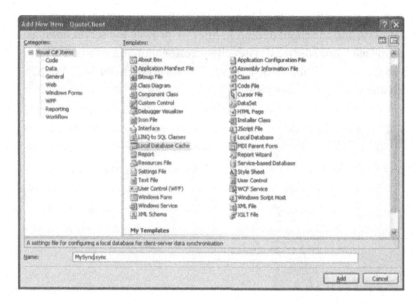

Figure 8-6. *Adding Local Database Cache*

Choose the Local Database cache and name it **MySync**. Click Add and a wizard displays (see Figure 8-7). The wizard exposes the properties used to configure data synchroniza-tion. We will discuss each item in detail.

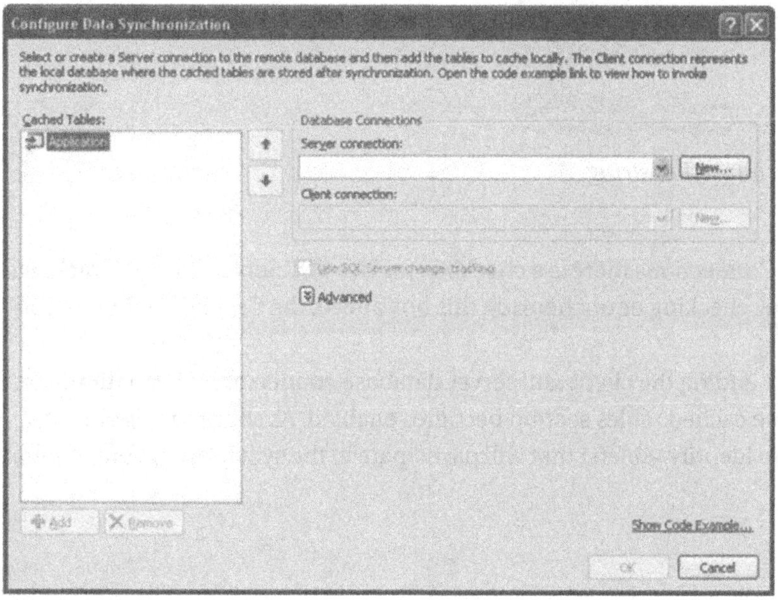

Figure 8-7. *Data Synchronization Wizard*

The section for database connections is used to provide database connection information for both the server database and the client database. After we provide the server database connection information (see Figure 8-8), a default client connection information is automatically generated with a client database (SQL Server CE) added to the project. We can modify it to point it to an existing local database.

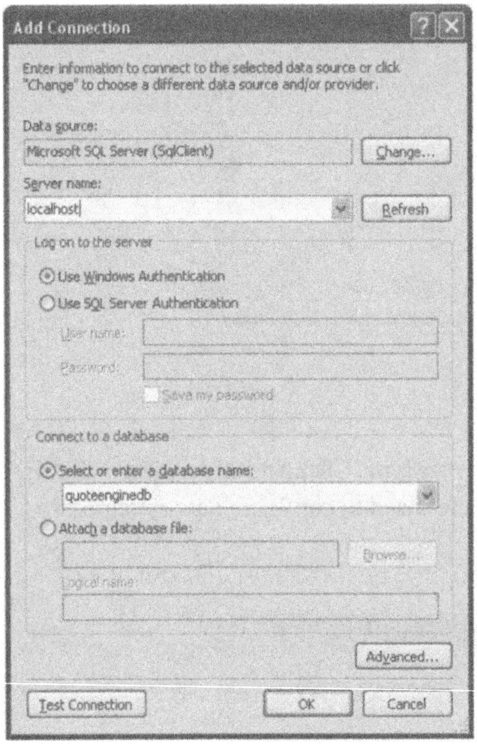

Figure 8-8. *Database connection string*

Under Database Connections there is a checkbox for Use SQL Server Change Tracking. You will see next how checking or unchecking this box affects the Cached Tables section on the left side.

Once we are done adding the client and server database connection information, the Add button under the cached tables section becomes enabled. As shown in Figure 8-9, this section is used to identify table(s) that will participate in the synchronization process.

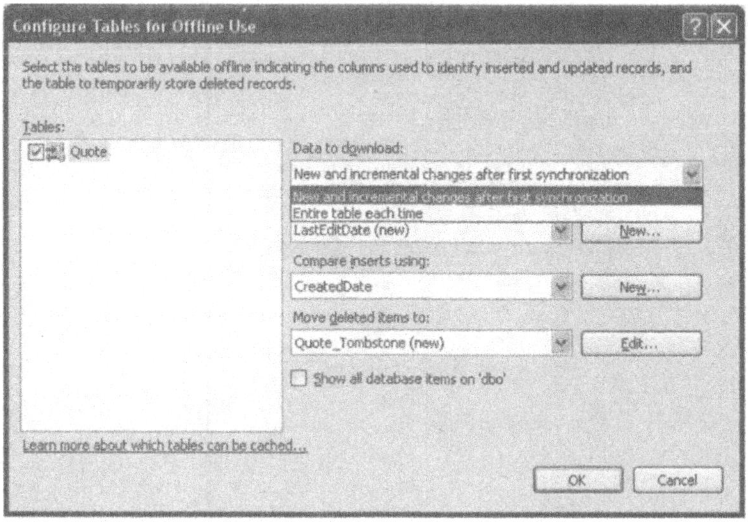

Figure 8-9. *Adding cached tables*

In our scenario, because there is only one table it will show up in the Add Cached Tables screen. From the Tables section, we can choose the tables you want to synchronize. On the Data To Download drop-down list, we can specify whether we want to synchronize new and incremental changes after the synchronization is done for the first time or whether we want a entire table refresh each time the client and server are synchronized. If Use SQL Server Change Tracking is checked in the wizard, the other three drop-down lists are disabled. SQL Server change tracking is now a built-in feature of SQL Server 2008, so SQL Server will take care of the change tracking (we don't have to specify columns for synchronizing updates and inserts or maintain the Tombstone table for deleted data).

In the Compare Updates Using and Compare Inserts Using drop-down lists, you can specify whether to use an existing column or create a new column for tracking inserts and updates. In this case, because we don't have a column to track updates, we will specify a new column, LastEditDate, and specify the existing column CreatedDate for inserts.

We will specify a new table, Quote_Tombstone, which will store the deleted items. Once the Quote table is added for change tracking, we can specify additional properties by clicking on the Quote table under the Cached Tables section. Figure 8-10 shows what it looks like.

The Creation Option property, found under the Client Configuration section, can specify how to generate the schema changes and synchronize data in the client.

Figure 8-11 shows what the wizard looks like after all the configuration information is set. If the Advanced section is expanded, you will see additional information such as the server and client project location and whether you want to synchronize the tables in a single transaction.

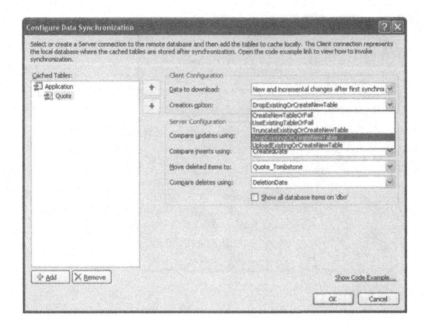

Figure 8-10. *Cached table configuration*

Figure 8-11. *Configure Data Synchronization Wizard*

Once you are done with the configuration, click OK. The server and client connection string settings entries are added to the Database Connections drop-down lists, as shown in Figure 8-11. The data synchronization automatically performs the following tasks:

- Adds references of the SyncFramework.dll for ADO.NET data services (Microsoft.Synchronization.Data.dll, Microsoft.Synchronization.Data.Server.dll, and Microsoft.Synchronization.Data.SqlServerCe.dll)

- Adds a local database: quoteenginedb.sdf

- Adds scripts used to prepare the database for synchronization

- Adds undo scripts to reverse the changes

Once these changes are made, you are prompted for the Data Source configuration, which will define the way you want to interact with the database objects. As seen in Figure 8-12, you can specify a name for the dataset (**quoteDataSet** in this example). This process will add the quoteDataSet.xsd file to the project.

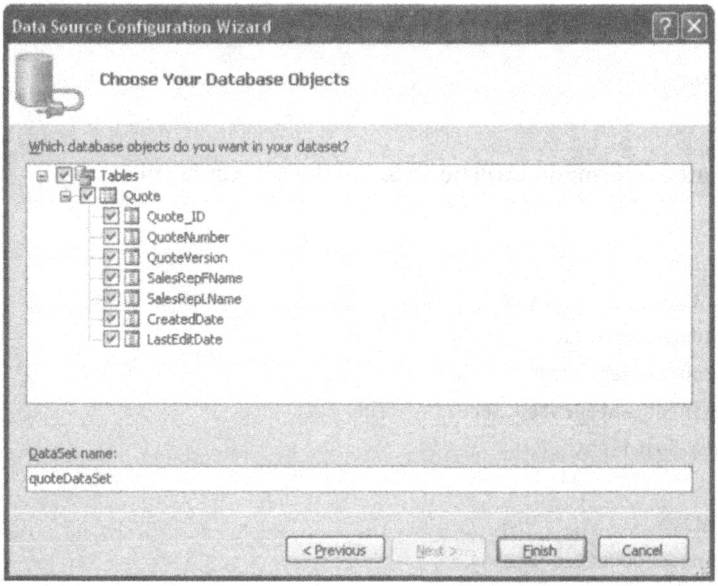

Figure 8-12. *Data Source configuration*

Figure 8-13 illustrates what the solution structure will look like once the wizard is done with the configuration.

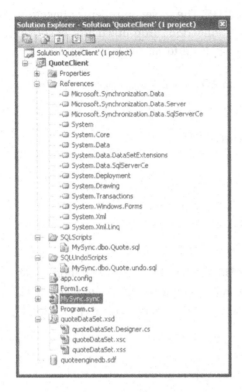

Figure 8-13. *Solution structure*

All the connection-related information will be added to the App.config file:

```
<connectionStrings>
        <add
name="QuoteClient.Properties.
Settings.ServerquoteenginedbConnectionString"
connectionString="Data Source=localhost;
Initial Catalog=quoteenginedb;Integrated Security=True"
providerName="System.Data.SqlClient" />
        <add
name="QuoteClient.Properties.
Settings.ClientquoteenginedbConnectionString"
connectionString="Data
Source=|DataDirectory|\quoteenginedb.sdf;Max Database Size=2047"

        providerName="Microsoft.SqlServerCe.Client.3.5" />
    </connectionStrings>
```

Let's now examine the contents of the local database cache file MySync.sync.

MySync.sync

To examine the contents of this class, first we will create a class diagram from the MySync.
designer.cs file. To do that, right-click on the designer file and click View Class Diagram.
A screen shot of the class diagram is presented in Figure 8-14.

Figure 8-14. *Class diagram*

Let's now examine each of these classes in detail.

QuoteSyncTable Class

QuoteSyncTable, which is a nested subclass of the MySyncSyncAgent class, inherits Microsoft.
Synchronization.SyncTable.

In the QuoteSyncTable class, we specify the table name and the creation option:

```
public partial class QuoteSyncTable : Microsoft.Synchronization.Data.SyncTable {

        partial void OnInitialized();

        public QuoteSyncTable() {
            this.InitializeTableOptions();
            this.OnInitialized();
        }

        [System.Diagnostics.DebuggerNonUserCodeAttribute()]
        private void InitializeTableOptions() {
            this.TableName = "Quote";
            this.CreationOption =
             Microsoft.Synchronization.Data.
             TableCreationOption.DropExistingOrCreateNewTable;
        }
    }
}
```

MySyncSyncAgent Class

This class inherits from the Microsoft.Synchronization.SyncAgent. The core goal of this class is to initialize sync providers and the sync tables and groups.

For sync providers, SyncAgent exposes two properties:

- LocalProvider: Specifies the provider for the local database cache

- RemoteProvider: The central database provider

Code for the InitializeSyncProvider() method is the following:

```
private void InitializeSyncProviders() {
        // Create SyncProviders.
        this.RemoteProvider = new MySyncServerSyncProvider();
        this.LocalProvider = new MySyncClientSyncProvider();
    }
```

The InitializeSyncTables() method creates a new instance of the QuoteSyncTable class and assigns it to the SyncAgent configuration:

```
private void InitializeSyncTables() {
        // Create SyncTables.
        this._quoteSyncTable = new QuoteSyncTable();
        this._quoteSyncTable.SyncGroup = new
         Microsoft.Synchronization.Data.
           SyncGroup("QuoteSyncTableSyncGroup");
        this.Configuration.SyncTables.Add(this._quoteSyncTable);
    }
```

A SyncGroup is also specified for the SyncTable. Let's now complete the MySyncSyncAgent class.

In the constructor of MySyncSyncAgent, the Initialize() methods are called:

```
public MySyncSyncAgent() {
        this.InitializeSyncProviders();
        this.InitializeSyncTables();
        this.OnInitialized();
    }
```

MySyncClientSyncProvider Class

This class inherits from the Microsoft.Synchronization.Data.SqlServerCe. SqlCeClientSyncProvider and specifies the connection string information for the local data store.

MySyncServerSyncProvider Class

This class inherits from the `Microsoft.Synchronization.Data.Server.DbServerSyncProvider` class and does the following three things:

- Specifies the connection string information for the remote central database.

- Initializes the `SyncAdapters`.

- Initializes the `NewAnchorCommand`. The anchor value is stored in the client database and is used by the commands to synchronize changes between the client and the server.

```
[System.Diagnostics.DebuggerNonUserCodeAttribute()]
    private void InitializeSyncAdapters() {
        // Create SyncAdapters.
        this._quoteSyncAdapter = new QuoteSyncAdapter();
        this.SyncAdapters.Add(this._quoteSyncAdapter);
    }


    [System.Diagnostics.DebuggerNonUserCodeAttribute()]
    private void InitializeNewAnchorCommand() {
        // selectNewAnchorCmd command.
        this.SelectNewAnchorCommand = new System.Data.SqlClient.SqlCommand();
        this.SelectNewAnchorCommand.CommandText = "Select
            @sync_new_received_anchor = GETUTCDATE()";

        this.SelectNewAnchorCommand.CommandType = System.Data.CommandType.Text;
        System.Data.SqlClient.SqlParameter
            selectnewanchorcommand_sync_new_received_anchorParameter = new
            System.Data.SqlClient.SqlParameter("@sync_new_received_anchor",
            System.Data.SqlDbType.DateTime);
        selectnewanchorcommand_sync_new_received_anchorParameter.Direction =
            System.Data.ParameterDirection.Output;

        this.SelectNewAnchorCommand.Parameters.Add
(selectnewanchorcommand_sync_new_received_anchorParameter);

    }
```

This is what the constructor for the `MySyncServerSyncProvider` looks like:

```
public MySyncServerSyncProvider(string connectionString) {
        this.InitializeConnection(connectionString);
        this.InitializeSyncAdapters();
        this.InitializeNewAnchorCommand();
        this.OnInitialized();
    }
```

QuoteSyncAdapter Class

The `QuoteSyncAdapter` class inherits from the `Microsoft.Synchronization.Data.Server.SyncAdapter` class and specifies commands for the synchronization process. All the CRUD (create, read, update, and delete) operation commands are specified in the `InitializeCommand()` method of the adapter:

- `InsertCommand`: Creates a command for inserting the rows into the Quote table. The sync adapter fires the `InsertCommand` when inserted records need to be synchronized between the client and the server. The following code generated by the wizard shows the `InsertCommand` for the records that are inserted in the Quote table (client or server):

  ```
  this.InsertCommand = new System.Data.SqlClient.SqlCommand();
          this.InsertCommand.CommandText = @"INSERT INTO dbo.Quote
  ([Quote_ID], [QuoteNumber], [QuoteVersion], [SalesRepFName],
  [SalesRepLName], [CreatedDate], [LastEditDate]) VALUES (@Quote_ID,
  @QuoteNumber, @QuoteVersion, @SalesRepFName, @SalesRepLName,
  @CreatedDate, @LastEditDate) SET @sync_row_count = @@rowcount";
  ```

  The following code shows that the `InsertCommand` takes seven input parameters and one output parameter where the row count is returned. It is used to determine whether the insert was successful, and the value is passed to `SyncStatistics` (discussed in detail later in this chapter).

  ```
          this.InsertCommand.CommandType = System.Data.CommandType.Text;
          this.InsertCommand.Parameters.Add(new
  System.Data.SqlClient.SqlParameter("@Quote_ID",
  System.Data.SqlDbType.BigInt));

          this.InsertCommand.Parameters.Add(new
  System.Data.SqlClient.SqlParameter("@QuoteNumber",
  System.Data.SqlDbType.BigInt));
  ```

```
        this.InsertCommand.Parameters.Add(new
System.Data.SqlClient.SqlParameter("@QuoteVersion",
System.Data.SqlDbType.BigInt));

        this.InsertCommand.Parameters.Add(new
System.Data.SqlClient.SqlParameter("@SalesRepFName",
System.Data.SqlDbType.VarChar));

        this.InsertCommand.Parameters.Add(new
System.Data.SqlClient.SqlParameter("@SalesRepLName",
System.Data.SqlDbType.VarChar));

        this.InsertCommand.Parameters.Add(new
System.Data.SqlClient.SqlParameter("@CreatedDate",
System.Data.SqlDbType.DateTime));

        this.InsertCommand.Parameters.Add(new
System.Data.SqlClient.SqlParameter("@LastEditDate",
System.Data.SqlDbType.DateTime));

        System.Data.SqlClient.SqlParameter
insertcommand_sync_row_countParameter = new
System.Data.SqlClient.SqlParameter("@sync_row_count",
System.Data.SqlDbType.Int);

        insertcommand_sync_row_countParameter.Direction =
System.Data.ParameterDirection.Output;

        this.InsertCommand.Parameters
.Add(insertcommand_sync_row_countParameter);
```

- DeleteCommand: Creates a command for deleting rows from the Quote table. Like
  InsertCommand, the sync adapter will fire DeleteCommand if a delete operation takes
  place at the client or the server. DeleteCommand is slightly challenged because there
  might be conflicts in synchronizing the delete operation between the client and the
  server. A conflict occurs if a record deleted in the client has been updated in the
  server, for example. Conflict detection is discussed later in this chapter.

```
this.DeleteCommand = new System.Data.SqlClient.SqlCommand();
                this.DeleteCommand.CommandText = "DELETE FROM dbo.Quote
WHERE ([Quote_ID] = @Quote_ID) AND (@sync_force_write = 1 OR ([LastEditDate] <=
        @sync_last_received_anchor)) SET
@sync_row_count = @@rowcount";
                this.DeleteCommand.CommandType = System.Data.CommandType.Text;
                this.DeleteCommand.Parameters.Add(new
System.Data.SqlClient.SqlParameter("@Quote_ID",
System.Data.SqlDbType.BigInt));
                this.DeleteCommand.Parameters.Add(new
System.Data.SqlClient.SqlParameter("@sync_force_write",
System.Data.SqlDbType.Bit));

                 this.DeleteCommand.Parameters.Add(new
System.Data.SqlClient.SqlParameter("@sync_last_received_anchor",
System.Data.SqlDbType.DateTime));

                System.Data.SqlClient.SqlParameter
deletecommand_sync_row_countParameter = new
System.Data.SqlClient.SqlParameter("@sync_row_count",
System.Data.SqlDbType.Int);

                deletecommand_sync_row_countParameter.Direction =
System.Data.ParameterDirection.Output;

    this.DeleteCommand.Parameters.Add
                (deletecommand_sync_row_countParameter);
```

- UpdateCommand: Creates a command for updating the rows into the Quote table.
  UpdateCommand is very similar to DeleteCommand because it can also cause conflicts
  in the database.

```
this.UpdateCommand = new System.Data.SqlClient.SqlCommand();
                this.UpdateCommand.CommandText = @"UPDATE dbo.Quote SET
[QuoteNumber] = @QuoteNumber, [QuoteVersion] = @QuoteVersion,
[SalesRepFName] = @SalesRepFName, [SalesRepLName] = @SalesRepLName,
[CreatedDate] = @CreatedDate, [LastEditDate] = @LastEditDate WHERE
([Quote_ID] = @Quote_ID) AND (@sync_force_write = 1 OR ([LastEditDate] <=
@sync_last_received_anchor)) SET @sync_row_count = @@rowcount";
                this.UpdateCommand.CommandType = System.Data.CommandType.Text;
                this.UpdateCommand.Parameters.Add(new
```

```
            System.Data.SqlClient.SqlParameter("@QuoteNumber",
System.Data.SqlDbType.BigInt));

                    this.UpdateCommand.Parameters.Add(new
            System.Data.SqlClient.SqlParameter("@QuoteVersion",
            System.Data.SqlDbType.BigInt));

                    this.UpdateCommand.Parameters.Add(new
            System.Data.SqlClient.SqlParameter("@SalesRepFName",
            System.Data.SqlDbType.VarChar));

                    this.UpdateCommand.Parameters.Add(new
            System.Data.SqlClient.SqlParameter("@SalesRepLName",
            System.Data.SqlDbType.VarChar));

                    this.UpdateCommand.Parameters.Add(new
            System.Data.SqlClient.SqlParameter("@CreatedDate",
System.Data.SqlDbType.DateTime));

                    this.UpdateCommand.Parameters.Add(new
            System.Data.SqlClient.SqlParameter("@LastEditDate",
            System.Data.SqlDbType.DateTime));

                    this.UpdateCommand.Parameters.Add(new
            System.Data.SqlClient.SqlParameter("@Quote_ID",
            System.Data.SqlDbType.BigInt));
```

UpdateCommand takes all the column values for the Quote table as parameters. There are two additional parameters in the DeleteCommand:

- @sync_force_write: This value indicates whether the command should retry the logic with force applying the change.

- @sync_last_received_anchor: This variable is used by the tracking columns to select changes from and apply to the server database. Depending on what data type the tracking column uses, it could hold a date time or a timestamp. SQL Server 2005 sp2 introduces MIN_ACTIVE_ROWVERSION, which returns a timestamp value. In this case, the tracking columns use the DateTime data type.

```
                    this.UpdateCommand.Parameters.Add(new
        System.Data.SqlClient.SqlParameter("@sync_force_write",
        System.Data.SqlDbType.Bit));

                    this.UpdateCommand.Parameters.Add(new
        System.Data.SqlClient.SqlParameter("@sync_last_received_anchor",
        System.Data.SqlDbType.DateTime));

                    System.Data.SqlClient.SqlParameter
        updatecommand_sync_row_countParameter = new
        System.Data.SqlClient.SqlParameter("@sync_row_count",
        System.Data.SqlDbType.Int);

                    updatecommand_sync_row_countParameter.Direction =
        System.Data.ParameterDirection.Output;
                        this.UpdateCommand.Parameters.Add
                        (updatecommand_sync_row_countParameter);
```

There are two types of select commands exposed by the adapter.

- Select conflict detection commands for updates and deletes

- Select incremental commands for inserts, updates, and deletes

The conflict detection command will return all the rows that are having a conflicting delete and update:

```
// QuoteSyncTableSelectConflictDeletedRowsCommand command.
        this.SelectConflictDeletedRowsCommand = new
System.Data.SqlClient.SqlCommand();

        this.SelectConflictDeletedRowsCommand.CommandText = "SELECT
[Quote_ID], [DeletionDate] FROM dbo.Quote_Tombstone WHERE ([Quote_ID] =
@Quote_ID)";

        this.SelectConflictDeletedRowsCommand.CommandType =
System.Data.CommandType.Text;

        this.SelectConflictDeletedRowsCommand.Parameters.Add(new
System.Data.SqlClient.SqlParameter("@Quote_ID",
System.Data.SqlDbType.BigInt));
```

```
    // QuoteSyncTableSelectConflictUpdatedRowsCommand command.
    this.SelectConflictUpdatedRowsCommand = new
System.Data.SqlClient.SqlCommand();

    this.SelectConflictUpdatedRowsCommand.CommandText = "SELECT
[Quote_ID], [QuoteNumber], [QuoteVersion], [SalesRepFName],
[SalesRepLName], [CreatedDate], [LastEditDate] FROM dbo.Quote WHERE
([Quote_ID] = @Quote_ID)";

    this.SelectConflictUpdatedRowsCommand.CommandType =
System.Data.CommandType.Text;

    this.SelectConflictUpdatedRowsCommand.Parameters.Add(new
System.Data.SqlClient.SqlParameter("@Quote_ID",
System.Data.SqlDbType.BigInt));
```

Conflicts can be of the following types:

- ClientInsertServerInsert: Occurs when both client and server try to insert a record with the same primary key

- ClientUpdateServerUpdate: Occurs when both client and server try to update the same record

- ClientUpdateServerDelete: Occurs when the same record being updated by the client is deleted by the server

- ClientDeleteServerUpdate: Occurs when the same record being deleted by the client is updated by the server

- ErrorsOccurred: Occurs when changes are prevented from being applied because of an exception

The SqlCeClientSyncProvider exposes a ConflictResolver property that can be used to resolve conflicts in the client. It can take three possible values:

- ClientWins: Directs the synchronization process to ignore the conflict and continue the process

- ServerWins: Allows the process to retry with force applying the change

- FireEvent: Fires the ApplyChangeFailed event

The ConflictResolver property is an easy way to resolve conflicts at the client level. For advanced conflict resolution, the client and the server sync providers expose the ApplyChangeFailed event, which can be used to detect the conflict and take necessary action. The ApplyChangeFailed is raised by the client sync provider if a conflict occurs during the download and is raised by the server sync provider if it occurred during the upload.

The SelectConflictDeletedRowsCommand returns the rows involved in conflicts of type ClientUpdateServerDelete, and the SelectConflictUpdatedRowsCommand returns the rows that are involved in the conflicts of type ClientInserServerInsert, ClientUpdateServerUpdate, and ClientDeleteServerUpdate.

The ApplyChangeFailedEventArgs object exposes the Action property, which can be used to take one of the following actions when the ApplyChangeFailed event is raised:

- Continue: SyncServices ignores the conflict and continues the synchronization process.

- RetryApplyingRow: SyncServices tries again to apply the row. If the retry fails, it will keep trying to apply the change until the conflict is resolved.

- RetryWithForceWrite: Depending on the value of the @sync_force_write parameter, this option lets the synchronization process retry with force applying the change.

The following section describes the incremental insert, update, and delete commands. The SelectIncrementalInsertsCommand does the following:

- Downloads the initial and incremental inserts for Snapshot, Download Only, and Bidirectional synchronization

- Retrieves the table schema from the server database

```
this.SelectIncrementalInsertsCommand = new System.Data.SqlClient.SqlCommand();
        this.SelectIncrementalInsertsCommand.CommandText = "SELECT
[Quote_ID], [QuoteNumber], [QuoteVersion], [SalesRepFName], [SalesRepLName],
    [CreatedDate], [LastEditDate] FROM dbo.Quote WHERE
([CreatedDate] > @sync_last_received_anchor AND [CreatedDate] <=
@sync_new_received_anchor)";

        this.SelectIncrementalInsertsCommand.CommandType =
System.Data.CommandType.Text;

        this.SelectIncrementalInsertsCommand.Parameters.Add(new
System.Data.SqlClient.SqlParameter("@sync_last_received_anchor",
System.Data.SqlDbType.DateTime));
```

```
            this.SelectIncrementalInsertsCommand.Parameters.Add(new
    System.Data.SqlClient.SqlParameter("@sync_new_received_anchor",
    System.Data.SqlDbType.DateTime));
```

The SelectIncrementalDeletesCommand and SelectIncrementalUpdatesCommand are
used in Download Only and Bidirectional synchronization. These commands are used to
get the deletes and updates from the server:

```
            // QuoteSyncTableSelectIncrementalDeletesCommand command.
            this.SelectIncrementalDeletesCommand = new
System.Data.SqlClient.SqlCommand();

            this.SelectIncrementalDeletesCommand.CommandText = "SELECT
[Quote_ID], [DeletionDate] FROM dbo.Quote_Tombstone WHERE (@sync_initialized = 1 AND
    [DeletionDate] > @sync_last_received_anchor AND
[DeletionDate] <= @sync_new_received_anchor)";

            this.SelectIncrementalDeletesCommand.CommandType =
System.Data.CommandType.Text;

            this.SelectIncrementalDeletesCommand.Parameters.Add(new
System.Data.SqlClient.SqlParameter("@sync_initialized",
System.Data.SqlDbType.Bit));

            this.SelectIncrementalDeletesCommand.Parameters.Add(new
System.Data.SqlClient.SqlParameter("@sync_last_received_anchor",
System.Data.SqlDbType.DateTime));

            this.SelectIncrementalDeletesCommand.Parameters.Add(new
System.Data.SqlClient.SqlParameter("@sync_new_received_anchor",
System.Data.SqlDbType.DateTime));

            // QuoteSyncTableSelectIncrementalUpdatesCommand command.
            this.SelectIncrementalUpdatesCommand = new
System.Data.SqlClient.SqlCommand();

            this.SelectIncrementalUpdatesCommand.CommandText = @"SELECT
[Quote_ID], [QuoteNumber], [QuoteVersion], [SalesRepFName], [SalesRepLName],
[CreatedDate], [LastEditDate] FROM dbo.Quote WHERE ([LastEditDate] >
@sync_last_received_anchor AND [LastEditDate] <= @sync_new_received_anchor
AND [CreatedDate] <= @sync_last_received_anchor)";
```

```
        this.SelectIncrementalUpdatesCommand.CommandType =
System.Data.CommandType.Text;

        this.SelectIncrementalUpdatesCommand.Parameters.Add(new
System.Data.SqlClient.SqlParameter("@sync_last_received_anchor",
System.Data.SqlDbType.DateTime));
        this.SelectIncrementalUpdatesCommand.Parameters.
        Add(new System.Data.SqlClient.SqlParameter
        ("@sync_new_received_anchor", System.Data.SqlDbType.DateTime));
```

Complete Synchronization Code Sample

After the wizard finishes the configuration process, the changes are automatically applied to the server database, and all synchronization changes are applied to the local data store for the first time. Figure 8-15 shows an additional table, Quote_Tombstone, created to maintain the deleted data. Additional columns and triggers are also created.

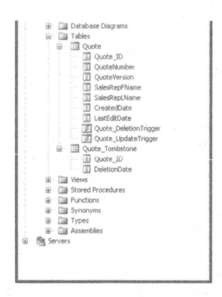

Figure 8-15. *Modifications for synchronization*

Now that the wizard has finished configuring the client and server, and the application is ready for synchronization, let's create a simple two-tier implementation of synchronizing the Quote database between the client and the server. Open the QuoteClient solution from the following location: Sync\Chapter VIII\Code\ExploreSyncAPI\QuoteClient.

Note The associated code is provided for review purpose only and is not supposed to run as is. The success of the synchronization process depends on the proper configuration of the client and the server database by the wizard, which needs to be set up on the local environment.

Synchronization Direction

There is one more configuration step before you can create the sample application: providing the SyncDirection for the SyncTable. This code sample specifies the SyncDirection:

```
public partial class MySyncSyncAgent {

    partial void OnInitialized(){
                this.Quote.SyncDirection = Microsoft.Synchronization.Data.
                SyncDirection.Bidirectional;
    }
 }
```

You can specify Bidirectional, Snapshot, Download Only, or Upload Only. In this case, Bidirectional is chosen.

You're now set to create the sample application. From the Data Sources Explorer, drag and drop the Quote table available under quoteDataSet on the Form1 designer. An editable grid will be created with a toolbar to update the changes. If you run the application, you will see that the records from the central data store are displayed in the grid. Because all changes are synchronized the first time you create the local data store, the entire server data is downloaded into the client cache.

In the form grid, you can see the only record added in the server database displayed (Figure 8-16). Next we will make some changes and see how to synchronize them using the Synchronize command.

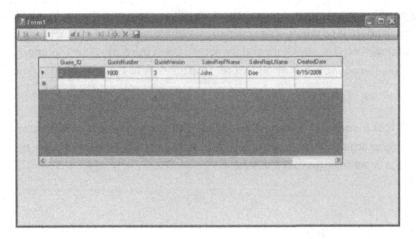

Figure 8-16. *Records displayed in Form1*

Synchronize Command

Drag and drop a button on the form and place it below the grid. Write the following piece of code in the event handler:

```
MySyncSyncAgent quoteSyncAgent = new MySyncSyncAgent();
Microsoft.Synchronization.Data.SyncStatistics quoteSyncStat =
quoteSyncAgent.Synchronize();
```

To refresh the form, call the following piece of code in the button click event handler:

```
this.quoteTableAdapter.Fill(this.quoteDataSet.Quote);
```

Every time you click the button, changes will be synchronized between the client and server. Because SyncDirection is Bidirectional, changes made in the server will also get pushed to the client.

The SyncStatistics object can be used to analyze the results of the synchronization process. We will discuss the properties exposed by SyncStatistics shortly.

Let's make the following changes to the records in the grid:

1. In the first record, change the SalesRepFName to Jane from John.

2. Add another record to the grid. You will see that this record got added with Quote_ID as 1. This happens because it is the first record getting added to the local data store, and 1 is not yet used there. Notice that in the server the first record had an ID of 2. This is deliberately done to show how Sync Services for ADO.NET 2.0 will synchronize the changes and push the record with Quote_ID 1 from client to server.

Click the Save button on the toolbar. The changes are now saved locally.

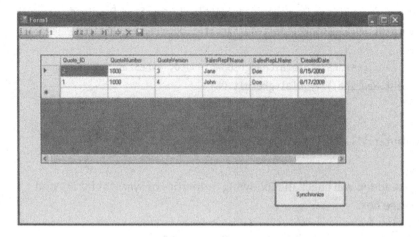

Figure 8-17. *Modifications saved in the local data store*

Click the Synchronize button and go back to SQL Server to verify the changes. The changes are now visible there, as shown in Figure 8-18. A record has been added with Quote_ID = 1, and the SalesRepFName in the record with Quote_ID = 2 has been changed from John to Jane.

Quote_ID	QuoteNumber	QuoteVersion	SalesRepFName	SalesRepLName	CreatedDate	LastEditDate
1	1000	4	John	Doe	2008-08-17 00:...	NULL
2	1000	3	Jane	Doe	2008-08-15 00:...	2008-08-17 17:...
* NULL	NULL	NULL	NULL	NULL	NULL	NULL

Figure 8-18. *Changes are synchronized with the database.*

Let's now examine the properties exposed by SyncStatistics.

SyncStatistics

Add the following piece of code in the Synchronize button event handler:

```
if (MessageBox.Show(
                    string.Format(@"Start Time:
{0}{8}Completed Time: {1}{8}No of Changes Applied (Downloaded / Failed):
{2}/{3}{8}No of Changes Applied (Uploaded / Failed): {4}/{5}{8}Total
(Downloaded / Uploaded): {6}/{7}",

                    syncStat.SyncStartTime,
syncStat.SyncCompleteTime,
```

```
                            syncStat.DownloadChangesApplied, syncStat.Download
ChangesFailed, syncStat.UploadChangesApplied, syncStat.UploadChangesFailed,

                            syncStat.TotalChangesDownloaded, syncStat.TotalChanges
Uploaded, Environment.NewLine)) == DialogResult.OK)


    {
this.quoteTableAdapter.Fill(this.quoteDataSet.Quote);
    }
```

The code you just added will check the following properties of SyncStatistics and display it in a message box:

- SyncStarTime: Shows the time the sync process was started.

- SyncCompleteTime: Shows the time the sync process was completed.

- DownloadChangesApplied: Shows the number of records that were successfully down-loaded from the server. (In the case of UploadOnly synchronization, this will be zero.)

- DownloadChangesFailed: Shows the number of records that failed to download.

- UploadChangesApplied: Shows the number of records that were successfully uploaded to the server. (For DownloadOnly synchronization, this number is zero.)

- UploadChangesFailed: Shows the number of records that failed to be applied to the server.

- TotalChangesDownloaded: Shows the total number of changes that were downloaded.

- TotalChangesDownloaded: Shows the total number of changes that were applied to the server.

Now go to SQL Server Management Studio, add another record to the Quote table, and save the changes (see Figure 8-19).

Quote_ID	QuoteNumber	QuoteVersion	SalesRepFName	SalesRepLName	CreatedDate	LastEditDate
1	1000	4	John	Doe	2008-08-17 00:...	NULL
2	1000	3	Jane	Doe	2008-08-15 00:...	2008-08-17 17:...
6	2000	1	Sam	Crystal	2008-08-18 00:...	2008-08-17 19:...
* NULL	NULL	NULL	NULL	NULL	NULL	NULL

Figure 8-19. *Adding a record in the server database*

Now run the application. You will see that the additional record is not displayed in the grid. Click the Synchronize button; the dialog box shown in Figure 8-20 displays.

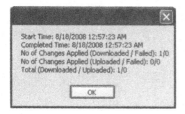

Figure 8-20. *Synchronization statistics*

You can clearly see in the figure that the number of changes downloaded is 1. Click OK and you will see the record you just added to the database being refreshed in the grid.

Summary

This chapter discussed how Sync Services for ADO.NET 2.0 can be used to synchronize data between two data sources and support OCS in a client-server scenario. To rapidly build the synchronization systems, Sync Services for ADO.NET 2.0 is integrated with SQL Server 2008 and Visual Studio 2008.

We created a sample application using Visual Studio 2008 to showcase a synchronization process in a simple two-tier environment. The next chapter explores how Sync Services for ADO.NET 2.0 can be used in collaboration scenarios for peer-to-peer synchronization.

CHAPTER 9

Synchronization Services for ADO.NET 2.0: Peer-to-Peer Synchronization

Synchronization Services for ADO.NET 2.0, which is part of the Microsoft Sync Framework, enables synchronization between ADO.NET-enabled databases. As we discussed, in offline scenarios, the data is stored directly on the user's device in an offline cache such as a SQL Server Compact Edition (CE) database, and users can access data directly from the local device. Users can then synchronize this local client database with a server database such as a SQL Server database.

Now consider a scenario in which there are multiple clients requesting data from a server that is not reachable or offline. Sync Services for ADO.NET 2.0 provides a solution for this scenario by allowing clients or peers to share data with each other. This scenario, in which peers can synchronize data with other peers without having to go through a central server, is called a *collaboration scenario*. This chapter explores how to use Sync Services for ADO.NET 2.0 for collaboration scenarios.

Sync Services for ADO.NET 2.0 is designed based on the ADO.NET data access application programming interfaces (APIs) and can synchronize not only SQL Server databases but also any other ADO.NET-enabled databases such as Oracle, for which an ADO.NET provider is available. One of the common goals of offline and collaboration scenarios is to enable synchronization for databases that do not have a reliable or consistent network connection. This synchronization is made possible by Sync Services for ADO.NET 2.0.

We start this chapter with an overview of collaboration scenarios for Sync Services for ADO.NET 2.0 and then explore the key classes in the APIs and their use. Then we will explore the architecture of two-tier and N-tier peer-to-peer synchronization with code samples.

Collaboration Scenario: Peer-to-Peer Synchronization

To understand the collaboration scenario, let's consider an example of a group of sales representatives who are onsite at their customer's office. All salespeople have their own devices that contain data they need: laptops and Windows mobile devices. They need to share data with each other and they do so by synchronizing this data with a central server of their company.

Now imagine a scenario in which one of the salespeople (Sales Rep A) is at a customer's office, and the central server is not accessible because of a network issue or planned server maintenance. Sales Rep A needs the changes from another representative (Sales Rep B), but the central server is offline. Wouldn't it be great if Sales Rep A could synchronize the data with Sales Rep B without depending on the central server? This scenario, in which one sales representative (peer) can synchronize data with another peer without a central server is called *peer-to-peer synchronization* or a *collaboration scenario*. This scenario is illustrated in Figure 9-1.

Sync Services for ADO.NET 2.0 contains the necessary APIs to support peer-to-peer synchronization. But before we dig into the classes and APIs for peer-to-peer synchronization, let's discuss how peer-to-peer synchronization works.

A peer represents an endpoint or replica such as a SQL Server database participating in synchronization. In a standard sync session, data from one peer is synchronized with data from another peer. The peer that initiates the synchronization is called the *local peer;* the other is called the *remote peer.* To enable peer-to-peer synchronization using Sync Services for ADO.NET 2.0, a peer should contain the following two components:

- Application code that manipulates (retrieves, inserts, updates, or deletes) data against the local database stored on the device

- Sync Services code that enables synchronization with the other peer

Imagine that there are three sales representatives (represented by Peer A, Peer B, and Peer C), and each peer wants to share data with the others. You can synchronize the data of each of three peers using three synchronization sessions. For example, Peer A can synchronize with Peer B and then Peer B can synchronize with Peer C. Finally, Peer A can synchronize with Peer C or Peer B to finish the synchronization process.

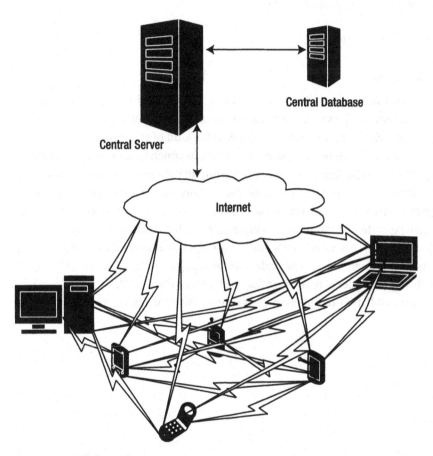

Figure 9-1. *Collaboration scenario: peer-to-peer synchronization*

Sync Services for ADO.NET 2.0 APIs for Collaboration

The `Microsoft.Synchronization.Data` namespace contains the classes required for peer-to-peer synchronization.

Using Sync Services for ADO.NET 2.0, you can synchronize two peers in two ways:

- Two-tier peer-to-peer synchronization

- N-tier peer-to-peer synchronization

Two-Tier Synchronization

Two-tier synchronization can be used when two peers participating in peer-to-peer synchronization are within the same network. For example, two peers can connect to each other by using a virtual private network (VPN).This kind of synchronization is typically used by companies that have a corporate network in which users can access others' data by dialing into the VPN. A good example is a group of software developers working together on the same project from different locations. Consider Team A, Team B, and Team C, which are working on the same project but from different branches of the organization. The central code and database are located in the head office. Each member of the team can dial into the company's VPN and access other team members' code or databases without going through the central code/database repository.

The architecture of two-tier synchronization is shown in Figure 9-2.

As shown in Figure 9-2, two-tier peer-to-peer synchronization consists of the following components:

- Peer database

- Change tracking table

- Sync adapter

- Sync provider

- Sync agent

- Sync application

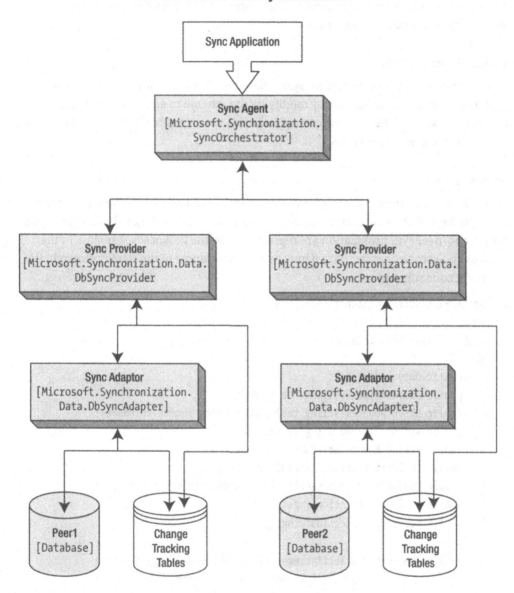

Figure 9-2. *Two-tier peer-to-peer synchronization*

Peer Database

Each peer has its own database (which can be any ADO.NET-enabled database) that will be synchronized with the other peer.

Change Tracking Table

Stores the sync metadata required for synchronization. The metadata can be stored directly in the tables within the database by modifying the schema to add new sync metadata columns. However, if the schema of the database is not extensible, the sync metadata can also be stored in separate tables.

Sync Adapter

Sync adapters are hooked to the peer database and metadata tables. The sync adapter contains the ADO.NET commands for manipulating data as well as metadata. Sync adapters for peer-to-peer synchronization are represented by the DbSyncAdapter class in the Microsoft.Synchronization.Data namespace. The anatomy of the class is shown in the following code snippet:

```
namespace Microsoft.Synchronization.Data
{
    public class DbSyncAdapter
    {
        public DbSyncAdapter();
        public DbSyncAdapter(string tableName);
        public DbSyncAdapter(string tableName, string remoteTableName);
        public string TableName { get; set; }
        public string RemoteTableName { get; set; }
        public Collection<string> RowIdColumns { get; }
        public DbSyncColumnMappingCollection ColumnMappings { get; }
        public string Description { get; set; }
        public override string ToString();

        public IDbCommand SelectIncrementalChangesCommand { get; set; }
                        public IDbCommand InsertCommand { get; set; }
        public IDbCommand UpdateCommand { get; set; }
        public IDbCommand DeleteCommand { get; set; }

        public IDbCommand InsertMetadataCommand { get; set; }
        public IDbCommand UpdateMetadataCommand { get; set; }
        public IDbCommand DeleteMetadataCommand { get; set; }
        public IDbCommand SelectMetadataForCleanupCommand { get; set; }
        public IDbCommand SelectRowCommand { get; set; }
    }
}
```

The sync adapter class can be broken down to the following three components:

- It has constructors and properties that can be used to hook the adapter to a base table in the peer database. You have to create one adapter for each base table that you want to synchronize.

- It allows developers to specify ADO.NET commands for retrieving, inserting, updating, and deleting data from the base table. It's a good practice to create store procedures to manipulate the data and hook them to the commands of the sync adapter. However, you can use any ADO.NET-supported command structure such as Transact SQL queries, views, functions, and so on.

- It allows developers to specify ADO.NET commands for retrieving, inserting, updating, and deleting data from the metadata tables just like the base tables. It also contains commands for selecting conflicting rows and deleting the old metadata from the metadata tables.

We will explore all these ADO.NET commands in more detail later in this chapter.

Sync Provider

Sync providers contain one sync adapter for each table. They execute the ADO.NET commands on the adapter when invoked by the sync agent (sync orchestrator). Sync providers provide abstraction because the sync agent communicates only with the sync provider, and the provider hides the implementation detail of the peer database. This abstraction allows sync developers to synchronize between two different types of databases or between a database and a nondatabase peer. For example, you can create a sync provider for a SQL Server database and synchronize it with an Oracle database by creating a sync provider for the Oracle database. You can also synchronize a SQL Server database with contents of an XML file or a nondatabase system. For this example of synchronizing a SQL Server database with XML file, you can create one sync provider for a SQL Server database and another for XML files.

The sync provider for peer-to-peer synchronization is represented by the DbSyncProvider class in the Microsoft.Synchronization.Data namespace. As shown in the following code listing, the DbSyncProvider class inherits from the KnowledgeSyncProvider class (this is the same class used when creating a custom sync provider):

```
public class DbSyncProvider : KnowledgeSyncProvider, IDisposable
```

The structure of the DbSyncProvider class can be divided into the following categories: metadata commands, providers, overridden methods from the KnowledgeSyncProvider class, events, and CleanupMetadata methods.

- *Metadata commands*: Besides specifying the commands for the sync adapter, you can also specify the following commands for the provider:

```
public IDbCommand SelectNewTimestampCommand { get; set; }
public IDbCommand SelectScopeInfoCommand { get; set; }
public IDbCommand UpdateScopeInfoommand { get; set; }
```

Don't concern yourself too much with these commands; we will cover them in detail in the later part of this chapter. For right now, understand that these commands are used to retrieve and update the sync timestamp and scope information.

Scope represents the logical grouping of the base tables. For example, if you want to synchronize only customers and their contacts between two databases, you can group them under a single scope called Customer Scope. Scope is represented by the Microsoft.Synchronization.Data.DbSyncScope class.

Sync Services for ADO.NET 2.0 makes use of timestamps to determine changes between two synchronization sessions. During each sync session a new timestamp value is created. This value is then used during the next sync session to determine what changes have been made between the sync sessions. So metadata commands are basically used by sync providers to maintain the knowledge of the peers.

- *Properties*: The sync provider contains the following properties:

```
public string ScopeName { get; set; }
public ChangeTrackingModel ChangeTracking { get; set; }
public IDbConnection Connection { get; set; }
public DbSyncAdapterCollection SyncAdapters { get; }
```

- ScopeName defines scope for the sync provider.

- ChangeTrackingModel implements change tracking using the sync provider.

```
public enum ChangeTrackingModel
{
    Decoupled = 0,
    Coupled = 1,
}
```

In *decoupled* change tracking, the change tracking information is stored in a separate table. In *coupled* change tracking, the base table is extended to include new columns to store the change tracking information.

■**Note** In coupled change tracking, even though the change tracking info is stored within the base table itself, you would still require a separate table to store *tombstones* (metadata about deleted data).

- Connection specifies a System.Data.IDbConnection object used by the sync provider to connect to the peer database.

- SyncAdapters attaches sync providers to sync adapters.

- *Overridden methods from the* KnowledgeSyncProvider *class*: Sync providers inherit from the KnowledgeSyncProvider class so they contain overridden methods from this class, as shown in the following code snippet. (These methods were discussed in detail in Chapter 3.)

```
public override void BeginSession(SyncProviderPosition position,
SyncSessionContext syncSessionContext);
public override void EndSession(SyncSessionContext syncSessionContext);
public override ChangeBatch GetChangeBatch(uint batchSize, SyncKnowledge
destinationKnowledge, out object  changeDataRetriever);
public override FullEnumerationChangeBatch GetFullEnumerationChange
Batch(uint batchSize, SyncId lowerEnumerationBound, SyncKnowledge
knowledgeForDataRetrieval, out object changeDataRetriever);
public override void GetSyncBatchParameters(out uint batchSize, out
SyncKnowledge knowledge);
public override void ProcessChangeBatch(ConflictResolutionPolicy resolution
Policy, ChangeBatch sourceChanges, object changeDataRetriever, SyncCallbacks
syncCallbacks, SyncSessionStatistics sessionStatistics);
public override void ProcessFullEnumerationChangeBatch(ConflictResolution
Policy resolutionPolicy, FullEnumerationChangeBatch sourceChanges, object
changeDataRetriever, SyncCallbacks syncCallbacks, SyncSessionStatistics
sessionStatistics);
public override SyncIdFormatGroup IdFormats { get; }
```

- *Events:* Sync providers also contain events raised during synchronization. These events and their delegates are listed here:

```
public event EventHandler<DbApplyChangeFailedEventArgs> ApplyChangeFailed;
public event EventHandler<DbApplyingChangesEventArgs> ApplyingChanges;
public event EventHandler<ApplyMetadataFailedEventArgs>
ApplyMetadataFailed;
public event EventHandler<DbChangesAppliedEventArgs> ChangesApplied;
public event EventHandler<DbChangesSelectedEventArgs> ChangesSelected;
public event EventHandler<DbSelectingChangesEventArgs> SelectingChanges;
public event EventHandler<DbOutdatedEventArgs> SyncPeerOutdated;
public event EventHandler<DbSyncProgressEventArgs> SyncProgress;

protected virtual void OnApplyChangeFailed
  (DbApplyChangeFailedEventArgs value);
protected virtual void OnApplyingChanges(DbApplyingChangesEventArgs value);
protected virtual void OnApplyMetadataFailed
  (ApplyMetadataFailedEventArgs value);

protected virtual void OnChangesApplied(DbChangesAppliedEventArgs value);
protected virtual void OnChangesSelected(DbChangesSelectedEventArgs value);
protected virtual void OnPeerOutdated(DbOutdatedEventArgs value);
protected virtual void OnSelectingChanges
  (DbSelectingChangesEventArgs value);
protected virtual void OnSyncProgress(DbSyncProgressEventArgs value);
```

These events are raised by the sync provider while applying changes to the base table, selecting the changes to be applied on the base table, or in case there is any error while applying changes to the base table or updating the metadata table. These events are very useful when detecting and resolving conflicts, as you will see in the later part of this chapter.

- CleanupMetadata *methods:* Methods called on the provider to execute the SelectMetadataForCleanupCommand on the sync adapter. It returns true if the metadata was cleaned up successfully.

To summarize, the sync provider is responsible for talking to sync metadata tables directly or indirectly via the sync adapter. It's responsible for change enumeration, change tracking, handling conflicts, and applying changes to the data.

Sync Agent

The sync agent is represented by the Microsoft.Synchronization.SyncOrchestrator class. It is responsible for the following:

- Establishing and managing the sync session.

- In peer-to-peer synchronization, each peer's sync provider is hooked to a sync agent, which calls the methods on these providers to synchronize data between two peers.

Sync Application

The sync application creates a new instance of the sync agent (SyncOrchestrator class) and attaches the local peer sync provider and remote peer sync provider to the sync agent. It then calls the Synchronize() method on the sync agent (as shown following), which creates a link between the local peer sync provider and remote peer sync provider:

```
syncAgent.Synchronize();
```

Now that you understand the bits and pieces required for two-tier peer-to-peer synchronization, let's connect them into the flow. Two-tier peer-to-peer synchronization flow can be described by following steps:

1. In two-tier peer-to-peer sync, there are two peers (databases) that synchronize data with each other using two sync sessions.

2. In a typical sync session, each peer contains a sync adapter and a sync provider. Sync adapters contain commands to manipulate base table data and sync metadata. The sync provider also contains commands to manipulate the sync metadata and is responsible for storing knowledge of each peer. Sync adapters are hooked to sync providers.

3. There are two sync providers in a sync session. One provider is attached to a local peer, and the other is attached to a remote peer. The peer requesting the change data is known as the local peer; the peer supplying the data is known as the remote peer. These two providers are hooked to a sync agent, which is responsible for establishing and maintaining a sync session.

4. The sync application initiates synchronization by calling the Synchronize() method on the sync agent.

5. The sync agent invokes the commands on the sync provider, which invokes the method on the sync adapter for implementing change tracking, change enumeration, handling conflicts, and selecting and applying changes to the peer database.

N-Tier Synchronization

N-tier synchronization is the most common method of peer-to-peer synchronization. Recall that two-tier synchronization can be used when two peers participating in peer-to-peer synchronization are within the same network. For example, two peers can connect to each other by using VPN. In a real-world scenario, this is rarely possible, however, and peers need to synchronize their data over the Internet instead of an intranet.

To understand N-tier synchronization, let's consider an example of sales representatives who are onsite at a customer's office. They all have devices, such as laptops or Windows Mobile devices, which contain the data they need. They need to share data with each other and with a central server of the company.

If the salespeople are in the office, they can have direct connection to their company's central server and they can also access their peers' data because they are all within the same intranet network. If they are working from home, they can use a VPN connection to connect to the central server. If they are at a customer's office, however, they might not be able to access the central server because of DMZs or firewalls preventing direct access to the corporate network.

So how can sales representatives synchronize their data with peers or the central server if they have access only to the Internet, not to the corporate network? Peer-to-peer synchronization over the Internet can be achieved by implementing N-tier synchronization. The architecture of N-tier synchronization is illustrated in Figure 9-3.

All the components are similar to those in the two-tier synchronization, except that

- There is a new sync proxy on the client side at the local peer database. This proxy acts as a remote sync provider for the sync agent.

- There is a new sync service on the remote peer. This service talks to the sync proxy and returns the data to the sync proxy from the remote sync provider.

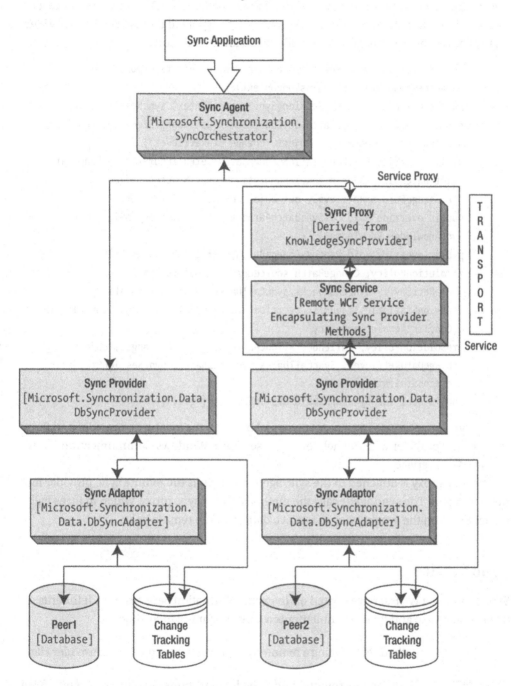

Figure 9-3. *N-tier peer-to-peer synchronization*

Sync Proxy

The sync proxy is not supplied by Sync Services for ADO.NET 2.0; it is created by developers by inheriting the KnowledgeSyncProvider class. Recall that KnowledgeSyncProvider class requires the derived calls to override the following methods:

```
public override void BeginSession(SyncProviderPosition position,
 SyncSessionContext syncSessionContext);
public override void EndSession(SyncSessionContext syncSessionContext);
public override ChangeBatch GetChangeBatch(uint batchSize, SyncKnowledge
destinationKnowledge, out object  changeDataRetriever);
public override FullEnumerationChangeBatch GetFullEnumerationChangeBatch
(uint batchSize, SyncId lowerEnumerationBound, SyncKnowledge
 knowledgeForDataRetrieval, out object changeDataRetriever);
public override void GetSyncBatchParameters(out uint batchSize, out
SyncKnowledge knowledge);
public override void ProcessChangeBatch(ConflictResolutionPolicy
resolutionPolicy, ChangeBatch sourceChanges, object change
 DataRetriever, SyncCallbacks syncCallbacks, SyncSessionStatistics
sessionStatistics); public override void ProcessFullEnumerationChangeBatch
(ConflictResolutionPolicy
resolutionPolicy, FullEnumerationChangeBatch sourceChanges, object
changeDataRetriever, SyncCallbacks syncCallbacks, SyncSessionStatistics
sessionStatistics);
public override SyncIdFormatGroup IdFormats { get; }
```

The sync proxy creates a transport channel between the local sync provider and the remote sync provider with the help of a sync service: a Windows Communication Foundation (WCF) service.

The sync proxy is attached to the sync agent and acts as the remote sync provider for the sync agent. The sync agent calls the methods on the sync proxy, which in turns calls the methods on the sync service to retrieve data from the remote peer.

Sync Service

Sync service is a WCF service hosted on Internet Information Services (IIS). It inherits from an interface and thereby implements a contract for the following:

- Providing methods for creating a remote sync provider from the DbSyncProvider class

- Calling methods on this remote sync provider in response to request received from sync proxy

Now that you know the classes involved in two-tier and N-tier synchronization, it's time to create the sample application implementing two-tier peer-to-peer synchronization. We will first synchronize a database between two peers using the peer-to-peer synchronization and then we will extend the same example to implement N-tier synchronization.

Sample Application for Two-Tier Peer-to-Peer Synchronization

In this section, we will cover creating a sample application for synchronizing three SQL Server databases using Sync Services for ADO.NET 2.0 in two-tier architecture. The entire code for this sample application is located in Sync\Chapter IX\Code\SyncPeers.

Database Structure for the Sample Application

The databases are named Collaboration_Peer1, Collaboration_Peer2, and Collaboration_Peer3. The structure of the databases is shown in Figure 9-4.

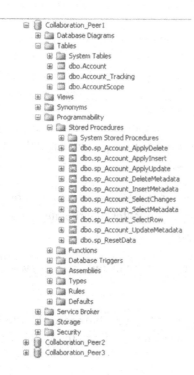

Figure 9-4. *Database structure for peer-to-peer synchronization*

Each database contains three tables:

- *Account table*: The base table will be synchronized between the three databases. The structure of the Account table is shown in Figure 9-5.

- *Account_Tracking table*: Holds the metadata required for synchronization. The structure of this table is shown in Figure 9-6.

Figure 9-6. *Account_Tracking table*

- AccountId: The primary ID from the Account table; it also serves as the primary ID in the Account_Tracking table to uniquely identify a row in the metadata table. It helps identify the metadata record for an account.

- sync_row_is_tombstone: Determines whether the metadata record is for deleted records from the base (Account) table. A value of 1 indicates that the metadata row is for a deleted record from the Account table.

- sync_row_timestamp: Represents the timestamp when the metadata record was inserted.

- sync_update_peer_key: Identifies which peer has updated the base record for the metadata row. A value of 1 indicates the remote peer, and 0 indicates the local peer.

- `sync_update_peer_timestamp`: Represents the timestamp when the base data record was updated.

- `sync_create_peer_key`: Identifies which peer has created the base record for the metadata row. A value of 1 indicates the remote peer, and 0 indicates the local peer.

- `sync_create_peer_timestamp`: Represents the timestamp when the base data record was inserted.

- `last_change_datetime`: Represents the last date time when the record in metadata table was changed.

■**Note** The names of these columns need not be same as shown here. You can select any names you like as long as they match the queries that you specify for commands of the sync adapter and sync provider.

- *AccountScope table*: Contains the scope information (logical grouping of tables). The structure of the AccountScope table is shown in Figure 9-7.

RSINGH02.Coll...o.AccountScope		
Column Name	Data Type	Allow Nulls
scope_id	uniqueidentifier	☑
scope_name	nvarchar(100)	☑
scope_sync_knowledge	varbinary(MAX)	☑
scope_tombstone_cleanup_knowledge	varbinary(MAX)	☑
scope_timestamp	timestamp	☐

Figure 9-7. *AccountScope table*

Although we are synchronizing only one table, Scope can contain multiple tables. You can insert a new record in the AccountScope table for each additional scope. You can assume AccountScope table as a place to hold the knowledge required for synchronization.

Peer-to-Peer Synchronization Tasks

Now that you have a fairly decent understanding of the base table and metadata tables, let's go through the steps involved in synchronizing tables between databases in peer-to-peer synchronization.

As a developer who is trying to synchronize two peers using Sync Services for ADO.NET 2.0, you need to do the following at each peer:

1. Implement change tracking and change enumeration. In this step you have to create the following:

   a. Change tracking tables (such as Account_Tracking) for each base table.

   b. Sync scope tables for each sync scope (such as AccountScope), which helps in change enumeration. Sync scope information helps to identify what has changed between two sync sessions.

   c. Create insert/update/delete triggers on the base table (Account) for updating the metadata tracking tables with these changes.

3. Create SQL objects (T-SQL queries, store procedures, or views) or methods to select incremental changes from the base table; insert, update, or delete rows from each base table and metadata tables.

4. Create a sync adapter for each table and assign these SQL objects (created in step 2) as commands to the sync adapter.

5. Create a sync provider and assign a scope to the sync provider. Scope determines the set of tables that will be synchronized.

6. Specify a connection for the sync provider to connect to the peer database.

7. Attach one sync adapter for each table in the scope to the sync provider.

8. Create SQL objects (T-SQL queries, store procedures, or views) or methods to retrieve and update the knowledge of each of the peers.

9. Attach the SQL objects created in the preceding step to the sync provider as commands.

After creating the sync adapters and providers at each peer, do the following to synchronize the peer databases:

1. Create a sync agent.

2. Determine which peer will request data from another peer. The peer requesting data is known as the local peer, and the peer supplying data is known as the remote peer. Attach the local sync provider and the remote sync provider to the sync agent.

3. Set the direction for the sync agent. The possible values for the sync direction are specified by the SyncDirectionOrder enum in the Microsoft.Synchronization.dll:

   ```
   public enum SyncDirectionOrder
   {
       UploadAndDownload = 0,
       DownloadAndUpload = 1,
       Upload = 2,
       Download = 3,
   }
   ```

4. Call the Synchronize() method on the sync agent to begin synchronizing the peers.

Additional Tasks

In most scenarios, developers should do the following:

- *Handle conflicts and errors*: Conflicts are automatically detected by the Sync Framework if you specify the SelectRowCommand for the sync adapter. You also need to create a SQL object (T-SQL query, store procedure, or view) to select the conflicting row from the table. This SQL object is then attached to the sync adapter via the SelectRowCommand property.

  Errors during synchronization are also automatically detected by Sync Services for ADO.NET 2.0. Most often these errors are due to constraint violation, bad data, or network issues.

Sync Services for ADO.NET 2.0 detect the conflict and errors during synchronization and raises the ApplyChangeFailed event of the sync provider in which the conflict or error was detected. You need to create a subscriber for this event if you want to handle the conflicts and errors during synchronization. Information about the conflict and error is passed as an event argument of type DbApplyChangeFailedEventArgs.

We will cover conflict handling and error handling in more detail while implementing the sample application.

- *Report sync progress*: Sync Services for ADO.NET 2.0 also lets you know the status and statistics about synchronization with the help of the SyncOperationStatistics class whose structure is shown here:

```
public class SyncOperationStatistics
{
    public int DownloadChangesApplied { get; }
    public int DownloadChangesFailed { get; }
    public int DownloadChangesTotal { get; }
    public DateTime SyncEndTime { get; internal set; }
    public int UploadChangesApplied { get; }
    public int UploadChangesFailed { get; }
    public int UploadChangesTotal { get; }
}
```

As shown in the code, the SyncOperationStatistics class contains the following:

- Properties for getting the integer count of number of changes applied during synchronization

- The DateTime property, which indicates sync start and end time

Solution Structure of the Sample Peer-to-Peer Sync Application

Let's create a sample application that synchronizes three databases in a peer-to-peer format using Synchronization Services for ADO.NET. The entire code for this sample application is located in Sync\Chapter IX\Code\SyncPeers.

The solution structure for this sample application is shown in Figure 9-8.

Figure 9-8. *Solution structure for sample application*

As shown in the figure, the solution consists of five projects:

- `RemoteProvider`: Contains the sync service (a WCF service encapsulating methods of the remote sync provider) and sync contract for implementing N-tier peer-to-peer synchronization. (We will cover N-tier peer-to-peer synchronization shortly.)

- SyncAdapter: Creates a sync adapter and associates ADO.NET commands with the adapter. It contains the following two class files:

  - SyncAdapterCommandHelper: Creates ADO.NET commands for select incremental changes from the base table; inserts, updates, or deletes rows from base tables and metadata tables.

  - SyncAdapterHelper: Creates a sync adapter and associates the ADO.NET commands with the adapter via properties of the sync adapter.

- SyncPeerDataHelper: Contains a helper class (DBHelper) that has utility methods for populating various controls used in the SyncPeers application.

- SyncPeers: A Windows form project that acts like a sync application. It contains Windows forms and it is used to achieve the following goals:

  - Demonstrate two-tier and N-tier peer-to-peer synchronization

  - Allow selection of different scenarios (creating/updating/deleting records from base tables) for synchronizing the three pairs

  - Demonstrate conflict handling

  - Display status and statistics of synchronization

- SyncProvider: Creates a sync provider and associates ADO.NET commands with the sync provider. It contains the following two class files:

  - SyncProviderCommandHelper: Creates ADO.NET commands for selecting the new high watermark for the current synchronization session, and selecting and updating sync scope and knowledge.

  - SyncProviderHelper: Creates a sync provider and associates the ADO.NET commands with the provider, attaches the sync adapter to the provider, and sets the sync scope.

Now let's start implementing the peer-to-peer required synchronization tasks discussed earlier in the chapter.

Implementing Change Tracking and Change Enumeration

This task is implemented by creating the metadata tables and sync scope tables. We are synchronizing the Account table between three SQL Server databases.

The following SQL script creates three SQL Server databases representing three peers:

```
USE master
GO
IF EXISTS (SELECT [name] FROM [master].[sys].[databases]
                WHERE [name] = N'Collaboration_Peer1')
        BEGIN
                        DROP DATABASE Collaboration_Peer1
        END
CREATE DATABASE Collaboration_Peer1
GO
ALTER DATABASE Collaboration_Peer1 SET ALLOW_SNAPSHOT_ISOLATION ON
GO
IF EXISTS (SELECT [name] FROM [master].[sys].[databases]
                WHERE [name] = N'Collaboration_Peer2')
        BEGIN
                        DROP DATABASE Collaboration_Peer2
        END
CREATE DATABASE Collaboration_Peer2
GO
ALTER DATABASE Collaboration_Peer2 SET ALLOW_SNAPSHOT_ISOLATION ON
GO
IF EXISTS (SELECT [name] FROM [master].[sys].[databases]
                WHERE [name] = N'Collaboration_Peer3')
        BEGIN
                        DROP DATABASE Collaboration_Peer3
        END
CREATE DATABASE Collaboration_Peer3
GO
ALTER DATABASE Collaboration_Peer3 SET ALLOW_SNAPSHOT_ISOLATION ON
GO
```

Tip It is strongly recommended that you use ALLOW_SNAPSHOT_ISOLATION ON. It is one of the easiest ways to ensure consistency of all change tracking information and prevent potential race conditions while running background cleanup tasks. For more information on this option, visit SQL Server 2008 Books Online.

This script is located in the sample application here: Sync\Chapter IX\Code\SyncPeers\ SyncPeers\SQL\00CreateDBPeers.sql.

We will use the decoupled change tracking method, so we will create a separate table for storing metadata.

The following SQL script creates the base, change tracking, and sync cope tables. It also inserts a record in the sync scope table that represents the AccountScope. This script needs to be run at each peer database:

```
Use Collaboration_Peer1
GO
--Create Data Table [Account]
CREATE TABLE Account(
            AccountId uniqueidentifier NOT NULL PRIMARY KEY DEFAULT NEWID(),
            [Name] nvarchar(100) NOT NULL)
GO
--Create Metadata tables..
--Create Scope table
CREATE TABLE AccountScope(
    scope_id uniqueidentifier DEFAULT NEWID(),
    scope_name nvarchar(100) NULL,
    scope_sync_knowledge varbinary(max) NULL,
     scope_tombstone_cleanup_knowledge varbinary(max) NULL,
     scope_timestamp timestamp)
SET NOCOUNT ON
SET TRANSACTION ISOLATION LEVEL READ UNCOMMITTED
--Insert AccountScope in Scope table
INSERT INTO AccountScope(scope_name) VALUES ('AccountScope')
GO
--Create metadata table
-- Create metadata tracking tables for each base table in Peers
CREATE TABLE Account_Tracking(
    AccountId uniqueidentifier NOT NULL PRIMARY KEY,
    sync_row_is_tombstone int DEFAULT 0,
    sync_row_timestamp timestamp,
    sync_update_peer_key int DEFAULT 0,
    sync_update_peer_timestamp bigint,
    sync_create_peer_key int DEFAULT 0,
    sync_create_peer_timestamp bigint,
    last_change_datetime datetime DEFAULT GETDATE())
GO
```

This script is located in the sample application here: Sync\Chapter VI\Code\SyncPeers\ SyncPeers\SQL\01CreateDataAndMetadataTable.sql.

We also need to create insert/update/delete triggers on the base table (Account) to update the metadata tracking tables with these changes, as shown in this SQL script:

```
CREATE TRIGGER Account_InsertTrigger ON Account FOR INSERT
AS
            INSERT INTO Account_Tracking(AccountId, sync_update_peer_key,
                            sync_update_peer_timestamp, sync_create_peer_key,
                            sync_create_peer_timestamp)
            SELECT AccountId, 0, @@DBTS + 1, 0, @@DBTS + 1
            FROM inserted
GO
CREATE TRIGGER Account_UpdateTrigger ON Account FOR UPDATE
AS
    UPDATE a
            SET sync_update_peer_key = 0,
                            sync_update_peer_timestamp = @@DBTS + 1,
last_change_datetime = GETDATE()
            FROM Account_Tracking a JOIN inserted i ON a.AccountId = i.AccountId
GO
CREATE TRIGGER Account_DeleteTrigger ON Account FOR DELETE
AS
    UPDATE a
            SET sync_update_peer_key = 0,
                            sync_update_peer_timestamp = @@DBTS + 1,
                            sync_row_is_tombstone = 1,
                            last_change_datetime = GETDATE()
            FROM Account_Tracking a JOIN deleted d ON a.AccountId = d.AccountId
GO
```

All these triggers have a value of 1 for sync_update_peer_key, indicating that it's a local change. This script is located in the sample application here: Sync\Chapter VI\Code\ SyncPeers/SyncPeers\SQL/03 CreateTriggers.sql.

This script needs to be run at each peer database.

Configuring the Sync Adapter

The sync adapter allows developers to specify ADO.NET commands to retrieve, insert, update, and delete data from the base table. It's a good practice to create store procedures to manipulate the data and hook them to the commands of the sync adapter. However, you can use any ADO.NET-supported command structure such as Transact SQL queries, views, functions, and so on. In the sample application, we will use SQL store procedures to manipulate data and metadata.

The two basic tasks involved in configuring the sync adapter are as follows:

- Create store procedures for retrieving, inserting, updating, and deleting data from the base table.

- Create ADO.NET commands for these store procedures and assigning them to sync adapters as properties.

The SyncAdapter project contains two classes for creating and configuring the sync adapter: SyncAdapterCommandHelper and SyncAdapterHelper.

SyncAdaperCommandHelper Class

This class creates the ADO.NET commands for retrieving, inserting, updating, and deleting data from the base table. It can be further divided into two sections: data commands for the Account (base) table and metadata commands for the Account_Tracking (metadata) table:

Data Commands (Account):

- The SelectIncrementalChangesCommand class selects the incremental changes from the base table. This process is called change enumeration.

  The SyncAdapterCommandHelper class contains the method that creates this command, GetSelectIncrementalChangesCommand(), as shown in the following code snippet:

```
public static SqlCommand GetSelectIncrementalChangesCommand()
{
    SqlCommand cmdSelectIncrementalChanges = new SqlCommand();
    cmdSelectIncrementalChanges.CommandType = CommandType.StoredProcedure;
    cmdSelectIncrementalChanges.CommandText = "sp_Account_SelectChanges";
    cmdSelectIncrementalChanges.Parameters.Add("@" +
    DbSyncSession.SyncMetadataOnly, SqlDbType.Int);
    cmdSelectIncrementalChanges.Parameters.Add("@" +
    DbSyncSession.SyncMinTimestamp, SqlDbType.BigInt);
    cmdSelectIncrementalChanges.Parameters.Add("@" +
    DbSyncSession.SyncInitialize,
    SqlDbType.Int);
    return cmdSelectIncrementalChanges;
}
```

The DbSyncSession class provides a set of session variables that specifies the values of the parameters for the command. It contains the following constants that represent the sync session parameters:

```
public const string SyncCheckConcurrency = "sync_check_concurrency";
public const string SyncCreatePeerKey = "sync_create_peer_key";
public const string SyncCreatePeerTimestamp = "sync_create_peer_timestamp";
public const string SyncForceWrite = "sync_force_write";
public const string SyncInitialize = "sync_initialize";
public const string SyncMetadataOnly = "sync_metadata_only";
public const string SyncMinTimestamp = "sync_min_timestamp";
public const string SyncNewTimestamp = "sync_new_timestamp";
public const string SyncRowCount = "sync_row_count";
public const string SyncRowCreateTimestamp = "sync_row_create_timestamp";
public const string SyncRowIsTombstone = "sync_row_is_tombstone";
public const string SyncRowTimestamp = "sync_row_timestamp";
public const string SyncScopeCleanupKnowledge
        = "sync_scope_cleanup_knowledge";
public const string SyncScopeId = "sync_scope_id";
public const string SyncScopeKnowledge = "sync_scope_knowledge";
public const string SyncScopeName = "sync_scope_name";
public const string SyncScopeTimestamp = "sync_scope_timestamp";
public const string SyncSessionId = "sync_session_id";
public const string SyncStageName = "sync_stage_name";
public const string SyncUpdatePeerKey = "sync_update_peer_key";
public const string SyncUpdatePeerTimestamp = "sync_update_peer_timestamp";
```

You can directly use the string represented by these constants. Values of these sync session variables are set by Sync Services for ADO.NET 2.0 during synchronization.

The SQL script for the sp_Account_SelectChanges store procedure is as follows:

```
CREATE PROCEDURE sp_Account_SelectChanges (
                    @sync_min_timestamp bigint,
                    @sync_metadata_only int,
                    @sync_initialize int)
AS
            SELECT  at.AccountId,
                                a.Name,
                                at.sync_row_is_tombstone,
                                at.sync_row_timestamp,
                                at.sync_update_peer_key,
                                at.sync_update_peer_timestamp,
```

```
                                        at.sync_create_peer_key,
                                        at.sync_create_peer_timestamp
                    FROM Account a RIGHT JOIN Account_Tracking at ON a.AccountId =
                                        at.AccountId
                    WHERE at.sync_row_timestamp > @sync_min_timestamp
                    ORDER BY at.AccountId ASC
GO
```

This store procedure is used to select incremental changes from the Account table using metadata information from the Account_Tracking table.

- InsertCommand inserts the incremental changes into the base table.

The SyncAdapterCommandHelper class contains the GetInsertCommand() method, which creates this command:

```
public static SqlCommand GetInsertCommand()
{
    SqlCommand cmdInsert = new SqlCommand();
    cmdInsert.CommandType = CommandType.StoredProcedure;
    cmdInsert.CommandText = "sp_Account_ApplyInsert";
    cmdInsert.Parameters.Add("@AccountId", SqlDbType.UniqueIdentifier);
    cmdInsert.Parameters.Add("@Name", SqlDbType.NVarChar);
    cmdInsert.Parameters.Add("@" + DbSyncSession.SyncRowCount,
     SqlDbType.Int).Direction = ParameterDirection.Output;
    return cmdInsert;
}
```

The SQL script for the sp_Account_ApplyInsert store procedure is as follows:

```
CREATE PROCEDURE sp_Account_ApplyInsert (
        @AccountId uniqueidentifier,
                        @Name nvarchar(100),
                        @sync_row_count int OUT)
AS
    IF NOT EXISTS (SELECT AccountId FROM Account_Tracking
     WHERE AccountId =    @AccountId)
                INSERT INTO Account (AccountId, Name)
                VALUES (@AccountId, @Name)
                SET @sync_row_count =
@@rowcount

GO
```

This store procedure is used to inserting incremental changes into the Account table using the metadata information from the Account_Tracking table.

- UpdateCommand updates the incremental changes into the base table.

The SyncAdapterCommandHelper class contains the GetUpdateCommand() method, which creates this command:

```
public static SqlCommand GetUpdateCommand()
{
    SqlCommand cmdUpdate = new SqlCommand();
    cmdUpdate.CommandType = CommandType.StoredProcedure;
    cmdUpdate.CommandText = "sp_Account_ApplyUpdate";
    cmdUpdate.Parameters.Add("@AccountId", SqlDbType.UniqueIdentifier);
    cmdUpdate.Parameters.Add("@Name", SqlDbType.NVarChar);
    cmdUpdate.Parameters.Add("@" + DbSyncSession.SyncMinTimestamp,
      SqlDbType.BigInt);
    cmdUpdate.Parameters.Add("@" + DbSyncSession.SyncRowCount,
      SqlDbType.Int).Direction = ParameterDirection.Output;
    cmdUpdate.Parameters.Add("@" + DbSyncSession.SyncForceWrite,
      SqlDbType.Int);
    return cmdUpdate;
}
```

The SQL script for the sp_Account_ApplyUpdate store procedure is shown following:

```
CREATE PROCEDURE sp_Account_ApplyUpdate (
        @AccountId uniqueidentifier,
                        @Name nvarchar(100),
                        @sync_min_timestamp bigint ,
                        @sync_row_count int OUT,
                        @sync_force_write int)
AS
            UPDATE a
            SET a.Name = @Name
            FROM Account a JOIN Account_Tracking at ON a.AccountId = at.AccountId
            WHERE ((at.sync_row_timestamp <= @sync_min_timestamp) OR
                        @sync_force_write = 1)
                        AND at.AccountId = @AccountId
            SET @sync_row_count = @@rowcount
GO
```

This store procedure is used to update incremental changes from the Account table using metadata information from the Account_Tracking table.

- DeleteCommand deletes changes from the base table.

The SyncAdapterCommandHelper class contains the GetDeleteCommand() method, which creates this command:

```
public static SqlCommand GetDeleteCommand()
{
    SqlCommand cmdDelete = new SqlCommand();
    cmdDelete.CommandType = CommandType.StoredProcedure;
    cmdDelete.CommandText = "sp_Account_ApplyDelete";
    cmdDelete.Parameters.Add("@AccountId", SqlDbType.UniqueIdentifier);
    cmdDelete.Parameters.Add("@" + DbSyncSession.SyncMinTimestamp,
     SqlDbType.BigInt);
    cmdDelete.Parameters.Add("@" + DbSyncSession.SyncRowCount,
     SqlDbType.Int).Direction = ParameterDirection.Output;
    return cmdDelete;
}
```

The SQL script for the sp_Account_ApplyDelete store procedure is as follows:

```
CREATE PROCEDURE sp_Account_ApplyDelete(
            @AccountId uniqueidentifier ,
            @sync_min_timestamp bigint ,
            @sync_row_count int OUT)
AS
        DELETE a
        FROM Account a JOIN Account_Tracking at ON a.AccountId = at.AccountId
          WHERE at.sync_row_timestamp <= @sync_min_timestamp
                    AND at.AccountId = @AccountId
          SET @sync_row_count = @@rowcount
GO
```

This store procedure deletes changes from the Account table using metadata information from the Account_Tracking table.

Metadata Commands (Account_Tracking)

- InsertMetadataCommand inserts the metadata information into the metadata table. This command is called when changes from one peer are applied to another peer.

The SyncAdapterCommandHelper class contains the GetInsertMetadataCommand() method, which creates this command:

```
public static SqlCommand GetInsertMetadataCommand()
{
    SqlCommand cmdInsertMetadata = new SqlCommand();
    cmdInsertMetadata.CommandType = CommandType.StoredProcedure;
    cmdInsertMetadata.CommandText = "sp_Account_InsertMetadata";
    cmdInsertMetadata.Parameters.Add("@AccountId",
      SqlDbType.UniqueIdentifier);
    cmdInsertMetadata.Parameters.Add("@" + DbSyncSession.SyncCreatePeerKey,
        SqlDbType.Int);
    cmdInsertMetadata.Parameters.Add("@" +
        DbSyncSession.SyncCreatePeerTimestamp, SqlDbType.BigInt);
    cmdInsertMetadata.Parameters.Add("@" + DbSyncSession.SyncUpdatePeerKey,
        SqlDbType.Int);
    cmdInsertMetadata.Parameters.Add("@" +
      DbSyncSession.SyncUpdatePeerTimestamp, SqlDbType.BigInt);
    cmdInsertMetadata.Parameters.Add("@" + DbSyncSession.SyncRowIs
      Tombstone,
      SqlDbType.Int);
    cmdInsertMetadata.Parameters.Add("@" + DbSyncSession.SyncRowCount,
      SqlDbType.Int).Direction = ParameterDirection.Output;

    return cmdInsertMetadata;
}
```

The SQL script for the sp_Account_InsertMetadata store procedure is as follows:

```
CREATE PROCEDURE sp_Account_InsertMetadata (
                    @AccountId uniqueidentifier,
                    @sync_create_peer_key int ,
                    @sync_create_peer_timestamp bigint,
                    @sync_update_peer_key int ,
                    @sync_update_peer_timestamp bigint,
                    @sync_row_is_tombstone int,
                    @sync_row_count int OUT)
AS
            INSERT INTO Account_Tracking (AccountId, sync_update_peer_key,
                    sync_update_peer_timestamp,
                      sync_create_peer_key, sync_create_peer_timestamp,
                    sync_row_is_tombstone)
```

```
                    VALUES (@AccountId, @sync_update_peer_key,
                    @sync_update_peer_timestamp,
                    @sync_create_peer_key, @sync_create_peer_timestamp,
                    @sync_row_is_tombstone)
                    SET @sync_row_count = @@rowcount
    GO
```

This store procedure inserts a new record in the Account_Tracking table.

- UpdateMetadataCommand updates the metadata information into the metadata table.
  This command is called when changes from one peer are applied to another peer.

The SyncAdapterCommandHelper class contains the GetUpdateMetadataCommand()
method, which creates this command:

```
public static SqlCommand GetUpdateMetadataCommand()
{
    SqlCommand cmdUpdateMetadata = new SqlCommand();
    cmdUpdateMetadata.CommandType = CommandType.StoredProcedure;
    cmdUpdateMetadata.CommandText = "sp_Account_UpdateMetadata";
    cmdUpdateMetadata.Parameters.Add("@AccountId",
    SqlDbType.UniqueIdentifier);
    cmdUpdateMetadata.Parameters.Add("@" + DbSyncSession.SyncCreatePeerKey,
    SqlDbType.Int);
    cmdUpdateMetadata.Parameters.Add("@" +
    DbSyncSession.SyncCreatePeerTimestamp, SqlDbType.BigInt);
    cmdUpdateMetadata.Parameters.Add("@" + DbSyncSession.SyncUpdatePeerKey,
    SqlDbType.Int);
    cmdUpdateMetadata.Parameters.Add("@" +
    DbSyncSession.SyncUpdatePeerTimestamp, SqlDbType.BigInt);
    cmdUpdateMetadata.Parameters.Add("@" +
    DbSyncSession.SyncCheckConcurrency, SqlDbType.Int);
    cmdUpdateMetadata.Parameters.Add("@" + DbSyncSession.SyncRowTimestamp,
    SqlDbType.BigInt);
    cmdUpdateMetadata.Parameters.Add("@" + DbSyncSession.SyncRowCount,
    SqlDbType.Int).Direction = ParameterDirection.Output;

    return cmdUpdateMetadata;
}
```

The SQL script for the sp_Account_UpdateMetadata store procedure is as follows:

```
CREATE PROCEDURE sp_Account_UpdateMetadata (
                        @AccountId uniqueidentifier,
                        @sync_create_peer_key int,
                        @sync_create_peer_timestamp bigint,
                        @sync_update_peer_key int,
                        @sync_update_peer_timestamp timestamp,
                        @sync_row_timestamp timestamp,
                        @sync_check_concurrency int,
                        @sync_row_count int OUT)
AS
            UPDATE Account_Tracking SET
                        sync_create_peer_key = @sync_create_peer_key,
                        sync_create_peer_timestamp =
                                            @sync_create_peer_timestamp,
                        sync_update_peer_key = @sync_update_peer_key,
                        sync_update_peer_timestamp =
                                            @sync_update_peer_timestamp
            WHERE AccountId = @AccountId AND
                        (@sync_check_concurrency = 0 OR sync_row_timestamp =
                        @sync_row_timestamp)
            SET @sync_row_count = @@rowcount
GO
```

This store procedure updates the record in the Account_Tracking table.

- DeleteMetadataCommand deletes the metadata information in the metadata table. This command is called when changes from one peer are applied to another peer.

The SyncAdapterCommandHelper class contains the GetDeleteMetadataCommand() method, which creates this command:

```
public static SqlCommand GetDeleteMetadataCommand()
{
    SqlCommand cmdDeleteMetadata = new SqlCommand();
    cmdDeleteMetadata.CommandType = CommandType.StoredProcedure;
    cmdDeleteMetadata.CommandText = "sp_Account_DeleteMetadata";
    cmdDeleteMetadata.Parameters.Add("@AccountId",
      SqlDbType.UniqueIdentifier);
```

```
            cmdDeleteMetadata.Parameters.Add("@" +
            DbSyncSession.SyncCheckConcurrency, SqlDbType.Int);
            cmdDeleteMetadata.Parameters.Add("@" + DbSyncSession.SyncRowTimestamp,
            SqlDbType.BigInt);
            cmdDeleteMetadata.Parameters.Add("@" + DbSyncSession.SyncRowCount,
            SqlDbType.Int).Direction = ParameterDirection.Output;
            return cmdDeleteMetadata;
        }
```

The SQL script for sp_Account_DeleteMetadata store procedure is shown as follows:

```
GO
CREATE PROCEDURE sp_Account_DeleteMetadata(
    @AccountId uniqueidentifier,
            @sync_row_timestamp timestamp,
            @sync_check_concurrency int,
            @sync_row_count int OUT)
AS

            DELETE at
            FROM Account_Tracking at
            WHERE at.AccountId = @AccountId
                        AND (@sync_check_concurrency = 0 OR
                        at.sync_row_timestamp = @sync_row_timestamp)
            SET @sync_row_count = @@rowcount
GO
```

This store procedure deletes the record in the Account_Tracking table.

SyncAdapterHelper Class

This class contains a static method, CreateSyncAdapters(), which creates a new sync adapter and assigns the ADO.NET commands to the adapter. The code for this method is as follows:

```
        public static DbSyncAdapter CreateSyncAdapters()
        {
            DbSyncAdapter syncAdapter = new DbSyncAdapter("Account");
            syncAdapter.RowIdColumns.Add("AccountId");
            syncAdapter.SelectIncrementalChangesCommand =
                SyncAdapterCommandHelper.GetSelectIncrementalChangesCommand();
            syncAdapter.InsertCommand = SyncAdapterCommandHelper.GetInsertCommand();
            syncAdapter.UpdateCommand = SyncAdapterCommandHelper.GetUpdateCommand();
            syncAdapter.DeleteCommand = SyncAdapterCommandHelper.GetDeleteCommand();
            syncAdapter.SelectRowCommand =
                SyncAdapterCommandHelper.GetSelectRowCommand();
```

```
        syncAdapter.InsertMetadataCommand =
            SyncAdapterCommandHelper.GetInsertMetadataCommand();
        syncAdapter.UpdateMetadataCommand =
            SyncAdapterCommandHelper.GetUpdateMetadataCommand();
        syncAdapter.DeleteMetadataCommand =
            SyncAdapterCommandHelper.GetDeleteMetadataCommand();
        syncAdapter.SelectMetadataForCleanupCommand =
            SyncAdapterCommandHelper.GetSelectMetadataForCleanupCommand(100);
        return syncAdapter;
    }
```

As shown in the code snippet, the sync adapter needs to be created for each table. Because we are synchronizing only the Account table, the adapter is created for the Account table, and the RowIdColumn for the adapter is set to the primary key (AccountId) of the table.

All the store procedure for sync adapter commands are contained in a script called 04 SelectAndApplyChanges.sql, which is located here: Sync\Chapter VI\Code\SyncPeers/ SyncPeers\SQL/04 SelectAndApplyChanges.sql.

Configuring the Sync Provider

The sync provider is configured with the help of two classes in the SyncProvider project:

SyncProviderCommandHelper Class

Creates the ADO.NET commands for the sync provider to select and manipulate knowledge and sync scope information.

- SelectNewTimestampCommand selects the new high watermark for the current synchronization session.

  The SyncProviderCommandHelper class contains the GetSelectNewTimestampCommand() method, which creates this command:

```
    public static SqlCommand GetSelectNewTimestampCommand()
    {
        SqlCommand cmdSelectNewTimestamp = new SqlCommand();
        string newTimestamp = "@" + DbSyncSession.SyncNewTimestamp;
        cmdSelectNewTimestamp.CommandText = "SELECT " + newTimestamp + " =
        @@DBTS ";
cmdSelectNewTimestamp.Parameters.Add(newTimestamp, SqlDbType.Timestamp);
        cmdSelectNewTimestamp.Parameters[newTimestamp].Direction =
        ParameterDirection.Output;
        return cmdSelectNewTimestamp;
    }
```

Sync Services for ADO.NET 2.0 uses timestamps to determine the changes between two synchronization sessions. During each sync session a new timestamp value is created. This timestamp value is then used during the next sync session to determine what changes have been made between the sync sessions.

- SelectScopeInfoCommand selects sync knowledge, cleanup knowledge, and a scope version (timestamp).

The SyncProviderCommandHelper class contains the GetSelectScopeInfoCommand() method, which creates this command:

```
public static SqlCommand GetSelectScopeInfoCommand()
{
    SqlCommand cmdSelectScopeInfo = new SqlCommand();
    cmdSelectScopeInfo.CommandType = CommandType.Text;
    cmdSelectScopeInfo.CommandText = "SELECT " +
                        "@" + DbSyncSession.SyncScopeId + " =
                    scope_id, " +
                        "@" + DbSyncSession.SyncScopeKnowledge
                    + " = scope_sync_knowledge, " +
                        "@" + DbSyncSession.SyncScopeCleanup-
                    Knowledge + " = scope_tombstone_cleanup_
                    knowledge, " +
                        "@" + DbSyncSession.SyncScopeTimestamp
                    + " = scope_timestamp " +
                      "FROM AccountScope " +
                      "WHERE scope_name = @" +
                    DbSyncSession.SyncScopeName;

    cmdSelectScopeInfo.Parameters.Add("@" + DbSyncSession.SyncScopeName,
    SqlDbType.NVarChar, 100);
    cmdSelectScopeInfo.Parameters.Add("@" + DbSyncSession.SyncScopeId,
    SqlDbType.UniqueIdentifier).Direction = ParameterDirection.Output;

    cmdSelectScopeInfo.Parameters.Add("@" +
    DbSyncSession.SyncScopeKnowledge,
    SqlDbType.VarBinary,
    10000).Direction = ParameterDirection.Output;
    cmdSelectScopeInfo.Parameters.Add("@" +
     DbSyncSession.SyncScopeCleanupKnowledge, SqlDbType.VarBinary,
            10000).Direction = ParameterDirection.Output;
```

```
        cmdSelectScopeInfo.Parameters.Add("@" + DbSyncSession.SyncScope-
        Timestamp, SqlDbType.BigInt).Direction = ParameterDirection.Output;

        return cmdSelectScopeInfo;
    }
```

- UpdateScopeInfoCommand updates sync knowledge and cleanup knowledge.

  The SyncProviderCommandHelper class contains the GetUpdateScopeInfoCommand()
  method, which creates this command:

```
public static SqlCommand GetUpdateScopeInfoCommand()
{
    SqlCommand cmdUpdateScopeInfo = new SqlCommand();
    cmdUpdateScopeInfo.CommandType = CommandType.Text;
    cmdUpdateScopeInfo.CommandText = "UPDATE  AccountScope SET " +
                        "scope_sync_knowledge = @" +
                          DbSyncSession.SyncScopeKnowledge + ", " +

                        "scope_tombstone_cleanup_knowledge = @" +
                        DbSyncSession.SyncScopeCleanupKnowledge
                        + " " + "WHERE scope_name = @" +
                        DbSyncSession.SyncScopeName +
                          " AND " +
                        " ( @" + DbSyncSession.SyncCheckConcurrency
                        + " = 0 or scope_timestamp = @" +
                        SyncSession.SyncScopeTimestamp + "); " +
                        "SET @" + DbSyncSession.SyncRowCount + "
                          = @@rowcount";
    cmdUpdateScopeInfo.Parameters.Add("@" +
                        DbSyncSession.SyncScopeKnowledge,
                        SqlDbType.VarBinary, 10000);
    cmdUpdateScopeInfo.Parameters.Add("@" +
        DbSyncSession.SyncScopeCleanupKnowledge,
      SqlDbType.VarBinary, 10000);

    cmdUpdateScopeInfo.Parameters.Add("@" + DbSyncSession.SyncScopeName,
    SqlDbType.NVarChar, 100);
    cmdUpdateScopeInfo.Parameters.Add("@" +
                        DbSyncSession.SyncCheckConcurrency,
```

```
        SqlDbType.Int);
        cmdUpdateScopeInfo.Parameters.Add("@" +
                                DbSyncSession.SyncScopeTimestamp,
          SqlDbType.BigInt);
        cmdUpdateScopeInfo.Parameters.Add("@" + DbSyncSession.SyncRowCount,
          SqlDbType.Int).Direction = ParameterDirection.Output;
        return cmdUpdateScopeInfo;
    }
```

SyncProviderHelper Class

This class contains a static method called CreateSyncProvider(), which implements the
following tasks from the sync provider:

- Create a new sync provider

- Associate ADO.NET commands with the sync provider

- Assign a scope to the sync provider

- Assign the SQL connection for the sync provider

The code for the method is as follows:

```
    public static DbSyncProvider CreateSyncProvider(int peerID)
    {
        DbSyncProvider syncProvider = new DbSyncProvider();
        syncProvider.ScopeName = "AccountScope";
        syncProvider.Connection = new
          SqlConnection(DBHelper.GetPeerConncetionStringByPeerID(peerID));
        syncProvider.SyncAdapters.Add(SyncAdapterHelper.CreateSyncAdpters());
        syncProvider.SelectNewTimestampCommand =
        SyncProviderCommandHelper.GetSelectNewTimestampCommand();
        syncProvider.SelectScopeInfoCommand =
        SyncProviderCommandHelper.GetSelectScopeInfoCommand();
        syncProvider.UpdateScopeInfoCommand =
        SyncProviderCommandHelper.GetUpdateScopeInfoCommand();
        return syncProvider;
    }
```

The peerId parameter represents an integer value, indicating at which end the provider
needs to be created. A value of 1 indicates Peer1; that is, Collaboration_Peer1 database;
2 indicates Collaboration_Peer2 database, and 3 indicates Collaboration_Peer3 database.

The CreateSyncProvider() method makes use of the GetPeerConnectionStringByPeerID()
method of the DBHelper class to get the connection string for connecting to the peer database.

The code for GetPeerConnectionStringByPeerID is shown following:

```
public static string GetPeerConnectionStringByPeerID(int peerID)
{
    switch (peerID)
    {
        case 1:
            return Properties.Settings.Default.
                        Collaboration_Peer1ConnectionString;
        case 2:
            return Properties.Settings.Default.
                        Collaboration_Peer2ConnectionString;
        case 3:
            return Properties.Settings.Default.
                        Collaboration_Peer3ConnectionString;
        default:
            return string.Empty;
    }
}
```

GetPeerConnectionStringByPeerID retrieves the connection string from the Settings
file of the SyncPeerDataHelper project, which in turn returns the values stored in the App.
config file, as shown following:

```
<?xml version="1.0"?>
<configuration>
    <configSections>
    </configSections>
    <connectionStrings>
        <add name="SyncPeers.Properties.Settings.Collaboration_Peer1ConnectionString
                    " connectionString="Data Source=RSINGH02;Initial
                        Catalog=Collaboration_Peer1;Integrated Security=True"
                            providerName="System.Data.SqlClient"/>
        <add name="SyncPeers.Properties.Settings.Collaboration_Peer2ConnectionString"
                        connectionString="Data Source=RSINGH02;Initial
                        Catalog=Collaboration_Peer2;Integrated Security=True"
                        providerName="System.Data.SqlClient"/>
        <add name="SyncPeers.Properties.Settings.Collaboration_Peer3ConnectionString"
                        connectionString="Data Source=RSINGH02;Initial
                        Catalog=Collaboration_Peer3;Integrated Security=True"
                        providerName="System.Data.SqlClient"/>
    </connectionStrings>
</configuration>
```

Recall that a sync adapter needs to be created for each table at each peer database. The sync provider needs to be created at each peer for each database, and all the sync adapters for the current scope are attached to the sync provider.

Synchronizing the Application

After creating sync adapters and providers, the next task is to create a sync agent and hook the sync providers to the agent. The synchronizing application then calls the Synchronize() method on the sync agent to begin synchronization.

In the sample application, the sync application is represented by the SyncPeers project, which is a Windows form project and contains references to following projects:

- SyncAdapter

- SyncPeerDataHelper

- RemoteProvider

- SyncProvider

SyncPeers contains two main components that allow users to create different peer-to-peer synchronization scenarios:

- The PeersData.cs user control contains three gridviews to display the Account table from each peer.

  Public methods: This class contains a RefreshGrids() public method that refreshes the data in each grid:

  ```
  public void RefreshGrids()
  {
      string query = " SELECT * FROM Account";
      BindDataGridView(Properties.Settings.Default.
                  Collaboration_Peer1ConnectionString, query, grdViewA);
      BindDataGridView(Properties.Settings.Default.
                  Collaboration_Peer2ConnectionString, query, grdViewB);
      BindDataGridView(Properties.Settings.Default.
                  Collaboration_Peer3ConnectionString, query, grdViewC);
  }
  ```

  PeersData.cs also contains the GetSelectedRecord() method, which returns the AccountId for the selected account record from the grid.

```
public Guid GetSelectedRecord(int peerId)
{
    switch (peerId)
    {
        case 1:
            return new Guid(grdViewA.SelectedCells[0].Value.ToString());
        case 2:
            return new Guid(grdViewB.SelectedCells[0].Value.ToString());
        case 3:
            return new Guid(grdViewC.SelectedCells[0].Value.ToString());
        default:
            return Guid.Empty;
    }
}
```

- `frmMain.cs` allows users to create different sync scenarios and synchronize data between different peers (see Figure 9-9).

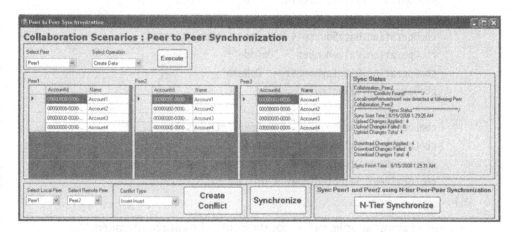

Figure 9-9. *Peer-to-peer sync form*

Let's examine the code for this form in more detail.

Form Load

As shown in the following code listing, the `IntializeControls()` method is called during the form load event:

```
private void frmMain_Load(object sender, EventArgs e)
{
    IntializeControls();
}
```

The IntializeControls() method initializes various combo box controls on the form with the help of public static methods from the DBHelper class:

```
private void IntializeControls()
{
    cboPeer.DataSource = DBHelper.GetPeers();
    cboPeer.ValueMember = "PeerID";
    cboPeer.DisplayMember = "PeerName";
    cboPeer.SelectedIndex = 0;

    cboConflictType.DataSource = DBHelper.GetConflictType();
    cboConflictType.ValueMember = "ConflictTypeID";
    cboConflictType.DisplayMember = "ConflictTypeName";
    cboConflictType.SelectedIndex = 0;

    cboOperation.DataSource = DBHelper.GetOperations();
    cboOperation.ValueMember = "OpCode";
    cboOperation.DisplayMember = "OpName";
    cboOperation.SelectedIndex = 0;

    cboLocalPeer.DataSource = DBHelper.GetPeers();
    cboLocalPeer.ValueMember = "PeerID";
    cboLocalPeer.DisplayMember = "PeerName";
    cboLocalPeer.SelectedIndex = 0;
}
```

To keep the example simple, values for the combo box are hard-coded. The IntializeControls() method makes use of the GetPeers(), GetConflictType(), and GetOperations() methods from the DBHelper class. These methods are very straightforward and simple.

GetPeers() returns a data table containing peers:

```
public static DataTable GetPeers()
{
    DataTable dt = new DataTable();
    dt.Columns.Add("PeerID", typeof(int));
    dt.Columns.Add("PeerName", typeof(string));
    DataRow dr = dt.NewRow();
    dr["PeerID"] = 1;
```

```
        dr["PeerName"] = "Peer1";
        dt.Rows.Add(dr);
        dr = dt.NewRow();
        dr["PeerID"] = 2;
        dr["PeerName"] = "Peer2";
        dt.Rows.Add(dr);
        dr = dt.NewRow();
        dr["PeerID"] = 3;
        dr["PeerName"] = "Peer3";
        dt.Rows.Add(dr);
        return dt;
    }
```

GetConflictType() returns a data table containing conflict types:

```
    public static DataTable GetConflictType()
    {
        DataTable dt = new DataTable();
        dt.Columns.Add("ConflictTypeID", typeof(int));
        dt.Columns.Add("ConflictTypeName", typeof(string));
        DataRow dr = dt.NewRow();
        dr["ConflictTypeID"] = 1;
        dr["ConflictTypeName"] = "Insert-Insert";
        dt.Rows.Add(dr);
        dr = dt.NewRow();
        dr["ConflictTypeID"] = 2;
        dr["ConflictTypeName"] = "Update-Update";
        dt.Rows.Add(dr);
        dr = dt.NewRow();
        dr["ConflictTypeID"] = 3;
        dr["ConflictTypeName"] = "Update-Delete";
        dt.Rows.Add(dr);
        return dt;
    }
```

GetOperations returns a data table containing operations that can be performed at each peer:

```
    public static DataTable GetOperations()
    {
        DataTable dt = new DataTable();
        dt.Columns.Add("OpCode", typeof(int));
        dt.Columns.Add("OpName", typeof(string));
        DataRow dr = dt.NewRow();
```

```
        dr["OpCode"] = 1;
        dr["OpName"] = "Create Data";
        dt.Rows.Add(dr);
        dr = dt.NewRow();
        dr["OpCode"] = 2;
        dr["OpName"] = "Updtate Data";
        dt.Rows.Add(dr);
        dr = dt.NewRow();
        dr["OpCode"] = 3;
        dr["OpName"] = "Delete Data";
        dt.Rows.Add(dr);
        dr = dt.NewRow();
        dr["OpCode"] = 4;
        dr["OpName"] = "Clean Data";
        dt.Rows.Add(dr);
        dr = dt.NewRow();
        dr["OpCode"] = 5;
        dr["OpName"] = "Clean MetaData";
        dt.Rows.Add(dr);
        return dt;
    }
```

We will explore all these conflict types in detail later in the chapter.

Synchronizing Peers

The final piece remaining for synchronizing peers is to initialize and configure the sync agent. Synchronization is initiated by clicking the Synchronize button on the Main form. The code for the click event of this button is the following:

```
private void btnSync_Click(object sender, EventArgs e)
{
    txtStatus.Text = string.Empty;
    Synchronize(int.Parse(cboLocalPeer.SelectedValue.ToString()),
      int.Parse(cboRemotePeer.SelectedValue.ToString()));
    ctlPeersData.RefreshGrids();
}
```

The btnSync_Click event calls the private helper method Synchronize() to synchronize the two peers selected by local peers and remote peers drop-down list. After synchronization, the RefreshGrids() method is called on the Peers data control to show the result of synchronization. The code for the Synchronize() method is shown following:

```
private void Synchronize(int localPeerID, int remotePeerID)
{
    try
    {
        localSyncProvider = SyncProviderHelper.
            CreateSyncProvider(localPeerID);
        localSyncProvider.SyncProviderPosition = SyncProviderPosition.Local;
        localSyncProvider.ApplyChangeFailed += new
            EventHandler<DbApplyChangeFailedEventArgs>(HandleConflicts);

        remoteSyncProvider = SyncProviderHelper.
            CreateSyncProvider(remotePeerID);
        remoteSyncProvider.SyncProviderPosition =
            SyncProviderPosition.Remote;
        remoteSyncProvider.ApplyChangeFailed += new
            EventHandler<DbApplyChangeFailedEventArgs>(HandleConflicts);

        collaborationSyncAgent = new SyncOrchestrator();
        collaborationSyncAgent.LocalProvider = localSyncProvider;
        collaborationSyncAgent.RemoteProvider = remoteSyncProvider;
        collaborationSyncAgent.Direction = SyncDirectionOrder.
         UploadAndDownload;
        syncStatistics = collaborationSyncAgent.Synchronize();

        DisplaySyncStatus(syncStatistics);
    }
    catch (DbOutdatedSyncException ex)
    {
        throw new Exception("Peer Database is outdated.Please run the
        CleanData.sql script
          in SQL or execute Clean Data Command from UI" + ex.ToString());
    }
    catch (Exception ex)
    {
        txtStatus.Text += ex.ToString();
        //TODO Exception handling
    }
}
```

The Synchronize() method performs the following tasks:

1. Creates a local and remote sync provider with the help of the SyncProviderHelper class.

2. Sets the SyncProviderPosition for remote and local providers.

3. Registers the ApplyChangeFailed event on the sync providers for handling conflicts and synchronization errors.

4. Creates a new sync agent with the help of the SyncOrchestrator class.

5. Attaches the local and remote sync providers to the sync agent.

6. Sets the direction for synchronization by using the values from the SyncDirectionOrder enum.

7. Calls the Synchronize() method on the sync agent to synchronize the two peers specified by input parameters localPeerID and remotePeerID.

8. Calls the DisplaySyncStatus() method to display the status of synchronization by passing syncStatistics as the input parameter.

Reporting Sync Progress

As shown in the following code listing, the DisplaySyncStatus method displays the sync status in the txtStatus text box:

```
private void DisplaySyncStatus(SyncOperationStatistics
        syncOperationStatistics)
{
    txtStatus.Text += "/*********************Sync Status*********************
    *******/" + Environment.NewLine;
    txtStatus.Text += "Sync Start Time : " +
        syncOperationStatistics.SyncStartTime.ToString() +
        Environment.NewLine;
    txtStatus.Text += "Upload Changes Applied : " +
        syncOperationStatistics.UploadChangesApplied.ToString() +
        Environment.NewLine;
    txtStatus.Text += "Upload Changes Failed : " +
        syncOperationStatistics.UploadChangesFailed.ToString() +
        Environment.NewLine;
```

```
        txtStatus.Text += "Upload Changes Total: " +
          syncOperationStatistics.UploadChangesTotal.ToString() +
          Environment.NewLine;
        txtStatus.Text += Environment.NewLine;
        txtStatus.Text += "Download Changes Applied : " +
          syncOperationStatistics.DownloadChangesApplied.ToString() +
          Environment.NewLine;
        txtStatus.Text += "Download Changes Failed : " +
          syncOperationStatistics.DownloadChangesFailed.ToString() +
            Environment.NewLine;
        txtStatus.Text += "Download Changes Total: " +
          syncOperationStatistics.DownloadChangesTotal.ToString() +
          Environment.NewLine;
        txtStatus.Text += Environment.NewLine;
        txtStatus.Text += "Sync Finish Time : " +
          syncOperationStatistics.SyncEndTime.ToString();
    }
```

Executing Operations

As shown in Figure 9-10, the Select Peer drop-down list, Select Operation drop-down list, and Execute button allow the user to perform the following operations on the peer database:

1. Create/update/delete records in the Account table.

2. Reset the data in the Account table to the initial state.

3. Clean data from the metadata table (Account_Tracking).

Figure 9-10. *Execute operations*

The code for the click event of the Execute button is the following:

```
    private void btnExecute_Click(object sender, EventArgs e)
    {
        int peerId =  int.Parse(cboPeer.SelectedValue.ToString());
        int operationCode = int.Parse(cboOperation.SelectedValue.ToString());
```

```
        if (operationCode != 5)
        {
            Guid slectedGuid = ctlPeersData.GetSelectedRecord(peerId);
            DBHelper.ExecuteOperation(operationCode ,peerId,slectedGuid);
            ctlPeersData.RefreshGrids();
        }
        else
        {
            CleanMetadata(peerId);
        }
    }
```

btnExecute_Click makes use of the DBHelper class to create/update/delete and reset the rows in the Account table at the specified peer.

The code for ExecuteOperation is as follows:

```
public static void ExecuteOperation(int operationCode, int peerID,
  Guid slectedGuid)
{
    switch (operationCode)
    {
        case 1:
            string sql = "INSERT INTO Account(Name) VALUES ('TestAccount" +
                DateTime.Now.ToLongTimeString() + "')";
            ExecuteSqlQuery(sql, peerID);
            break;
        case 2:
            sql = "UPDATE Account SET Name = 'TestAccount" +
                DateTime.Now.ToLongTimeString() + "' WHERE AccountId = '" +
                slectedGuid.ToString() + "'";
            ExecuteSqlQuery(sql, peerID);
            break;
        case 3:
            sql = "DELETE FROM Account WHERE AccountId = '" +
                        slectedGuid.ToString() + "'";
            ExecuteSqlQuery(sql, peerID);
            break;
        case 4:
            CleanPeers(peerID);
            break;
        default:
            break;
    }
}
```

ExecuteOperation calls the ExecuteSqlQuery() method to execute the query against the database:

```
public  static void ExecuteSqlQuery(string query, int peerID)
{
    using (SqlConnection con = new
      SqlConnection(GetPeerConncetionStringByPeerID(peerID)))
    using (SqlCommand cmd = new SqlCommand(query, con))
    {
        con.Open();
        cmd.ExecuteNonQuery();
    }
}
```

If the clean data operation was selected, ExecuteOperation calls the CleanPeers() method to execute the sp_ResetData store procedure:

```
public static void CleanPeers(int peerID)
{
    ExecuteSqlQuery("EXEC ('sp_ResetData')", peerID);
}
```

The sp_ResetData store procedure is contained in the CleanData.sql script in the folder Sync\Chapter VI\Code\SyncPeers\SyncPeers\SQL.

The CleanData.sql script initializes the Account table with four records:

```
CREATE PROCEDURE sp_ResetData
AS

            SET NOCOUNT ON
            SET TRANSACTION ISOLATION LEVEL READ UNCOMMITTED
            DELETE FROM Account_Tracking
            DELETE FROM Account

            --INSERT INTO Account.
            INSERT INTO Account(AccountId,Name) VALUES ('00000000-0000-0000-
                        0000-000000000001','Account1')
INSERT INTO Account(AccountId,Name) VALUES ('00000000-0000-0000-0000-
            000000000002','Account2')
            INSERT INTO Account(AccountId,Name) VALUES ('00000000-0000-0000-
            0000-000000000003','Account3')
            INSERT INTO Account(AccountId,Name) VALUES ('00000000-0000-0000-
            0000-000000000004','Account4')
GO
```

This script creates a store procedure to insert test data in the Account table. It also resets the data back to its original state. This script needs to be run for each peer.

Running the Application for Two-Tier Peer-to-Peer Synchronization

To run the application, do the following:

1. Right-click on the SyncPeers project within the solution and select Set As Startup Project, as shown in Figure 9-11.

Figure 9-11. *Setting the startup project*

2. Run the SQL script CompleteSQL.sql located at Sync\Chapter VI\Code\SyncPeers\ SyncPeers\SQL.

OR

3. Run the following script from the same folder:

   `00 CreateDBPeers.sql`

   Now run following scripts for each peer database:

   `01 CreateDataAndMetadataTable.sql`

   `02 CleanData.sql`

   `03 CreateTriggers.sql`

   `04 SelectAndApplyChanges.sql`

4. Update the App.config file in the SyncPeerDataHelper project with the connection string to connect to peer databases:

```xml
<?xml version="1.0"?>
<configuration>
    <configSections>
    </configSections>
    <connectionStrings>
        <add name="SyncPeers.Properties.Settings.Collaboration_Peer1ConnectionString
                        " connectionString="Data Source=RSINGHO2;Initial
                        Catalog=Collaboration_Peer1;Integrated Security=True"
                        providerName="System.Data.SqlClient"/>
        <add name="SyncPeers.Properties.Settings.Collaboration_Peer2ConnectionString
                        " connectionString="Data Source=RSINGHO2;Initial
                        Catalog=Collaboration_Peer2;Integrated Security=True"
                        providerName="System.Data.SqlClient"/>
        <add name="SyncPeers.Properties.Settings.Collaboration_Peer3ConnectionString
                        " connectionString="Data Source=RSINGHO2;Initial
                        Catalog=Collaboration_Peer3;Integrated Security=True"
                        providerName="System.Data.SqlClient"/>
    </connectionStrings>
</configuration>
```

Now press F5. The main form displays the test data for each peer in gridview, as shown in Figure 9-12.

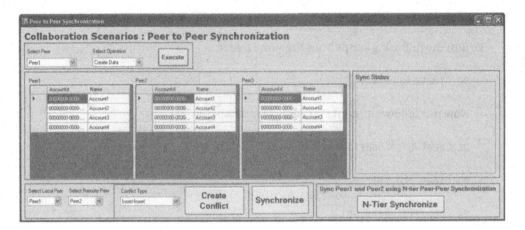

Figure 9-12. *Main form*

Click the Execute button to create a new account record in the Peer1 database. This will create a new record and refresh the gridview to reflect this new record (see Figure 9-13).

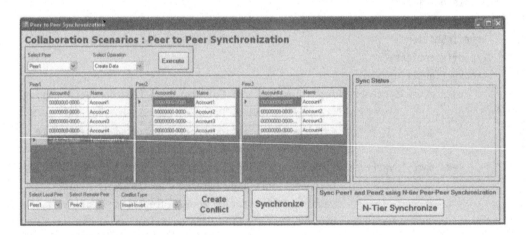

Figure 9-13. *Creating a new record*

Click the Synchronize button to synchronize the Account table between Peer1 and Peer2. After synchronization is finished, the new record is added into database for Peer2, and the sync status message is displayed in the sync status area, as shown in Figure 9-14.

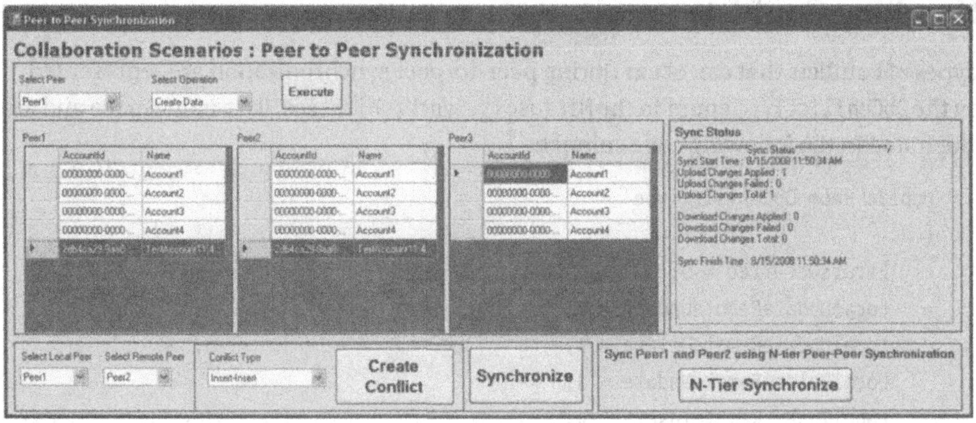

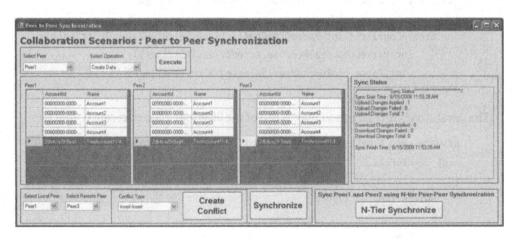

Figure 9-14. *Sync of Peer1 and Peer2*

Select Peer3 from the Select Remote Peer drop-down list and click Synchronize again to synchronize Peer1 and Peer3. The final synchronization result is shown in Figure 9-15.

Figure 9-15. *Sync of Peer1 and Peer3*

That's it; we have synchronized Peer1 and Peer2 and then Peer1 and Peer3 with each other using two-tier peer-to-peer synchronization architecture with the help of Sync Services for ADO.NET 2.0.

Now let's extend this application to handle conflicts as well.

Handling Conflicts

Types of conflicts that can occur during peer-to-peer synchronization are represented by the DbConflictType enum in the Microsoft.Synchronization.Data namespace and are illustrated in the following code snippet:

```
public enum DbConflictType
{
    ErrorsOccurred = 0,
    LocalUpdateRemoteUpdate = 1,
    LocalUpdateRemoteDelete = 2,
    LocalDeleteRemoteUpdate = 3,
    LocalInsertRemoteInsert = 4,
    LocalDeleteRemoteDelete = 5,
}
```

The sample application uses the Create Conflict button to create the conflicts. The code for the click event of this button is as follows:

```
private void btnConflict_Click(object sender, EventArgs e)
{
    CreateConflicts(int.Parse(cboConflictType.SelectedValue.ToString()),
        int.Parse(cboLocalPeer.SelectedValue.ToString()),
        int.Parse(cboRemotePeer.SelectedValue.ToString()));
}
```

The CreateConflict() method makes use of the DBHelper class to create conflicts:

```
private void CreateConflicts(int ConflictType, int localPeerID,
 int remotePeerID)
{
    switch (ConflictType)
    {
        case 1:
            DBHelper.ExecuteSqlQuery("INSERT INTO Account(Accountid,Name)
            VALUES
            ('00000000-0000-0000-0000-000000000010',
            'InsertConflictAccount')",
            localPeerID);
            DBHelper.ExecuteSqlQuery("INSERT INTO Account(Accountid,Name)
            VALUES
             ('00000000-0000-0000-0000-000000000010',
            'InsertConflictAccount')",
              remotePeerID);
            break;
```

```
        case 2:
            DBHelper.ExecuteSqlQuery("UPDATE Account SET Name =
            'UpdateConflictLocalPeerAccount' WHERE Name = 'Account1'",
            localPeerID);

            DBHelper.ExecuteSqlQuery("UPDATE Account SET Name =
             'UpdateConflictRemotePeerAccount' WHERE Name = 'Account1'",
    remotePeerID);
            break;
        case 3:
            DBHelper.ExecuteSqlQuery("UPDATE Account SET Name =
            'UpdateConflictLocalPeerAccount' WHERE Name = 'Account2'",
            localPeerID);
            DBHelper.ExecuteSqlQuery("DELETE Account WHERE
            Name = 'Account2'", remotePeerID);
            break;
        default:
            break;
    }
    ctlPeersData.RefreshGrids();
}
```

Handling conflicts involves three tasks:

1. Registering the ApplyChangeFailed event on the local and remote sync provider:

```
localSyncProvider.ApplyChangeFailed += new
    EventHandler<DbApplyChangeFailedEventArgs>(HandleConflicts);
remoteSyncProvider.ApplyChangeFailed += new
    EventHandler<DbApplyChangeFailedEventArgs>(HandleConflicts);
```

The code is added to the Synchronize() method in the frmMain.cs class.

2. Adding the ADO.NET commands to the sync adapter for selecting the conflicting rows.

The SyncAdapterCommandHelper class contains the GetSelectRowCommand() method, which creates this ADO.NET command:

```
public static SqlCommand GetSelectRowCommand()
{
    SqlCommand cmdSelectRow = new SqlCommand();
    cmdSelectRow.CommandType = CommandType.StoredProcedure;
    cmdSelectRow.CommandText = "sp_Account_SelectRow";
    cmdSelectRow.Parameters.Add("@AccountId",
```

```
SqlDbType.UniqueIdentifier);
                    return cmdSelectRow;
            }
        Code for the sp_Account_SelectRow is shown below
        CREATE PROCEDURE sp_Account_SelectRow
            @AccountId uniqueidentifier
        AS
          SELECT  at.AccountId,
                  a.Name,

                    at.sync_row_timestamp,
                    at.sync_row_is_tombstone,
                    at.sync_update_peer_key,
                    at.sync_update_peer_timestamp,
                    at.sync_create_peer_key,
                    at.sync_create_peer_timestamp
                  FROM Account a RIGHT JOIN Account_Tracking at ON a.AccountId =
                  at.AccountId
                  WHERE at.AccountId = @AccountId


        GO
```

This script creates a store procedure for selecting conflicting rows from the data and metadata table. This script needs to be run for each peer. This script can be found in the Sync\Chapter VI\Code\SyncPeers\SyncPeers\SQL folder.

Now this command is assigned to the SelectRowCommand property of the sync adapter in the CreateSyncAdapters() method of the SyncAdapterHelper class:

```
syncAdapter.SelectRowCommand = SyncAdapterCommandHelper.GetSelectRowCommand();
```

3. Resolving conflicts using custom logic or using one of the values of the ApplyAction enum.

```
public enum ApplyAction
{
    Continue = 0,
    RetryApplyingRow = 1,
    RetryWithForceWrite = 2,
    RetryNextSync = 3,
}
```

The sample application contains the HandleConflicts() method, which displays the information about the conflict and launches the dialog box for resolving the conflicts using the ResolveConflict form.

The code for HandleConflicts() is the following:

```
private void HandleConflicts(object sender, DbApplyChangeFailedEventArgs e)
{
    string conflictingPeerConnection;
    if (e.Connection.Database.ToString().Equals
        (localSyncProvider.Connection.Database))
    {
        conflictingPeerConnection = localSyncProvider.Connection.Database;
    }
    else
    {
        conflictingPeerConnection = remoteSyncProvider.Connection.Database;
    }
    string conflictInfo = "/***********Conflicts Found***********/ " +
        Environment.NewLine +
        e.Conflict.Type + " was detected at following Peer " +
        Environment.NewLine +
        conflictingPeerConnection + Environment.NewLine;
    txtStatus.Text += conflictInfo;
    SyncPeers.HandleConflicts.ResolveConflict rc = new
      SyncPeers.HandleConflicts.ResolveConflict(e, conflictInfo);
    switch (e.Conflict.Type)
    {
        case DbConflictType.LocalInsertRemoteInsert:
            rc.ShowDialog();
            break;
        case DbConflictType.LocalUpdateRemoteUpdate:
            rc.ShowDialog();
            break;
        case DbConflictType.LocalUpdateRemoteDelete:
            rc.ShowDialog();
            break;
        case DbConflictType.LocalDeleteRemoteUpdate:
            rc.ShowDialog();
            break;
        case DbConflictType.ErrorsOccurred:
            rc.ShowDialog();
            break;
```

```
            case DbConflictType.LocalDeleteRemoteDelete:
                break;
            default:
                break;
        }
        ctlPeersData.RefreshGrids();
    }
```

As shown in the following code snippet, the constructor of the ResolveConflict form initializes two gridviews to display local and remote changes that are causing the conflict:

```
public ResolveConflict(DbApplyChangeFailedEventArgs e,string conflictInfo)
{
    InitializeComponent();
    dbApplyChangeFailedEventArgs = e;
    txtConflictInfo.Text = conflictInfo;
    grdViewLocal.DataSource = dbApplyChangeFailedEventArgs.
      Conflict.LocalChange;
    grdViewRemote.DataSource =
        dbApplyChangeFailedEventArgs.Conflict.RemoteChange;
}
```

The conflicts are resolved when the user clicks the ResolveConflict button (its code is as follows):

```
private void btnResolveConflict_Click(object sender, EventArgs e)
{
    if (rbContinue.Checked)
    {
        dbApplyChangeFailedEventArgs.Action = ApplyAction.Continue;
    }
    else
    {
        if (rbRetryWithForceWrite.Checked)
        {
            dbApplyChangeFailedEventArgs.Action = ApplyAction.
            RetryWithForceWrite;
        }
        else
        {
```

```
            if (rbRetryApplyingRow.Checked)
            {
                dbApplyChangeFailedEventArgs.Action =
                ApplyAction.RetryApplyingRow;
            }
            else
            {
                if (rbRetryNextSync.Checked)
                {
                    dbApplyChangeFailedEventArgs.Action = ApplyAction.
                    RetryNextSync;
                }
            }
        }
    }
    Close();
}
```

To create a conflict, select a conflict type from the Conflict Type drop-down list on the main form and click the Create Conflict button. If the Insert-Insert conflict is selected, a new account record will be created in Peer1 and Peer3, as shown in Figure 9-16.

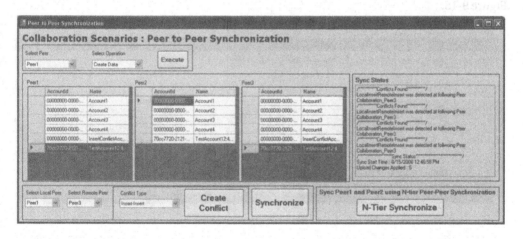

Figure 9-16. *Conflict*

Now click the Synchronize button, which will launch the ResolveConflict dialog box, as shown in Figure 9-17.

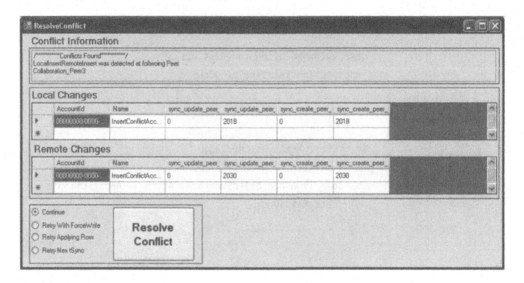

Figure 9-17. *Resolving the conflict*

The ResolveConflict dialog box displays the local and remote change and allows you to select a conflict resolution action to resolve the conflict.

Select Continue and click Resolve Conflict. The source change wins, as shown in Figure 9-18.

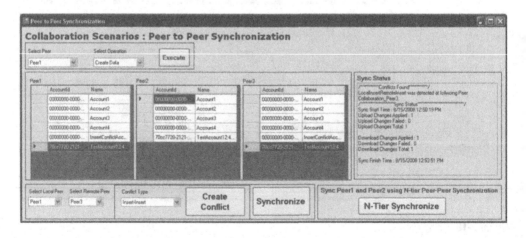

Figure 9-18. *Resolving the conflict*

As shown in Figure 9-18, the conflict is resolved by overwriting Peer3's changes with Peer1's changes.

Cleaning Metadata

It's sometimes necessary to clean metadata in old records, which helps synchronization. To clean metadata, we need to implement the following tasks:

1. Create an ADO.NET command to select the metadata rows to be deleted.

   The SyncAdapterCommandHelper class contains the GetSelectMetadataForCleanupCommand() method to create this command:

   ```
   public static SqlCommand GetSelectMetadataForCleanupCommand(int
     MetadataAgingInHours)
   {
       SqlCommand cmdSelectMetadataForCleanup = new SqlCommand();
       cmdSelectMetadataForCleanup.CommandType = CommandType.StoredProcedure;
       cmdSelectMetadataForCleanup.CommandText = "sp_Account_SelectMetadata";
       cmdSelectMetadataForCleanup.Parameters.
        Add("@metadata_aging_in_hours", SqlDbType.Int).Value =
        MetadataAgingInHours;
       return cmdSelectMetadataForCleanup;
   }
   ```

   The code for the sp_Account_SelectMetadata store procedure is the following:

   ```
   CREATE PROCEDURE sp_Account_SelectMetadata
               @metadata_aging_in_hours int
   AS
               IF @metadata_aging_in_hours = -1
                           BEGIN
                               SELECT AccountId,
                                   sync_row_timestamp,
                                   sync_update_peer_key,
                                   sync_update_peer_timestamp,
                                   sync_create_peer_key,
                                   sync_create_peer_timestamp
                               FROM Account_Tracking
                               WHERE sync_row_is_tombstone = 1
                           END
           ELSE
             BEGIN
               SELECT AccountId,
                 sync_row_timestamp,
                 sync_update_peer_key,
                 sync_update_peer_timestamp,
   ```

```
                         sync_create_peer_key,
                         sync_create_peer_timestamp
                        FROM Account_Tracking
                        WHERE sync_row_is_tombstone = 1 AND
                        DATEDIFF(hh, last_change_datetime, GETDATE()) >
                        @metadata_aging_in_hours
                          END
        GO
```

This script creates a store procedure to select the rows from the metadata table that can be cleaned up. This script needs to be run for each peer (you can find this script in the Sync\Chapter VI\Code\SyncPeers\SyncPeers\SQL folder).

2. Assign this command to the sync adapter via the SelectMetadataForCleanupCommand property:

```
syncAdapter.SelectMetadataForCleanupCommand =
    SyncAdapterCommandHelper.GetSelectMetadataForCleanupCommand(100);
```

3. Call the CleanMetadata() method on the sync provider as shown here:

```
private void CleanMetadata(int peerId)
{
    DbSyncProvider dbSyncProvider =SyncProviderHelper.
        CreateSyncProvider(peerId);
    if (!dbSyncProvider.CleanupMetadata())
    {
        txtStatus.Text = "Metadata for Peer " + peerId.ToString() +
            "Can not be deleted, Please try Again";
    }
    txtStatus.Text = "Metadata for Peer " + peerId.ToString() +
        " is Deleted";
}
```

N-Tier Peer-to-Peer Synchronization

Now let's extend the sample two-tier peer-to-peer sync application to also support N-tier synchronization.

To create an N-tier peer-to-peer synchronization solution, do the following:

1. Create a remote WCF service.

2. Add the service reference to the sync application.

3. Create a local proxy for the remote WCF service.

4. Attach the proxy as a remote provider to the sync agent.

5. Attach the local provider to the sync agent and call the Synchronize() method on the sync agent.

Creating the Remote WCF Service

This service is created in the RemoteProvider project. This project contains the service and the service contract.

The code for the IRemotePeerSyncContract service contract is shown here:

```
public interface IRemotePeerSyncContract
{
    [OperationContract(IsInitiating = true, IsTerminating = false)]
    void BeginSession();

    [OperationContract(IsInitiating = false, IsTerminating = false)]
    void GetKnowledge(out uint batchSize, out SyncKnowledge knowledge);

    [OperationContract(IsInitiating = false, IsTerminating = false)]
    ChangeBatch GetChanges(uint batchSize, SyncKnowledge destinationKnowledge,
        out object changeData);

    [OperationContract(IsInitiating = false, IsTerminating = false)]
    void ApplyChanges(ConflictResolutionPolicy resolutionPolicy, ChangeBatch
        sourceChanges, object changeData,
        ref SyncSessionStatistics sessionStatistics);

    [OperationContract(IsInitiating = false, IsTerminating = false)]
    void EndSession();
}
```

The RemotePeerSyncService WCF service inherits from this interface and implements a contract for the following:

1. Providing methods for creating a remote sync provider from the DbSyncProvider class.

2. Calling methods on this remote sync provider in response to a request received from the sync proxy. Because the sync provider itself inherits from the KnowledgeSyncProvider class, the service basically calls the methods of the KnowledgeSyncProvider class on the sync provider.

The code for the WCF service is as follows:

```
public class RemotePeerSyncService : IRemotePeerSyncContract
{
    private DbSyncProvider remoteSyncProvider = null;
    public void BeginSession()
    {
        remoteSyncProvider = SyncProviderHelper.CreateSyncProvider(2);//@:Peer2
    }
    public void GetKnowledge(
        out uint batchSize,
        out SyncKnowledge knowledge)
    {
        remoteSyncProvider.GetSyncBatchParameters(out batchSize, out knowledge);
    }
    public ChangeBatch GetChanges(
        uint batchSize,
        SyncKnowledge destinationKnowledge,
        out object changeData)
    {
        return remoteSyncProvider.GetChangeBatch(batchSize, destinationKnowledge,
            out changeData);
    }
    public void ApplyChanges(
        ConflictResolutionPolicy resolutionPolicy,
        ChangeBatch sourceChanges,
        object changeData,
        ref SyncSessionStatistics sessionStatistics)
    {
        SyncCallbacks syncCallback = new SyncCallbacks();
        remoteSyncProvider.ProcessChangeBatch(resolutionPolicy, sourceChanges,
            changeData, syncCallback,
            sessionStatistics);
    }
    public void EndSession()
    {
        remoteSyncProvider = null;
    }
}
```

Adding a Service Reference

To add the WCF service reference to the sync application (the SyncPeers project), follow these steps:

1. Right-click on the SyncPeers project and select Add Service Reference.

2. In the Add Service Reference dialog box, click Discover and enter the namespace as RemoteProviderProxy (see Figure 9-19).

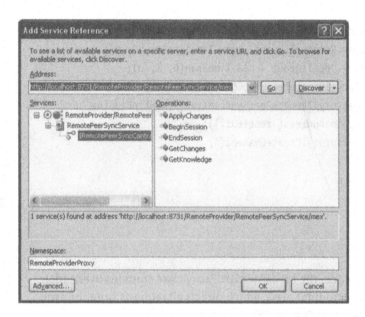

Figure 9-19. *Adding a service reference*

Creating a Local Proxy

A sync proxy is not supplied by Sync Services for ADO.NET 2.0; it's created by developers by inheriting the KnowledgeSyncProvider class:

```
public class LocalPeerSyncProxy : KnowledgeSyncProvider
```

As shown in the following code snippet, the sync proxy creates the remote sync provider inside the constructor of the class that is used later on by other overridden methods of the KnowledgeSyncProvider class.

It also creates a transport channel between the local sync provider and the remote sync provider with the help of the IRemotePeerSyncContract contract:

```
public LocalPeerSyncProxy(string remoteUri)
{
    _remoteUri = remoteUri;
    CreateProxyForRemoteProvider();
}

private void CreateProxyForRemoteProvider()
{
    try
    {
        WSHttpBinding wSHttpBinding = new WSHttpBinding();
        wSHttpBinding.ReceiveTimeout = new TimeSpan(0, 10, 0);
        wSHttpBinding.OpenTimeout = new TimeSpan(0, 1, 0);
        ChannelFactory<IRemotePeerSyncContract> factory = new
            ChannelFactory<IRemotePeerSyncContract>(wSHttpBinding,
            new EndpointAddress(_remoteUri));
        syncProxy = factory.CreateChannel();
    }
    catch (Exception ex)
    {
        throw ex;
    }
}
```

As shown in the following code, the LocalPeerSyncProxy class contains overridden methods of the KnowledgeSyncProvider class, which directs all requests from the sync agent to the remote RemotePeerSyncService WCF service.

```
public override void BeginSession(SyncProviderPosition position,
    SyncSessionContext syncSessionContext)
{
    syncProxy.BeginSession();
}
public override void EndSession(SyncSessionContext syncSessionContext)
{
    syncProxy.EndSession();
}
public override void GetSyncBatchParameters(out uint batchSize,
    out SyncKnowledge knowledge)
{
    batchSize = syncProxy.GetKnowledge(out knowledge);
}
```

```
public override ChangeBatch GetChangeBatch(uint batchSize, SyncKnowledge
    destinationKnowledge,
    out object changeDataRetriever)
{
    return syncProxy.GetChanges(out changeDataRetriever, batchSize,
     destinationKnowledge);
}
public override void ProcessChangeBatch(ConflictResolutionPolicy
     resolutionPolicy, ChangeBatch sourceChanges,

    object changeDataRetriever, SyncCallbacks syncCallback,
     SyncSessionStatistics sessionStatistics)
{
    SyncSessionStatistics remoteSessionStatistics = new
        SyncSessionStatistics();
    syncProxy.ApplyChanges(resolutionPolicy, sourceChanges,
        changeDataRetriever, ref remoteSessionStatistics);
    sessionStatistics.ChangesApplied = remoteSessionStatistics.
        ChangesApplied;
    sessionStatistics.ChangesFailed = remoteSessionStatistics.ChangesFailed;
}
public override SyncIdFormatGroup IdFormats
{
    get
    {
        if (syncIdFormatGroup == null)
        {
            syncIdFormatGroup = new SyncIdFormatGroup();
            syncIdFormatGroup.ChangeUnitIdFormat.IsVariableLength = false;
            syncIdFormatGroup.ChangeUnitIdFormat.Length = 1;
            syncIdFormatGroup.ReplicaIdFormat.IsVariableLength = false;
            syncIdFormatGroup.ReplicaIdFormat.Length = 16;
            syncIdFormatGroup.ItemIdFormat.IsVariableLength = true;
            syncIdFormatGroup.ItemIdFormat.Length = 10 * 1024;
        }
        return syncIdFormatGroup;
    }
}
```

Nonimplemented Methods

To keep the example short, the following methods were not implemented for the sample application:

```
public override FullEnumerationChangeBatch GetFullEnumerationChangeBatch
 (uint batchSize, SyncId lowerEnumerationBound, SyncKnowledge
 knowledgeForDataRetrieval, out object changeDataRetriever)
{
    throw new NotImplementedException();
}
public override void ProcessFullEnumerationChangeBatch(
ConflictResolutionPolicy resolutionPolicy,
FullEnumerationChangeBatch sourceChanges, object changeDataRetriever,
SyncCallbacks syncCallback, SyncSessionStatistics sessionStatistics)
{
    throw new NotImplementedException();
}
```

The GetFullEnumerationChangeBatch() and ProcessFullEnumerationChangeBatch() methods are used when an out-of-date synchronization destination is detected.

Configuring a Sync Agent for N-Tier Synchronization

The sync agent is configured in the click event of the N-Tier Synchronize button on the main form of the SyncPeers application:

```
private void btnN_TierSync_Click(object sender, EventArgs e)
{
    try
    {
        KnowledgeSyncProvider localKnowledgeSyncProvider;
        KnowledgeSyncProvider remoteKnowledgeSyncProvider;
        string remoteUri
            =@"http://localhost:8731/RemoteProvider/RemotePeerSyncService/";

        localKnowledgeSyncProvider =SyncProviderHelper.CreateSyncProvider(1);
        remoteKnowledgeSyncProvider = new
        LocalPeerProxy.LocalPeerSyncProxy(remoteUri);

        collaborationSyncAgent = new SyncOrchestrator();
        collaborationSyncAgent.LocalProvider = localKnowledgeSyncProvider;
        collaborationSyncAgent.RemoteProvider = remoteKnowledgeSyncProvider;
        collaborationSyncAgent.Direction = SyncDirectionOrder.
```

```
        UploadAndDownload;
        syncStatistics = collaborationSyncAgent.Synchronize();
        txtStatus.Text = string.Empty;
        DisplaySyncStatus(syncStatistics);
        ctlPeersData.RefreshGrids();
    }
    catch (DbOutdatedSyncException ex)
    {
        throw new Exception("Peer Database is outdated.
        Please run the CleanData.sql script
        in SQL or execute Clean Data Command from UI" + ex.ToString());
    }
    catch (Exception ex)
    {
        txtStatus.Text = ex.ToString();
        //TODO Exception handling
    }
}
```

The sync proxy is attached to the synchronization agent and acts as the remote sync provider for the sync agent. The sync agent calls the methods on the sync proxy, which in turn calls the methods on the sync service to retrieve data from the remote peer.

Running the Application

Run the SyncPeers application and create a new record in the Peer1 database. The main form will look similar to Figure 9-20.

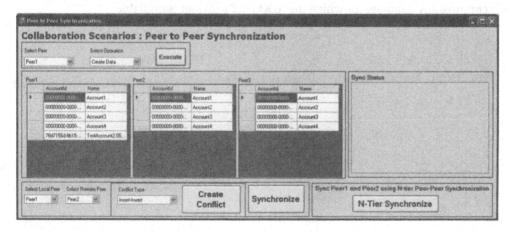

Figure 9-20. *N-tier sync start*

Click the N-Tier Synchronize button to synchronize Peer1 and Peer2. Figure 9-21 shows the result of N-tier synchronization with a new record added in Peer2.

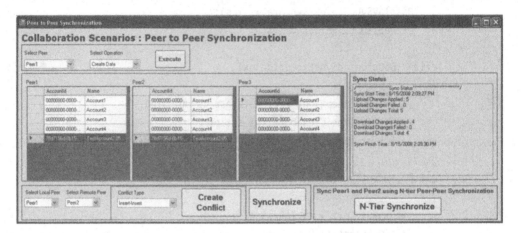

Figure 9-21. *N-tier sync finish*

Summary

Microsoft Sync Services for ADO.NET 2.0 provides developers with APIs to easily create sync ecosystems for two-tier and N-tier synchronization. In addition, Sync Services for ADO.NET 2.0 also offers developers an infrastructure for handling conflicts, reporting sync progress, and cleaning metadata. Sync Services for ADO.NET 2.0 relies heavily on sync adapters for creating ADO.NET commands to manipulate data and metadata and on sync providers for creating ADO.NET commands for manipulating replica knowledge. Sync Services for ADO.NET 2.0 not only works with SQL Server databases but can also synchronize any database for which the ADO.NET provider is available.

■■■

Sync Framework Library Reference

We are heading toward the end of our journey! We have had a detailed look at what the Microsoft Sync Framework is and how we can use it in our applications to synchronize data, files, and so on in our systems. The intent of this appendix is to give you a ready guide to the classes, interfaces, and enumerations in the Sync Framework library.

Here is a list of the major namespaces in the Sync Framework core class library:

- Microsoft.Synchronization

- Microsoft.Synchronization.Files

- Microsoft.Synchronization.FeedSync

- Microsoft.Synchronization.Data

- Microsoft.Synchronization.MetadataStorage

Microsoft.Synchronization Namespace

This section takes a look at the classes, interfaces, and enumerations of the Microsoft. Synchronization namespace.

The Microsoft.Synchronization namespace contains the following classes:

- ChangeBatch

- ChangeBatchBase

- ChangeBatchIsReadOnlyException

- ChangeBatchNeedsKnowledgeException

- ChangeCountMismatchException

- ChangeDataAdapter

- ChangeNeedsKnowledgeException

- ChangeNotExpectedException

- ChangeUnitChange

- ChangeUnitCountMismatchException

- ChangeVersionNotInKnowledgeException

- ClockVector

- ClockVectorElement

- CreateFailuresMustBeForEntireItemException

- DuplicateItemException

- FilterInfo

- ForgottenKnowledge

- FullEnumerationChangeBatch

- FullEnumerationNeededEventArgs

- IncompleteReplicaKeyMapException

- InvalidFeedException

- InvalidKnowledgeVersionException

- InvalidOrderException

- InvalidReplicaKeyException

- InvalidSyncTimeException

- ItemChange

- ItemChangeSkippedEventArgs

- ItemChangeUnitOverride

- ItemChangingEventArgs

- ItemConflictingEventArgs

- ItemDataModifiedConcurrentlyException

- ItemHasChangeUnitsException

- ItemHasNoChangeUnitsException

- ItemHasNoDataException

- ItemHasNoVersionDataException

- ItemListFilterInfo

- ItemMustExistException

- ItemNotInFeedMetadataException

- ItemOverride

- ItemRangeOverride

- KnowledgeBuilder

- KnowledgeDecreasedUnexpectedlyException

- KnowledgeInspector

- KnowledgeSyncProvider

- KnowledgeSyncProviderConfiguration

- LoadChangeContext

- NegativeRangeException

- NotifyingChangeApplier

- NotifyingChangeApplierIChangeDataRetrieverAdapter

- ObjectNeedsStateException

- Override

- RangeOutOfOrderException

- RecoverableErrorData

- ReplicaKeyMap

- ReplicaNotFoundException

- SaveChangeContext

- SaveChangeWithChangeUnitsContext

- SyncAbortedException

- SyncCallbacks

- SyncException

- SyncGlobalId

- SyncId

- SyncIdFormat

- SyncIdFormatGroup

- SyncIdFormatMismatchException

- SyncInvalidOperationException

- SyncKnowledge

- SyncOperationStatistics

- SyncOrchestrator

- SyncOrchestratorStateChangedEventArgs

- SyncProvider

- SyncRuntimeInternalErrorException

- SyncSessionContext

- SyncSessionStatistics

- SyncStagedProgressEventArgs

- SyncVersion

- UnmanagedSyncProviderWrapper

- UserLoadChangeContext

Table A-1 lists the names and purposes of the major classes from the preceding list.

Table A-1. *Microsoft.Synchronization Namespace Classes*

Class	Purpose
ChangeBatch	A sealed class that represents the metadata information for the changes made in a sync operation.
ChangeBatchBase	Represents the metadata for all changes made. This class can be overridden by its derived classes.
ChangeBatchIsReadOnlyException	Represents the exception that is thrown when an item changes or when there is a conflict that has been added to a ChangeBatch object.
ChangeBatchNeedsKnowledgeException	Represents the exception that is thrown if the ChangeBatch object doesn't know about a change.
ChangeCountMismatchException	Represents an exception that is thrown when the source and destination item versions don't match.
ChangeDataAdapter	An abstract class that can be overridden to convert data between a managed and an unmanaged provider.
ChangeNeedsKnowledgeException	Represents the exception that is thrown when an ItemChange instance doesn't know about a particular change.
ChangeNotExpectedException	Represents the exception that is thrown when the order of source and destination item versions don't match.
DuplicateItemException	Represents the exception that is thrown when there is an attempt to add an entry to a replica key map that already exists.
FilterInfo	Specifies the filter that can be used to restrict changes in a ChangeBatch instance.
InvalidFeedException	Represents the exception that is thrown when a FeedSync is invalid.
ItemChange	A sealed class used to represent change to an item participating in a synchronization operation.
ItemChangingEventArgs	Contains the necessary information for the ItemChanging event.
KnowledgeBuilder	Re-creates a SyncKnowledge instance.
ReplicaKeyMap	Represents the mapping between replica IDs and replica keys.

Table A-1. *Microsoft.Synchronization Namespace Classes (Continued)*

Class	Purpose
SyncException	Represents the exception that is thrown when an exception occurs during a synchronization process.
SaveChangeContext	Represents the information about the change that has been made before it is saved.
SyncKnowledge	Represents the sync knowledge that a replica contains.
SyncProvider	Represents the sync provider.
SyncVersion	Represents the item version.

Following is a list of the interfaces in the Microsoft.Synchronization namespace:

- IChangeDataRetriever

- IChangeDataRetrieverAdapter

- IClockVector

- IClockVectorElement

- INotifyingChangeApplierTarget

Table A-2 lists the names and purposes of the interfaces of the Microsoft. Synchronization namespace.

Table A-2. *Microsoft.Synchronization Namespace Interfaces*

Interface	Purpose
IChangeDataRetriever	Specifies how the destination provider will retrieve items from a source provider in a sync session.
IChangeDataRetrieverAdapter	Represents a change data retriever adapter.
IClockVector	Represents a clock vector that contains the changes that have occurred.
IClockVectorElement	Represents the clock element in a knowledge structure.
INotifyingChangeApplierTarget	Represents an object that is capable of saving the changes to a replica.

Following is a list of the enumerations in the Microsoft.Synchronization namespace:

- ChangeKind

- ConflictResolutionAction

- ConflictResolutionPolicy

- FilterType

- FullEnumerationAction

- SaveChangeAction

- SessionProgressStage

- SyncDirectionOrder

- SyncOrchestratorState

- SyncProviderPosition

Table A-3 lists the names and purposes of the major enumerations of the Microsoft.Synchronization namespace:

Table A-3. *Microsoft.Synchronization Namespace Enumerations*

Enumeration	Purpose
ChangeKind	Represents the change type of an item participating in the synchronization process.
FilterType	Represents the type of a filter used to restrict the files and folders participating in the synchronization process.
SaveChangeAction	Represents the action that follows a save operation.
SyncDirectionOrder	Represents the synchronization direction.
SyncOrchestratorState	Specifies various states that a sync session can possess.
SyncProviderPosition	Indicates the position of one sync provider relative to another provider of its kind in a sync session.

Microsoft.Synchronization.Files Namespace

The Microsoft.Synchronization.Files namespace contains the members that are required to synchronize files and folders in your system using the File Sync Provider. The Sync Services for file systems documentation from Microsoft states the following: "Microsoft Sync Framework is a comprehensive synchronization platform that enables collaboration and offline access for applications, services, and devices. It features technologies and tools that enable roaming, sharing of data, and taking data offline. By using Sync Framework, developers can build synchronization ecosystems that integrate any application with any data from any store that uses any protocol over any network."

Following is a list of the major classes in the Microsoft.Synchronization.Files namespace:

- AppliedChangeEventArgs

- ApplyingChangeEventArgs

- CopyingFileEventArgs

- DetectedChangesEventArgs

- DetectingChangesEventArgs

- FileData

- FileSyncInvalidOperationException

- FileSyncProvider

- FileSyncScopeFilter

- SkippedChangeEventArgs

- SkippedFileDetectEventArgs

The following are the enumerations:

- ChangeType

- FileSyncOptions

- SkipReason

FileSyncProvider Class

Table A-4 lists the important properties of the FileSyncProvider class.

Table A-4. *FileSyncProvider Class Members*

Member	Purpose
FileSyncOptions	Specifies how the FileSyncProvider will behave during the synchronization process.
PreviewMode	Gets or sets the preview mode of the FileSyncProvider. In the preview mode of operation, the AppliedChange event is not triggered.
ReplicaId	Returns the replica ID of the FileSyncProvider.
ScopeFilter	Returns the names of the files and directories in the current scope.
RootDirectoryPath	Returns the absolute path of the folder that contains the files and directories that will participate in the synchronization process.
TempDirectoryPath	Returns the location where the temporary files created during the synchronization process will be stored.
MetadataFileName	Returns the name of the metadata storage file.
MetadataDirectoryPath	Returns the location of the metadata storage file.

Table A-5 lists the important methods and events of the FileSyncProvider class.

Table A-5. *FileSyncProvider Class Methods and Events*

Member	Purpose
DetectChanges	This method knows the changes to the file(s) that participated in the synchronization process.
ApplyingChange	This event fires when a particular file participating in the synchronization process is about to change.
AppliedChange	This event fires after a changed has been applied to a file participating in the synchronization process.
CopyingFile	This event fires periodically to check the progress of file copying.
SkippedChange	This event fires when a particular file participating in the synchronization process has been skipped.

FileSyncScopeFilter Class

The FileSyncScopeFilter class is used to include or exclude files and folders that will be participating in the synchronization process.

Table A-6 lists the important members of the FileSyncScopeFilter class.

Table A-6. *FileSyncScopeFilter Class Members*

Member	Purpose
FileNameExcludes	A public property that collects names of files that will be excluded from the synchronization process.
FileNameIncludes	A public property that collects names of files that will be included from the synchronization process.
SubdirectoryExcludes	A public property that collects all relative paths of the directories that will be excluded from the synchronization process.
AttributeExcludeMask	Gets or sets the attributes used to exclude the files and folders in the synchronization process.

Microsoft.Synchronization.Data Namespace

The Sync Services for ADO.NET documentation from Microsoft states the following: "Sync Services for ADO.NET 2.0 is a part of Microsoft Sync Framework. Sync Framework is a comprehensive synchronization platform that enables collaboration and offline access for applications, services, and devices. It features technologies and tools that enable roaming, sharing, and taking data offline. By using Sync Framework, developers can build synchronization ecosystems that integrate any application with any data from any store that uses any protocol over any network."

The Microsoft.Synchronization.Data namespace contains the following classes:

- AnchorException
- ApplyChangeFailedEventArgs
- ApplyingChangesEventArgs
- ApplyMetadataFailedEventArgs
- ChangesAppliedEventArgs
- ChangesSelectedEventArgs
- ClientSyncProvider
- CreatingSchemaEventArgs
- DataSyncException

- DbApplyChangeFailedEventArgs

- DbApplyingChangesEventArgs

- DbChangesAppliedEventArgs

- DbChangesSelectedEventArgs

- DbMetadataSyncException

- DbOutdatedEventArgs

- DbOutdatedSyncException

- DbSelectingChangesEventArgs

- DbSyncAdapterCollection

- DbSyncColumnMapping

- DbSyncColumnMappingCollection

- DbSyncConflict

- DbSyncContext

- DbSyncException

- DbSyncProgressEventArgs

- DbSyncProvider

- DbSyncScope

- DbSyncScopeMetadata

- DbSyncScopeProgress

- DbSyncSession

- DbSyncSessionProgressEventArgs

- DbSyncTableProgress

- MetadataException

- SchemaCreatedEventArgs

- SchemaException

- SelectingChangesEventArgs

- ServerSyncProvider

- ServerSyncProviderProxy

- SessionVariableException

- SyncAnchor

- SyncConfiguration

- SyncConflict

- SyncConflictResolver

- SyncContext

- SyncGroup

- SyncGroupMetadata

- SyncGroupProgress

- SyncParameter

- SyncParameterCollection

- SyncProgressEventArgs

- SyncSchema

- SyncSchemaColumn

- SyncSchemaColumns

- SyncSchemaForeignKey

- SyncSchemaForeignKeys

- SyncSchemaTable

- SyncSchemaTables

- SyncSession

- SyncStatistics

- SyncTable

- SyncTableCollection

- SyncTableInfo

- SyncTableMetadata

- SyncTableProgress

- SyncTracer

Table A-7 lists the names and purpose of the important classes in the Microsoft. Synchronization.Data namespace.

Table A-7. *Microsoft.Synchronization.Data Namespace Members*

Class Name	Purpose
ClientSyncProvider	Abstracts a client sync provider and is responsible for communicating with the client data store.
DataSyncException	Represents the base exception class for all exceptions that are thrown during a synchronization process.
DbSyncAdapter	Represents commands that retrieve data and metadata changes and apply them.
DbSyncConflict	Represents a row-level synchronization conflict during a synchronization process.
DbSyncContext	Encapsulates changes to data and metadata during a synchronization process.
DbSyncProvider	Represents a generic sync provider.
DbSyncScope	Represents a group of objects that need to be synchronized during a sync session.
DbSyncScopeMetadata	Represents the metadata information of a DbSyncScope instance.
DbSyncScopeProgress	Represents the synchronization progress information for the objects in a DbSyncScope.
DbSyncSession	Represents a sync session.
ServerSyncProvider	Represents the generic server sync provider.
SyncSchema	Stores schema information of all tables necessary to create tables that are part of the synchronization process.
SyncTable	Contains the client settings for a table that would be part of the synchronization process.
SyncTableMetadata	Contains the metadata information of a SyncTable that is a part of the synchronization process.

Following is a list of the enumerations in the Microsoft.Synchronization.Data namespace:

- ApplyAction

- ChangeTrackingModel

- ConflictType

- DbConflictType

- DbOutdatedSyncAction

- DbResolveAction

- DbSyncStage

- ResolveAction

- SyncDirection

- SyncErrorNumber

- SyncSchemaForeignKeyRule

- TableCreationOption

Microsoft.Synchronization.FeedSync Namespace

Following are the classes of the Microsoft.Synchronization.FeedSync namespace:

- EndpointState

- FeedBuilder

- FeedClockVector

- FeedClockVectorElement

- FeedConsumer

- FeedIdConverter

- FeedItemConverter

- FeedItemHistory

- FeedItemMetadata

- FeedMetadata

- FeedProducer

- FeedSharingInformation

- FeedSyncServices

Table A-8 lists the names and purposes of the important classes in the Microsoft. Synchronization.FeedSync namespace.

Table A-8. *Microsoft.Synchronization.FeedSync Namespace Members*

Class Name	Purpose
EndpointState	Represents the FeedSync end point state.
FeedBuilder	Creates a FeedSync feed during a synchronization process.
FeedConsumer	Retrieves items from a FeedSync feed and passes them on to a sync provider.
FeedIdConverter	Can be overridden and then used to translate IDs in FeedSync format to corresponding IDs in the provider format.
FeedItemConverter	Can be overridden and then used to translate items in FeedSync format to corresponding items in the provider format.
FeedItemHistory	Represents the history information of a FeedSync item.
FeedItemMetadata	Contains the FeedSync metadata information for an item.
FeedMetadata	Represents metadata information for a FeedSync feed.
FeedSyncServices	Used as a service that can translate data from FeedSync XML to Sync Framework object format.

Microsoft.Synchronization.MetadataStorage Namespace

The Sync Framework documentation from Microsoft states the following: "Metadata Storage Service provides support for storing and handling synchronization metadata. Metadata Storage Service defines many of its classes as abstract so that storage service writers can implement a custom set of classes to store metadata in any kind of data store. Metadata Storage Service also provides an implementation of the classes that use a lightweight database to store synchronization metadata in a single database file in a file system."

Following are the classes in the Microsoft.Synchronization.MetadataStorage namespace:

- ChangeUnitMetadata

- DeleteDetector

- ExplicitTransactionRequiredException

- FieldSchema

- IndexSchema

- ItemMetadata

- ItemMetadataNotFoundException

- KeyUniquenessException

- MetadataFieldNotFoundException

- MetadataStorageEngineException

- MetadataStore

- MetadataStoreException

- MetadataStoreInvalidOperationException

- ReplicaMetadata

- ReplicaMetadataAlreadyExistsException

- ReplicaMetadataInUseException

- ReplicaMetadataNotFoundException

- SqlMetadataStore

- VersionNotSupportedException

Table A-9 shows the major classes of the Microsoft.Synchronization.MetadataStorage namespace and their purpose.

Table A-9. *Microsoft.Synchronization.MetadataStorage Namespace Members*

Class Name	Purpose
ChangeUnitMetadata	Represents metadata information of a change unit of a particular item.
MetadataStore	Represents a metadata store. You can use this class to retrieve the replica of a metadata instance.
ReplicaMetadata	Provides access to the replica metadata instance.
ReplicaMetadataAlreadyExistsException	This exception is thrown when you try to create a new replica metadata instance and the same metadata for that replica exists in the store. In other words, this exception is thrown when you attempt to create a duplicate metadata instance.
ReplicaMetadataInUseException	This exception is thrown when you try to create more than one active ReplicaMetadata object.
SqlMetadataStore	The metadata store actually stored in a light-weight database.
VersionNotSupportedException	This exception is thrown when you attempt to retrieve the replica metadata instance from a metadata store where the version of the metadata that you are trying to retrieve is not supported.
DeleteDetector	Determines the items that have been deleted from the replica.
ItemMetadata	Represents the metadata that is associated with an item.

Index

You Need the Companion eBook